Ideological Dilemmas
A Social Psychology of Everyday Thinking

Michael Billig
Susan Condor
Derek Edwards
Mike Gane
David Middleton
Alan Radley

SAGE Publications
London • Newbury Park • Beverly Hills • New Delhi

First published 1988

SAGE Publications Ltd
28 Banner Street
London EC1Y 8QE

SAGE Publications Inc
2111 West Hillcrest Drive
Newbury Park, California 91320

SAGE Publications Inc
275 South Beverly Drive
Beverly Hills, California 90212

SAGE Publications India Pvt Ltd
32, M-Block Market
Greater Kailash – I
New Delhi 110 048

British Library Cataloguing in Publication data

Ideological dilemmas: a social psychology
  of everyday thinking.
  1. Ideology related to social psychology
  2. Social psychology related to ideology
  I. Billig, Michael
  145

ISBN 0-8039-8095-7
ISBN 0-8039-8096-5 Pbk

Library of Congress catalog card number 88-061484

Typeset by System 4 Associates, Farnham Common, Bucks
Printed in Great Britain by J.W. Arrowsmith Ltd, Bristol

Contents

Acknowledgements

Some of the chapters draw upon work supported by various funding bodies. The authors would like to thank the following: the British Heart Foundation for grants 83/19 and 85/7 awarded to Alan Radley; the Economic and Social Research Council (ESRC) for grant C00232236 awarded to Derek Edwards, Neil Mercer and Janet Maybin for the project 'The development of joint understanding in the classroom'; and the Social Science Research Council (now the ESRC) for grant HG/11/24/8 to Michael Billig and Raymond Cochrane for the project 'Political identification and socialization in adolescents'.

1
Introduction

A teacher is giving a lesson on the way that a pendulum swings. A young girl is talking about a fight at a local dance. After a heart attack a man is pondering how to adjust to the limitations of his life. In a hospital for children a nurse asks a colleague for a piece of equipment. All these are mundane events, which seem to have little connection except for their mundaneness. Perhaps brief film of such scenes might be used to introduce the sort of serious television programme which likes to boast that it includes all human life. Beneath the programme's title, and in time to its theme music, the image will dart from scene to scene in a way that stresses the variety of the filmed episodes. The evocation of the scenes at the start of a social science book is a different matter. Far from announcing the possibility that all human life might make a guest appearance, it suggests that a single theoretical thread will pull the episodes along in a common intellectual direction.

The single thread is provided by the notion of ideological dilemmas. The episodes will feature as later chapters explore the dilemmatic aspects of everyday life, and ideologically dilemmatic themes will be explored in such mundane events. To say that this book is concerned with the way that ideological dilemmas appear in everyday thinking may be not particularly meaningful. The problem is not merely that the notion of 'ideological dilemmas' may be an unfamiliar one, which will need to be explained at length. There is also the problem that approaches in the social sciences, especially those which might introduce unfamiliar concepts, are often best understood, not so much in their own terms, but in relation to those notions which they seek to supplant. Therefore, it might be helpful to identify briefly at the outset the rival approaches to the study of social life and the claims of the dilemmatic approach.

In attacking the dominant theoretical trends of contemporary social psychology, Serge Moscovici (1984a) has argued that one of the prime tasks of contemporary social science is to study 'the thinking society'. The label 'the thinking society' is a deliberately provocative one, for in a literal sense societies do not think; only individuals do. However, Moscovici was drawing critical attention to those psychological theories of thinking which ignore the social context of thought, or the way that society provides the basis for thinking. Similarly he was criticizing those sociological theories which ignore the thinking of individuals. Our approach also stresses the importance of studying the 'thinking society', by exploring the way that thinking takes places through the dilemmatic aspects of ideology. In outlining these notions, we too will be criticizing those psychological and sociological approaches which overlook the thinking society.

On the one hand, dominant trends in cognitive psychology, including what is called cognitive social psychology, have studied in detail the way that individuals process information, draw inferences and categorize the social world. By and large, cognitive psychologists have looked at these processes in terms of the psychology of the individual. If the functions of categorization or inference are discussed, they will be in relation to tasks which these processes enable the individual to perform. It is as if the individual is an isolated Robinson Crusoe, who has been yanked out of the flow of historical time to be placed amongst the formidable equipment of the psychology laboratory. What tends to be overlooked is the social nature and content of thought. Cognitive psychologists have been notably remiss in examining how the processes of cultural and ideological history flow through the minds of their laboratory subjects.

However, it is not merely a matter of turning to experts in the study of ideology in order to find the 'thinking society'. Theorists of ideology typically do not ignore the processes of history, nor do they ignore how these processes create the norms and beliefs of particular societies. However, they often ignore the thinking of individuals, for individuals are often seen as the blinded bearers of a received ideological tradition. All the individual can do is to act according to these received constraints and to pass them on to the next generation. In this respect, ideology is seen as something which closes the mind and switches off thought.

In stressing the dilemmatic aspects of ideology, we hope to oppose the implications of both cognitive and ideological theory, which ignore the social nature of thinking. In contrast to the cognitive psychologists, we stress the *ideological* nature of thought; in contrast to theorists of ideology, we stress the *thoughtful* nature of ideology. This emphasis is achieved by stressing the dilemmatic aspects of ideology and of thinking generally. Ideology is not seen as a complete, unified system of beliefs which tells the individual how to react, feel and think. Instead ideology, and indeed common sense, are seen to comprise contrary themes. Without contrary themes, individuals could neither puzzle over their social worlds nor experience dilemmas. And without this, so much thought would be impossible.

These notions, and the critique of cognitive psychology and contemporary theories of ideology, are outlined in chapters 2 and 3. Chapter 2 discusses the notion of dilemmas in relation to the contrary themes of common sense. The existence of contrary maxims, or opposing pieces of folk wisdom, illustrates that common sense possesses a dilemmatic nature. These contrary themes are the preconditions for those dilemmas in which people are faced with difficult decisions. It is not our intention to explore how people cope with these situations and how decisions are made. Our concern is more with the dilemmatic preconditions, in other words with those contrary themes which under normal circumstances are reflected in people's thoughts. In fact, the existence of the contrary themes ensures that there is a need for thought. Individuals are not to be seen as being fully preprogrammed by neatly systematized plans of action, which are awaiting the appropriate triggering stimulus and which obviate the need for all deliberation. Rather, the contrary themes enable people to discuss and puzzle over their everyday life, and in this respect the rhetorical skills of argument are closely linked to the skills of thinking (Billig, 1987).

In chapter 3 the ideological nature of dilemmas is discussed. We are concerned not merely with the dilemmatic aspects of common sense in general, but particularly with those dilemmatic aspects which have ideological roots. Here the historical creation of thinking is emphasized. Our concepts and our ideas reflect our own times, and they also reflect the history which has produced these current moments. Of particular interest for a study of contemporary ideology is the ideology of liberalism. Not only have concepts of liberalism been transmitted into everyday thinking, but they are reproduced dilemmatically. Thus liberalism contains opposing themes, whose opposition enables endless debate and argument. If chapter 2 is aimed primarily at the cognitive psychologists who ignore the dilemmatic aspects of thinking, chapter 3 criticizes those sociological theorists who ignore the dilemmatic aspects of ideology. In consequence, passing criticisms will be made of such figures as Karl Mannheim and Louis Althusser, although some of the theoretical implications of this critique will be taken up again and developed in the final chapter of the the book.

Each of chapters 4 to 8 examines the ideas of the dilemmatic approach in relation to a particular empirical issue. A preliminary word of explanation needs to said about these chapters. They are all based upon research projects which were started and conducted in isolation from each other and from the development of the dilemmatic approach. The authors, who formed the Loughborough Discourse and Rhetoric Group, had been engaged upon these individual projects before they came together to work out common themes. Having discussed issues of theory which interested us, we decided to discover whether we could apply our theoretical notions to our particular projects. In one sense this constitutes a demanding test of theoretical ideas. It is the customary practice to design research projects in order to reveal the sorts of phenomena which the theorist believes to exist. Thus one might have expected us to design projects which would specifically reveal the dilemmatic aspects of social life; having found what we were searching for, we might then declare the theories proved. Theoretical opponents might then have the task of displaying those aspects of social reality which fail to contain the required dilemmatic characteristics.

However, in our case the projects came before the formulation of the dilemmatic approach. Therefore we set ourselves the task of going back to our data (or more precisely, going back to our transcripts) to see whether we could find ideologically dilemmatic elements. In each case, these elements were not difficult to find. Chapters 4 to 8 give examples of these interpretations. None of these chapters is a research report in the true sense of the term. All of the projects have been reported more fully elsewhere. Nor do the chapters stick closely to the details of the individual projects. Rather they draw upon examples from the projects in order to illustrate wider themes, as the dilemmatic perspective is used to illustrate some of the complexities of different aspects of modern life. Unlike the television producer, we can make no claim to have included all of modern life. Moreover, we must be aware of the arbitrary manner in which the substantive topics were selected for the book, or rather were thrust upon the book. We cannot say that the contrary themes of liberal ideology underwrite all aspects of modern life. What we can claim, however, is that ideological themes of a dilemmatic character can be found in the conversations, routines and interviews which we were studying. In all of these, we found more ideological influence than might have been expected by cognitive psychologists and more dilemmatic perplexity than might have been predicted by theorists of ideology.

The research projects, which the substantive chapters draw upon, share the characteristic of being based primarily on qualitative investigations. We shall not be citing the statistical analyses of vast surveys, or presenting tables of numerical data. We are interested in interpreting remarks and actions, often bringing to the surface counter-meanings. In this respect, our approach shares features with other qualitative approaches to social psychological investigations. In common with the approach of discourse analysis (Potter and Wetherell, 1987) we seek to elucidate social psychological processes through an understanding of discourse. In so doing, however, we do not seek to separate discourse from social action. Similarly the goal of understanding 'the thinking society' is one which is specifically adopted by the social representation approach of Moscovici (1984a and 1984b). The social representation theorists have identified the representation of scientific concepts in everyday discourse as a major issue to be studied by social psychologists (Moscovici, 1976; Jodelet, 1984). The general issue of the way that intellectual ideas can be translated into commonsensical ones appears in our research projects. They reveal how the philosophical concepts of liberalism appear in everyday contemporary discourse, often with complex and contrary meanings, so that liberalism, as experience, has a dilemmatic rather than systematized form. In fact, our approach can be seen as suggesting an extension to the social representation approach by stressing the role of argumentation in the thinking society (Billig, 1988a and in press).

In chapter 4 these notions are applied to the issue of education. The contrary themes of equality and authority are identified in the thinking of teachers. Moreover, the dilemmatic contrast between these themes is represented in the classroom practices of the teachers. Close observation of the ways in which teachers speak and behave in the classroom reveals the balancing of democratic and authoritarian elements, as teachers attempt simultaneously to impart knowledge as well as elicit it from the pupils. In all this, teaching is not itself a neutral act by which an ideology is transmitted, often by paid employees of the state. The act of teaching is itself a representation of the ideology and it is a dilemmatic representation. The teachers are aware of the dilemmatic themes in their discourse on education, for they themselves discuss the nature of education and the nature of their own role.

The same basic dilemma between equality and authority appears in chapter 5, which concentrates upon the behaviour of experts. In particular, examples are taken from a research project that looked at a child development unit attached to a hospital. The members of the unit had followed egalitarian principles in seeking to reduce the authoritarianism of rank in the position of the various qualified experts. In this, they were following the traditions of liberal ideology. However, as experts they were fulfilling non-egalitarian roles, and in the modern role of the expert we find ambivalences between democratic egalitarianism and authoritarian expertise. Again these ambivalences provide matters of debate and thought for the experts themselves, who are aware of the dilemmas of the position.

Chapter 6 focuses upon issues of health and illness, and in particular upon a group of men who, having suffered heart attacks, have undergone major heart surgery. These men are forced to contemplate their lives and the dialectic of being simultaneously a supposedly free agent but also a physical body, constrained by laws of material necessity. However, the dialectic between health and illness is not a simple one, for each concept implies the existence of the other. Moreover, these concepts are not ideologically neutral, for they draw upon conflicting themes of Enlightenment philosophy, which simultaneously stress the reality of free individual will and the necessity of bodily materialism. These contrary themes recur in ordinary discourse, and especially in the discourse of these men forced to confront the dilemmas of their own situation.

Again contrary themes from the Enlightenment surface in chapter 7, on prejudice and tolerance. The very notion of 'prejudice' is an Enlightenment concept and is one that has passed into everyday discourse. The dialectic of prejudice is not a simple one, but includes contrary themes. We find the concept of prejudice being used in a way that simultaneously claims a rationality for the speaker, by criticizing the irrational prejudices of others, and that permits the expression of discriminatory views against other groups. Instances are given of how adolescents who claim to support a racist political party use the discourse of the Enlightenment, which overtly appears to criticize the irrationalism of racism. However, the ambiguities and dilemmas are built deeply into the discourse of the Enlightenment. As previously, this analysis relies on an interpretive exercise to uncover the different and contrary themes in this dialectic of prejudice.

Chapter 8 – the final substantive chapter – concerns the discourse of gender. The liberal heritage of individualism is expressed in this discourse, as it is clear that all individuals are different, and thus women as individuals should be considered individually. Yet on the other hand there is a reality to the gender categorization, for there are similarities of identity and perceived common fate between women. In consequence, the question is raised of how far one can generalize across individuals. This question, and the answers offered, possess ideological roots, for the construction of gender categories can hardly be considered in the abstract, apart from the history of ideology and social power. Also in the discourse of gender there is the underlying ideological theme of competition, as speakers make their distinctions and categorizations in order to discuss who is better or superior to whom. In this respect, the dialectic between egalitarianism and authoritarianism again appears.

The different projects have yielded different sorts of data. Some have been based upon recordings of natural interaction, in which the observer has not intruded. Others have been based upon recorded in-depth interviews. Then there are recorded discussions, which may or may not have included the academic observer. Despite the methodological differences, and despite the differences in the original theoretical preoccupations of the research projects, some common themes emerge. It has been possible to see the reproduction of the great problems of philosophy, and in particular of liberal philosophy, in everyday discourse. This philosophy is reproduced neither as a series of philosophical solutions, nor as singular positions that people consistently occupy, but as dilemmas. Even when solutions are found by individuals – at least solutions for the everyday reproduction of the underlying dilemma – other problems emerge as the ideologically constituted dilemma expresses itself in other forms. In this way, the ideology is not reproduced as a closed system for talking about the world. Instead it is reproduced as an incomplete set of contrary themes, which continually give rise to discussion, argumentation and dilemmas.

It is hoped that this perspective bridges the gap between the individualism of much contemporary psychological theorizing about thinking and the social level of analysis contained in many theories of ideology. By stressing the dilemmatic and rhetorical nature of thinking, we see thinking as inherently social. In fact, thinking is frequently a form of dialogue within the individual (Billig, 1987). Yet the content of the dialogue has historical and ideological roots, for the concepts involved, and their meanings, are constructed through the history of social dialogue and debate. In this sense the social pattern of ideology is mapped on to individual consciousness. Similarly, because of its dilemmatic nature, ideology cannot preclude thought and debate. Thus, the paradox of the term 'the thinking society' describes the reality that our dilemmas of ideology are social dilemmas and that our ideology cannot but produce dilemmas to think about.

2

The Nature of Dilemmas

This chapter will discuss what is meant by the concept of 'the dilemmatic aspects of thinking'. In so doing, it will introduce a number of key themes in our approach, whilst offering criticisms of other social psychological approaches to the study of dilemmas. In social psychology, and indeed in other social sciences, it is customary to offer definitions for every official-sounding concept used and to offer these definitions at the earliest possible stage of a discussion. Thus, the reader might be expecting at this point a precisely worded sentence, explicating what we mean by 'the dilemmatic aspects of thinking'. Some readers might even be discomforted by the absence of such a definition, which might be seen as the only safe map reference on a journey through a terrain of dangerously shifting word meanings. However, it can be argued that a concept is best explicated in the course of a theoretical discussion about its possible uses, the sorts of phenomena which it might describe, and why competing concepts may be unsatisfactory. The simple map reference, for all its precision, may be less helpful than a discursive travelogue which offers reasons why one path and not another can be recommended and what views can be expected by travellers along the way.

Nevertheless, a general warning can be offered about the concept of 'the dilemmatic aspects of thinking'. Just as a guidebook might advise tourists not to expect glorious views on a forest walk or ancient archaeological ruins on a directed stroll around Manhattan, so a warning can be given about the present chapter. There will be no detailed analysis of the psychology of decision-making. The dilemmatic aspects of thinking do not refer to the agonized mental states of the decision-maker, who is faced with a difficult choice. Our concern is not with decision-making as such, but with the general preconditions of decision-making. In addition, the focus is upon social preconditions, as revealed in common sense or in ideology. As a consequence, attention is directed not to the individual thinker as such, but to those aspects of socially shared beliefs which give rise to the dilemmatic thinking of individuals. The discussion will start by considering how social psychologists have typically studied dilemmas. Because social psychologists have often restricted their attention to choice-making, they have overlooked the dilemmatic aspects of thinking. It will be suggested that common sense contains contrary themes, and these enable the emergence of social dilemmas. In this sense, common sense is dilemmatic. More than this, the contrary themes of common sense represent the materials through which people can argue and think about their lives, for people need to possess contrary themes if they are to think and argue. Therefore a consideration of these socially produced, dilemmatic aspects has implications for the psychological study of thinking.

Dilemmas and choices

Most social psychologists who have studied the topic of dilemmas have seen dilemmas in terms of individuals making difficult decisions. We will argue that this narrow focus has prevented social psychologists from appreciating the dilemmatic quality of much everyday thinking, which can be revealed whether or not individuals are actually faced with decisions to be made. Although our use of 'dilemmatic' is not confined to decision-making as such, it must be conceded that the term is derived from the narrower focus of choice. Semantically it could hardly be otherwise, because in normal speech dilemmas are associated with awkward decisions. According to the *Oxford English Dictionary*, a dilemma involves 'a choice between two (or, *loosely*, several) alternatives which are or appear equally unfavourable' (emphasis in original). A strict interpretation of this definition might imply that the choice is hardly a choice at all, for whatever the decision-maker decides, the outcome will be equally appalling. The lack of manoeuvrability is caught by the Latin proverb 'In front the precipice, behind the wolf.' However, the difficulty of a dilemma may not be confined to the inevitable unfavourability of the outcome. Aristotle in *Rhetoric* noted that dilemmas could often be turned around. He cited the example of the priestess warning her son against speaking in public: 'If you speak justly, you will be hated by men; if unjustly, by the gods' (II, xxiii, 15). The problem, according to Aristotle, could have been posed in positive terms: if just words are spoken the gods will love the speaker, whilst men will love him for his unjust speeches. Whether the choice is phrased in terms of the unfavourable outcome, or positively in terms of being loved, the choice is just as difficult. Either way, the dilemma still remains a dilemma.

The obvious psychological interest in dilemmas is to analyse the psychological state of the decision-maker. Others have described the troubled mind of the decision-maker, haunted by doubt and wishing to creep away from all the problems set by gods and man (Janis and Mann, 1977). Our concern, by contrast, is to examine the social preconditions for dilemmas in order to show how ordinary life, which seems far removed from the dramas of wolves and precipices, is shaped by dilemmatic qualities. It will be suggested that the mentality of the ordinary person, not placed in the dramatic situation of choosing between precipice and wolf, nevertheless contains the conflicting themes which surface so vividly in the dilemmatic situation *per se*. In order to show how these dilemmatic aspects of thinking characterize social beliefs, it may be helpful to give examples of dilemmas. Then, it will be possible to illustrate how particular dilemmas presuppose much more general dilemmatic aspects of thinking. For this purpose three different dilemmas will be considered.

The first dilemma is one which is recounted by the Epicurean philosopher Diogenes Laertius in his description of the life of Socrates. Apparently a young Athenian man was perplexed about whether or not to get married. He approached Socrates, hoping for sagacious advice to solve his dilemma. All he received from the great philosopher was the reply: 'Whichever you do, you will repent it' (1972: 163).

Socrates can provide a connection between the first example and our second one, whose general form, according to some social psychologists, resembles a much studied dilemma (Dawes, 1973; see below). This second example is that faced by soldiers in war: whether or not to flee from the prospect of death in battle. Socrates, when accused of corrupting the youth of Athens by his immoral philosophy, replied that he had stuck to his philosophical duties just as doggedly as he had remained at his post on the battlefield. He had not deserted the field of either military or philosophical conflict. Instead he had shown his firm decision in an age-old dilemma, which pits individual interest against collective interest. Individual soldiers can save their own skins by slipping away unobtrusively from the hubbub of the battlefield. However, if all the soldiers on a particular side follow this piece of self-interest, then the enemy can advance unimpeded, to slaughter the individually retreating army. Thus self-interest, if repeatedly followed by all members of one army (but not by the other side), would lead to collective loss and thereby, from the individual's point of view, would be self-defeating (Dawes, 1973).

The third illustrative dilemma is a purely hypothetical one. It is possible to imagine a person with a very particular and individual skill. Perhaps this is the skill of a potter, an interior decorator or a speciality cook. Whatever the particular skill, our craftsperson faces a problem. More products are suddenly required than the craftsperson in question can produce. Perhaps the speciality cook has been given an order by a regular customer for an unusually large number of consommés. Help could be summoned: family and friends might lend a hand in the emergency. However, the quality of the product is bound to decline were non-specialists, lacking the mysterious talents of the craftsperson, to be recruited at the last moment. If no help is accepted then the regular customer might be disappointed by the hungry wolf of empty plates; but if help is given, then there looms the precipice of declining quality.

In each of the three dilemmas the decision-maker is faced with a choice, in which the balance of profits and losses seem to be equally weighted between the alternative courses of action. There would be little dilemma if one possible choice promised much reward and few losses whilst the other held out nothing but the vista of precipices, wolves and the enmity of the gods. The dilemma arises from the difficulty in assessing the various possible gains and losses, and also from attempting to estimate the probabilities of obtaining the various profits and losses. Thus it is not just the prospect of losses which makes the choice so difficult. After all, the choice of certain death by plunging down a precipice or being mauled to death by wolves is not so difficult. What makes the choice so hard is the chance that the decision might matter. There might just be the faintest prospect of survival. Maybe the wolves are not hungry, or there is a concealed ledge on the precipice. All would depend upon making the right choice. And the right choice depends upon judging the likelihood of the unlikely fortune.

Of course, one person's dilemma may not be another's, should the profits and losses be perceived differently. Socrates so much valued honour, and so little his own life, that the soldier's dilemma hardly appeared as a dilemma to him. The balance was firmly tilted to one side: the matter was not worth a moment of the great man's thinking. It was the same when he was imprisoned, awaiting execution. Crito told him that an escape could be arranged, but Socrates was having nothing of that. Dismissively he declared that it was his duty to obey the decisions of the state (Plato, 1959: 44f). Socrates also dismissed, or appeared to dismiss, the dilemma of the young man. Effectively he was saying 'It doesn't matter what you do, so don't worry about the choice.' He dismissed the dilemma because of his knowledge of the male psyche, which ensures that the balance of profits and losses would be the same regardless of decision: whichever step was taken, the grass would always seem greener beyond the other precipice.

In all these examples, choices have to be made. Even inactivity is a choice, once the possibility of activity has been raised. Not getting married is a choice, when one has considered choosing marriage. So is refusing to desert one's regiment, or spurning the chance of escaping from the condemned cell. These situations are dilemmas if the choices are difficult to make because the balance of profits and losses seems to be evenly matched.

Psychological study of dilemmas

It is the choice-making aspects of dilemmas which have been extensively studied by psychologists. There have been hundreds of experiments which have put volunteer subjects in dilemmas and then have observed their responses. The curious thing about the majority of these studies is that the social nature and contents of the dilemmas have been abstracted from the situation. The subjects are left with the sparse forms of a dilemma, and the psychologists are interested in the resulting choices and the variables which effect the choice. Consequently, the type of psychological study to be described in this section has been concerned with the output of the choice-maker who has been placed in a dilemma. This sort of study takes the dilemma itself for granted by not inquiring how dilemmas might arise in the first place. In so doing, psychologists do not go beyond the narrowly defined situation of the dilemma to probe the more general dilemmatic aspects of thinking.

This point can be illustrated by returning to the second example of a dilemma given in the previous section. This was the dilemma of the soldier wondering whether to flee the battlefield to save his own skin. Dawes (1973) comments that this is a particularly dramatic instance of the commons dilemma. This is a much studied dilemma, and is based upon a real historical problem. In England during the eighteenth century, small farmers were faced with the problem of whether to exercise their ancient right to graze cattle on common land. Because of land enclosures much of this common land had been lost, so that there was insufficient common grazing land. Individual farmers might improve the state of their own herds by grazing them on the commons, but if all farmers did so, the grazing land would quickly become barren through overgrazing. As a result, everyone's cattle would suffer from hunger.

When the commons dilemma is studied experimentally by social psychologists, subjects are not asked to imagine that they are eighteenth-century small farmers. Nor are they required to see themselves as frightened foot soldiers in the middle of battle. In fact, they are not asked to imagine anything. They are instructed to press one of two buttons, in order to gain points, in a 'game' to be played by two persons. Depending on which button is pressed, the subject stands to gain a specified goodly number of points, unless the other subject, or 'game-player', also presses the equivalent button: then both will lose heavily a specified number of points. The balance of rewards and penalties is so arranged in order to represent the formal properties of the dilemma of the commons, in which individual interest conflicts with joint interest (see Colman, 1982 for a review of experimental gaming studies of this and other dilemmas).

In these laboratory studies, everything has been reduced to its barest form. The choices of the dilemma have been expressed in terms of payoffs of a single desired utility – whether points or, as in some well-appointed laboratories, actual money. The experimental subjects have to maximize profit by their choices. What is missing is the great moral and ideological complexities of the original dilemmas. The subject does not have to defend the ancient right to graze cattle, or to ponder upon the morality of cowardice. Everything has been given its price. The psychologist has abstracted the clash of historic values, and has subordinated wider issues to the discovery of what makes experimental subjects press one or other button in pursuit of a single value.

It would be misleading to suggest that social psychologists have only studied dilemmas in this abstracted form. For a number of years there was great interest shown by social psychologists in comparing group with individual decision-making. Much of this research used the choice dilemmas questionnaire of Kogan and Wallach (1964). This questionnaire set respondents a series of tricky dilemmas. Respondents were required to imagine hypothetical situations in which a choice had to made between risking much to achieve a highly desirable but uncertain outcome, or settling for a secure but definitely second-best outcome. For example, one hypothetical situation involved deciding about venturing an operation, which would result in a complete cure but which could kill the patient, or opting for an incapacitated life. Initially, research results suggested that groups made riskier decisions than individuals (for reviews see Cartwright, 1971, 1973; Doise and Moscovici, 1984; Fraser and Foster, 1984; Wetherell, 1987). There was much intellectual excitement about the possibility that groups were enhancing the value of risk in order to appear bold risk-takers (Brown, 1965). As so often happens in experimental social psychology, clear findings soon disappear under the accumulated rubble of contradictory results. Later studies produced the somewhat less exciting conclusion that sometimes groups produce riskier decisions than the lone decision-maker and sometimes more cautious ones, and that sometimes groups and individuals come to similar conclusions.

It is not the results of these studies which are of interest here, but two other factors. First, the social psychologists tended not to be interested in the dilemmas themselves. From the psychologists' perspectives the dilemmas were just means for studying the processes of decision-making. The precise contents of the dilemmas were unimportant, so long as they set the subjects tricky problems which involved choosing between risky and conservative options. There is a resemblance between this line of research and the gaming research: the content of dilemmas was less important than the output, or the subjects' decisions.

There is another point to note about the choice dilemmas research. The experimental subjects typically became quite involved in their discussions of the dilemmas. They would argue animatedly about the hypothetical situations. Although social psychologists have tended to analyse these arguments (Burnstein and Vinokur, 1975), we can ask what sorts of social knowledge the subjects were using to make these hypothetical dilemmas seem real. The subjects were not arguing about the particularities of a given case or about the personalities of the individuals involved, because the dilemmas involved hypothetical persons and situations. Rather the subjects were employing common sense, which, quite literally, is the sense commonly shared by a community. They were talking about the suitable ways of behaving, and about the worth of particular outcomes; whether, for example, the life of an invalid could be a satisfactory life. In so doing they were discussing the nature and relative merits of social values, just as Socrates and Crito discussed in the Athenian prison the relative value of sacrificing one's life for duty, as against the value of escaping from the law to continue one's philosophical calling. Such discussions centre upon socially shared beliefs, images, moral values and the sort of social knowledge which has been generally grouped under the label of 'social representations' (Moscovici, 1981, 1984a, 1984b).

These sorts of social knowledge are quite different from the mathematical calculations of gain and loss which the decision-maker in the abstracted gaming situation is presumed to employ. We are dealing here with the type of social knowledge which is often represented by well-known maxims and proverbs. When social psychologists believed that the group discussions enhanced the value of risk-taking, it was as if the discussions reaffirmed the common-sense maxim 'Nothing ventured nothing gained.' But when it was realized that the discussions could also offer the counsel of caution, it was as if reckless venturing were being restrained by the admonition to 'Look before you leap.' What, of course, provoked endless discussion was whether each situation was suitable for the daredevil venturing or for timid looking.

The three dilemmas discussed in the previous section can be seen as presenting situations which involve more than the mathematical calculation of profits and losses, as if the complex dilemmas of social life can be reduced to a single utility. In each of the three dilemmas, socially shared images, representations and values can be seen to conflict. It is this conflict which produces the difficulty of the dilemma. In fact, without the conflict of values the dilemma could not occur in social life.

The dilemma of the young man asking Socrates about marriage depends upon culturally shared images of bachelorhood and marriage. The dilemma would not operate in the same way if spinsterhood were substituted for bachelorhood, at least in those societies in which the unmarried woman was a figure of social stigma. The dilemma does not depend upon the particular character of the young man. Modern readers can smile at Diogenes Laertius's account, even though (or perhaps because) the young man is anonymous. The dilemma is a social dilemma, in that it refers to social images about male attitudes towards responsibility and freedom, love and lust, and about the wish to have all values, even when these so obviously conflict in life.

The second dilemma represents the clash between individual interest and social interest. Of course, in any real case of the soldier's dilemma, wider values are of direct relevance: for example, the value of the war itself and whether the soldier would be deserting a just or an unjust cause; or whether the soldier wished to avoid taking life just as much as losing life; or whether the soldier was aware of responsibilities to family at home, who would starve if he were to be slain by an enemy in an absurd conflict. All these considerations raise deep moral issues, and ordinary people can debate such matters, just as Socrates and Crito did in the prison cell.

Of all the three dilemmas, the one about the speciality cook seems to be the most narrowly economic. It would seem to be a dilemma in which value conflicts can be stripped away, in order to reduce the situation to those bare essentials with which game theorists feel most at ease. The dilemma can be seen in terms of choosing which course of action will produce the greatest payoff, or least damage, to the trade of the speciality cook. However, the dilemma need not be perceived in this way. The specialist cook may want to preserve a small enterprise which does not sacrifice the quality of the product, or the quality of the producer's life, to the pursuit of profit. One the other hand, the dilemma might refer to a particular emergency rather than to a long-term plan for the enterprise. Here again the situation can involve a clash of old maxims, or elements of what is commonly sensible. As our proverb will remind us, if the consommé is produced by many hands then the work will be lightened. But against this, as is known to all of us whether or not we are culinary experts, too many cooks spoil the consommé.

It is these bits and pieces of social knowledge which give rise to the three dilemmas, or to the social dilemmas depicted in the choice dilemmas questionnaire. These dilemmas can only arise because people share values, norms, social expectations, duties, guilt feelings, wishful hopes and so on. In this respect the individual decision-maker is not alone, although the act of choosing can itself be a lonely act. Social psychologists, who wish to study real dilemmas, need to reinstate the social elements which have been abstracted by the game-playing approach. However, it is not merely that the bits and pieces of social knowledge are themselves socially shared, but that what are shared are conflicting bits and pieces. The maxims and values, which are held by all, can be brought into conflict with each other. Because common sense comprises such potentially conflicting elements, it can be said to possess a dilemmatic quality. If common sense did not possess this quality, then the dilemmas of choice could not arise with the full force of moral and social dramas.

Contradictions of common sense

It might be thought that the dilemmas in the preceding sections have been carefully selected, in order to exaggerate the conflicting themes of common sense. Had other themes been chosen, a more unitary image of common sense might have resulted. However, it is fundamental to the present approach that the contrary themes of common sense are neither rare nor unimportant. Nor are they of recent origin. Francis Bacon, in *Of the Dignity and Advancement of Learning*, included an appendix which listed commonplace maxims arranged in antithetical pairs. For every maxim there was a counter-maxim which seemed to recommend the opposite. Bacon noted that in arguments people draw upon the maxims or upon the themes expressed by the maxims, and therefore the maxims he listed contained 'the *seeds*, not *flowers* of arguments' (Bacon, 1858: 492, emphasis in original).

The clash of common-sense beliefs has also been recognized by many social psychological textbooks. Typically, textbook writers cite contrary common-sense beliefs about people, such as 'Absence makes the heart grow fonder' and 'Out of sight, out of mind' (see Billig, 1987: 206f for examples taken from the textbooks). The existence of such contrary beliefs is then taken as evidence for the hopeless confusion of common sense, and the need for the methods and rigours of science to clear up matters once and for all. Unfortunately, experimentation has failed to sort common-sense maxims into the useful, partially useful and useless in a clear, unambiguous way. The research about group risk-taking seemed to suggest that the palm of victory was about to be awarded to the maxim 'Nothing ventured nothing gained' in its age-old competition with 'Look before you leap.' But then with further experimentation the old rival drew level, and bets are still being taken as the two continue galloping around their endless course.

It is quite appropriate that no palm of victory be awarded, for the social world is not divided into opposing camps, each supporting one or other of the antithetical maxims. 'Many hands make light work' does not have its zealous adherents, seeing nothing but truth in their chosen maxim, and looking with distaste upon these who muster beneath the false banner of 'Too many cooks spoil the broth.' Both maxims contain their own bits of truth and their own limitations, and both are shared by the same people. Thus they are both part of the common sense which is commonly shared by the English-speaking tradition. In the same way, everyone in a given society can admit to the desirability of looking after family responsibilities, as well as showing social responsibility. All can agree in principle with the maxims 'Charity begins at home' and 'Love thy neighbour.' The trouble starts not because one maxim has the monopoly of common sense, but because the various elements of common sense are seen to collide in a way which on occasions necessitates difficult decisions.

Not only does common sense contain maxims which conflict, but the very vocabulary at our disposal expresses conflicting themes. Many words are not mere labels which neutrally package up the world. They also express moral evaluations, and such terms frequently come in antithetical opposites which enable opposing moral judgements to be made. The risk-taker can be described as reckless or courageous: the conservative decision-maker can be labelled timid or prudent. The mere availability of these words encourages the dilemma whether to approve or disapprove of a given person. Should Socrates be labelled as morally courageous or stubbornly obstinate? It makes all the difference which term is chosen, and the moral evaluation can only be made because a commonly sensible alternative could also have been made.

It is not haphazard that common sense contains its contrary themes, or, to use the term introduced at the beginning of this chapter, that it possesses its dilemmatic character. The very existence of these opposing images, words, evaluations, maxims and so on is crucial, in that they permit the possibility not just of social dilemmas but of social thinking itself. Without these oppositions there would be no way of arguing about dilemmas or understanding how opposing values can come into collision. As Bacon noted, the contrary maxims provide the seeds of arguments. Here Bacon was drawing attention to the role which maxims play in rhetoric, for debaters about social issues commonly draw upon the commonplaces shared by themselves and their audiences.

There is a further implication. The contrary themes of common sense provide more than the seeds for arguments: they also provide the seeds for thought itself. The justification for suggesting this is based upon the notion that thinking and arguing are closely connected. When one thinks about a dilemma, wondering whether to pursue one or other course, one arranges the reasons as in an argument, sifting through the balance of justifications and criticisms using the pros as arguments against the cons and vice versa. In a real sense social argumentation can be seen as providing the model for social thinking (Billig, 1987). These are not necessarily the sort of acrimonious arguments which take place between different communities and whose acrimony derives from the lack of comprehension of each other's strangely nonsensical common sense. These are the arguments which arise *within* a particular common sense, as people debate about the common sense which they share.

Moreover, these are the sorts of arguments which people must have with themselves if they are to deliberate about matters. For example, if people are to wonder whether to marry or not, they must conduct some sort of internal debate. If they only echo the reasons for one action, they will not have deliberated properly. Or if they wonder whether to praise friends as courageous or to condemn them as reckless, they must weigh the different factors, going to the trouble to make sure that both sides are given a hearing in the debating chamber of the single mind. This sort of deliberation is, of course, possible only if the individual possesses the dilemmatic aspects of social belief. If all elements of social belief were in complete harmony, and there were no possibility of ever confusing recklessness with courage, then there would be no possibility for arguing about such matters. Nor would there be the possibility for deliberation about choice, for without the possibility of such deliberation an awareness of choice can disappear:

> If the process of spelling out in words through adopting different perspectives is a way that a person may deliberate upon possible courses of action, then repeated failure to spell out an alternative perspective will leave the person unaware of the possibility of there being any choice at all. (Radley, 1978)

There are a number of social psychological implications from this link between arguing and thinking and from linking both to the dilemmatic aspects of common sense. We consider these implications under the two following headings.

Universality of argumentation

It should not be thought that the dilemmatic aspects of common sense are confined to the social beliefs of particular communities, so that only some societies possess the conflicting elements which give rise to arguments, whilst the common sense of other societies exists in whole-hearted harmony. Much of this book will be concerned with the specific ideological dilemmas of modern society. However, at this stage a much more general point can be made. The common sense of all societies will possess contrary themes, which provide the possibility of argument and deliberation. Of course, the content of the contrary themes will vary from society to society. And it is not the case that all members of all societies think, argue and are perplexed about exactly the same things. In fact, the forms of the ideological dilemmas which are discussed later are often particular to contemporary society and its particular ideological traditions.

Here it is sufficient to make a general point about the psychological universality of rhetoric. If thinking and arguing are linked, then the capacity for using rhetoric is universal. In all societies one can expect people to justify themselves and to criticize the views of others, and in so doing they will be employing the rhetoric of argumentation (see Billig, 1988a). The fact that rhetorical capacities may be socially universal does not mean that rhetoric takes the same forms in all societies. What it does imply is that dilemmas about values and commonsensical beliefs are not confined to modern Western societies, in which consensus agreement about traditional truths may have collapsed. In suggesting the psychological importance of rhetoric, Billig (1987) specifically drew examples from the traditions of orthodox Judaism. Here is a community which seeks to live by fixed, agreed rules and which seeks to arrest the passage of historical progress by continually referring back to past authorities. Yet here also is a community whose culture is marked by dilemmatic argument, as, for example, the conflicting values of justice and mercy continually create and re-create the possibilities for further dilemmatic discussion. Even the Deity is believed to join in these discussions, as he argues with His prophets and even with Himself.

Perhaps it might be objected that orthodox Judaism represents a highly literate society, and that one should not expect rhetorical argument in simpler, preliterate societies. If this were so, the psychological implication would be that preliterate people do not, or indeed cannot, deliberate about their lives. Happily the implication is incorrect, for the anthropological evidence suggests that rhetoric is by no means confined to the literate

(Bloch, 1975). Even when formal oratory in preliterate societies seems to possess the character of set-piece speeches, rather than the cut-and-thrust of debate, there often have been lively arguments behind the scenes before the solemn oratorical ritual has been agreed upon (see for example Keenan's 1975 anthropology of Merinan oratory).

The person as argumentative debater

The stress upon argumentation and the dilemmatic aspects of common sense provides a different image of the person from that encountered in much current social psychological theorizing. Our view sees the individual as existing within a social context, in which all dilemmas and oppositions cannot possibly have been worked out. Moreover the individual, by possessing the common sense of the community, also possesses the contrary aspects of beliefs which permit debates to continue both internally and externally. This is a different image from that conveyed by psychological theories, which see thinking in terms of a desire for inner attitudinal harmony or in terms of the processing of incoming information.

One of the most influential theories in social psychology has been Festinger's (1957) theory of cognitive dissonance. This theory, as well as a number of similar 'balance theories', depicts thinkers as being motivated by the desire to maintain consistency in their thoughts. Inconsistency is seen as being essentially uncomfortable. The assumption of consistency can be detected in common social psychological terms such as 'attitudinal system' or 'value system'. These concepts imply that thoughts are well systematized within the human mind. Any belief which a person might hold is seen to be a reflection of an inner 'belief system'. If persons express an opinion on an issue, then they are revealing their 'attitudinal system'. Each thought we hold or action we perform will take its meaning from its place in the psychological system. If it is discrepant with the system, then the individual needs to engage in some attitudinal repair work in order to rectify the damage and restore the calmness of consistency. It is as if social psychologists imagine that locked up in the human head is some sort of blood-red silicon chip, which organizes thoughts and actions. This chip is the psychologist's Rosetta Stone: if only it could be discovered and then decoded, the hidden plan of the mind would be revealed.

Some social psychologists, interested in cognitive processes, have sought this silicon chip in the schemata which the mind is said to possess for the processing of information. The mind needs procedures and rules in order to organize the stimuli which are forever bombarding the sense organs. These schemata not only enable the person to make sense of the physical world, but provide the rules for directing actions and thoughts in the social world. Thus, in general, schemata 'tell the perceiver what to look for' (Taylor and Crocker, 1981: 90). Because people so often find what they look for, the schemata tend to ensure that people notice and receive information which confirms their original schematic assumptions (Bruner, 1957; Greenwald, 1980; Snyder, 1981). For example, those people who possess the schema that black people are aggressive are forever coming up with evidence to support their *idée fixe*, and seem unable to notice any information which might disturb their belief (Duncan, 1976). In this way, the schematic processing of information can aid the motivation to avoid inconsistency.

It cannot be denied that people have assumptions and that they frequently allow their thoughts to be directed by unthinking prejudices. However, what is at issue is whether the schematic or balance theories of social psychology overlook the dilemmatic aspects of thinking and whether, in so doing, they promote a different image of the thinker from that suggested here. The balance theories suggest that people will avoid thinking, for internal disharmony is uncomfortable, and all inner pressures are operating in the direction of producing a clean, shiny mental system. The schematic theories, when they equate cognition with the schematic processing of information, tend to view thinking as what we do unthinkingly. In this way they tend to demean thinking and overlook the dilemmatic, or deliberative, aspects (Billig, 1985; Edwards and Middleton, 1986, 1987).

By contrast the rhetorical approach does not start by considering individual motivations or individual information processing. It starts from the assumption that knowledge is socially shared and that common sense contains conflicting, indeed dissonant, themes. It is not neatly systematized in a way that permits the individual who has dutifully accepted society's values to generate automatically all necessary thoughts, actions and argumentative discourse. Instead, common sense provides the individual with the seeds for contrary themes, which can conflict dramatically in dilemmatic situations. Because these are seeds, not flowers, all is not fully systematized. Contained within the conflicting general principles are many different possibilities, which may on occasions give rise to argument and debate. Rather than apply their systems unthinkingly, people must also deliberate and argue about which seeds need planting at which times in order to develop into flowers. And when people so deliberate or argue, their thinking has a dilemmatic quality.

Explicit and implicit dilemmatic aspects

It is one thing to outline a general theoretical approach, but it is quite another to say how it might be applied to the study of social phenomena. The preceding discussion only conveys the broad notion that researchers ought to look for the contrary, or dilemmatic, aspects of social beliefs. It recommends the examination of beliefs from a social perspective which does not assume that individuals have systematized their thoughts. Over and above this, it does not tell researchers how they might possibly go about their quest for the dilemmatic aspects of thoughts. This is a matter not merely of recommending a favoured methodology, but also of giving hints about whether all dilemmatic aspects might be equally interesting or whether attention might be more profitably directed in one direction or another. For example, one might concentrate upon the discrepancies between actions and words or between theory and practice, or upon the inconsistencies between expressed ends and chosen means. Although the preceding discussion was phrased in general terms, it did hint that the hunters of the dilemmatic aspects might direct their hawks and hounds towards the conflicting themes within shared social images, beliefs, norms and above all values. There, amongst maxims and familiar bits and pieces of shared everyday knowledge, might lie the main dilemmatic quarry.

Particular interest will be paid to examining how contrary themes of social knowledge are revealed in everyday discourse. This will include analysing the meaning of pieces of discourse in order to interpret themes and counter-themes. This sort of interpretative task will involve what are conventionally called qualitative, rather than quantitative, analyses. In this respect, the analyses will be consistent with the broad outlines of Potter and Wetherell's (1987) recommendation that social psychologists should give especial attention to the study of discourse. However, this preference for the qualitative study of discourse should not be taken to imply that opinion surveys, which involve the administration of standard questionnaires to large samples of respondents, cannot be used to study the dilemmatic aspects of thinking. In fact, surveys can be analysed to reveal broad patterns of attitudinal inconsistency within populations (see for example Nilson, 1981). However, the discovery that people might agree to two questionnaire items, which appear at first sight inconsistent, leads to questions of meaning. One might wish to know how respondents interpret the items, and whether they give a reasoned justification which explains away the seeming inconsistency (see Heath, 1986 for a discussion of survey research and the study of attitudinal consistency).

In order to facilitate the study of the dilemmatic aspects of discourse, a rough distinction can be made between those conflicting themes which are explicitly expressed and those which are implicit (for a more detailed discussion of the theoretical differences between the explicit and the implicit aspects of social attitudes see Billig, 1988b). The distinction between the implicit and the explicit is not presented as being an absolute one, and in the later chapters both implicit and explicit aspects of ideological dilemmas will be analysed. In practice it may be difficult to determine where the explicit ends and the implicit starts. Nevertheless, it may be helpful to make such a distinction, in order to say a few words about the analysis of dilemmatic aspects.

The analysis of explicit dilemmatic aspects
Sometimes people can express quite explicitly their simultaneous adherence to the conflicting themes of common sense. According to *The New Rhetoric* of Perelman and Olbrechts-Tyteca (1971), it is a feature of rhetoric that both sides of an argument may be reasonable. An individual, even in an argumentative situation, may wish to express this rhetorical assumption by simultaneously asserting the reasonableness, or truth, of two rhetorically conflicting elements of social belief. For example, both maxims of an antithetical pair can simultaneously be upheld. Politicians, wishing to appeal to all the values of their audiences, often fill their speeches with this kind of thing: 'On the one hand one cannot gain without venturing, but on the other hand one must look before leaping.' Sometimes, whilst keeping the appearance of two-handed reasonableness, the speaker might wish to carry the weapon of argumentative assault in one or other hand: 'Whilst I fully appreciate that without venture there can be no gain, nevertheless we must be sure to look carefully and not leap into the dark.' Just subtly the edge is given to the latter maxim of the antithetical pair, although the audience may be reassured that the recommendation is only for this particular occasion: at other times, the speaker is suggesting, there may be a recommendation to venture all in a courageous, but not reckless, gesture.

The analyst, examining the dilemmatic aspects of discourse, must pay especial attention to the nuances of the different strategies which might be employed for the equal and unequal expression of conflicting themes (Wetherell, Stiven and Potter, 1987). Of course, the unequal expression can be used in order to ward off potential criticisms. The speaker, who fully appreciates the worth of venturing, will be seeking to avoid being branded as a timorous coward who undervalues boldness: a pledge is being offered for future, and perhaps past, risk-taking (see Billig, 1987, chapters 9 and 10 for a discussion of such rhetorical strategies). The analysis of the discourse of racial and gender inequality will show how these strategies can be employed so that the evocation of one value will ease the expression of the contrasting one. In this sort of analysis, one is essentially laying bare the meanings which are being expressed, and examining the dilemmatic aspects which are explicit in discourse or thought. However, as one probes deeper the negative meaning expressed, one is moving towards uncovering implicit meanings.

The analysis of implicit dilemmatic aspects
In examining the explicitly expressed dilemmatic aspects, the analyst can broadly follow the meanings which the communicator intended to express. However, the implicit meanings can go beyond the overt intentions of the communicator, for they can be contained within the semantic structure of the discourse itself. To bring these implicit meanings to the surface

the analyst faces a greater interpretative or hermeneutic task, for a counter-theme needs to be interpreted within discourse which seems *prima facie* to be arguing straightforwardly for a particular point. If contrary counter-themes can be said to be concealed within discourse, they are not hidden in the way that Freudian theorists believe that certain inconsistent themes are hidden by repression from the conscious mind. The concealment is not a deliberate or even subconscious concealment, but may operate within layers of meaning of language. Discourse which seems to be arguing for one point may contain implicit meanings which could be made explicit to argue for the counter-point. Thus discourse can contain its own negations, and these are part of its implicit, rather than explicit, meaning. The analyst should not be afraid to engage in hermeneutics in order to read these implicit meanings.

The maxim 'Too many cooks spoil the broth' can illustrate how a negative meaning can be contained implicitly within discourse. 'Too many' implies that the maxim is to be used to counter those who might be overdoing a multiplicity of production. In this way the phrase has an argumentative meaning, and can be expected to be used in debate when too many hands are being proposed. As Bacon realized, the maxims contain the seeds of argument: they are not infallible guides to conduct, but in their antithetical pairs they enable us to deliberate about conduct in a way which would not be possible if all we possessed were a single, unopposed and unopposable guide. The maxim 'Too many cooks' is not attacking multiplicity of production as such: many cooks are not taken to spoil the broth, only too many of them. The maxim could have been phrased with the specificity of 'Two's company, but three's a crowd', but significantly it is not. In fact, the maxim can be interpreted as supporting the multiplicity which it appears at first sight to attack: in counselling against the spoiling tendencies of 'too many', it explicitly avoids counselling against 'many'. The omission can be taken as having semantic significance. Implicitly the semantics concede the negative point that the hands of many cooks can lighten the load of producing unspoiled consommés. Thus implicitly it concedes the legitimacy of its old proverbial antithesis.

Chapter 4 will employ the hermeneutic approach to search for the implicit contrary themes within the liberal beliefs of education. In addition to the outward themes of egalitarianism, held both by theorists and also by practising teachers, are themes which contain their own implicit authoritarian meanings, as indeed do the egalitarian themes in the discourse of expertise discussed in chapter 5. The point behind this hermeneutic analysis is not to expose inconsistencies as signs of hypocrisy, or to undermine the intentions of the educationalists. In fact, the charge of hypocrisy is completely misplaced, because the counter-themes are implicit rather than explicit: as such, the person expressing the discourse may not be fully aware of these counter-meanings in the way that an out-and-out hypocrite would be. The purpose is not to undermine but to explore the complexities of meaning. To use an overused phrase, the aim is to explore the dialectic of discourse meanings. The meaning of the discourse of liberal educational philosophy, in its theoretical and everyday forms, is shown to be dialectical: it simultaneously contains its own dominant explicit meanings as well as its counter-meanings or negation. Thus the discourse combines its own thesis and antithesis. Similarly the discourse of 'prejudice' shows a similar dialectic, in that the concept of 'prejudice' is used in discourse to express the very same ideas as it ostensibly appears to contradict. And the discourse of illness presupposes an opposing discourse of health.

The examples reveal a further feature of the subsequent analyses. The dilemmatic aspects, with which we are principally concerned, are those which emerge from contemporary ideology. This is in contrast to most of the examples used earlier in the present chapter. These have referred to general dilemmas of common sense, with some being taken from the common sense of ancient societies. The purpose of these examples has been to illustrate general points of theory. In particular they have been used in support of the theme that the study of dilemmas should not be confined to actual choice-making behaviour. There is a need to recognize the dilemmatic aspects of thought, which are preconditions for any dilemmatic choice and which continue to exist in common sense, even in the absence of actual situations which necessitate the taking of difficult choices. However, the interest in ideological dilemmas means a narrowing of focus to particular dilemmatic themes, rather than dealing with all sorts of dilemmatic thinking. Because of this, it is unsatisfactory to continue talking in a non-specific way about common sense and its dilemmatic aspects. It is necessary to turn from the general discussion of common sense to an examination of the nature of ideology and its role in modern society. Only then will it be possible to analyse how ideology can shape the dilemmatic aspects of contemporary thinking.

3
Dilemmas of Ideology

The existence of dilemmatic thinking may well be universal, in that it is to be found in all social arrangements. Nevertheless, the content of dilemmas will vary from society to society and from epoch to epoch, and it will do so for a simple reason: varying patterns of cultural norms, beliefs and values will give rise to varying patterns of dilemmatic concerns. Modern consumers may not be beset by the problems of heaven and hell which troubled their medieval forebears. Yet each cultural and economic condition produces its own particular dilemmatic arguments. Our interest here is in modern society and its dilemmas. In particular, it is in those dilemmas which involve values and beliefs that could be said to be ideological.

At once this raises the difficult concept of 'ideology'. Most social scientific concepts lack clear and precise definitions which are accepted by all theorists, and the concept of 'ideology' has been particularly troublesome in this respect. Different theorists have used the concept in very different ways, whilst disputing each other's intellectual right to do so; moreover, the same theorists have often found themselves slipping into different meanings as they talk about 'ideology'. As Abercrombie, Hill and Turner (1980: 187) have remarked: 'It is widely agreed that the notion of ''ideology'' has given rise to more analytical and conceptual difficulties than almost any other in the social sciences'. In the same spirit, David McLellan begins his excellent book *Ideology* with the warning to readers that 'Ideology is the most elusive concept in the whole of social science' (1986: 1). (For conceptual and historial discussions of the concept see also Abercrombie, 1980; Larrain, 1979, 1983; Thompson, 1986.)

It is not the present intention to wade through the different definitions of 'ideology', or through the complex theoretical arguments underlying the definitions. Neither will it be the strategy to parade before the reader the various conceptions, stripped down to their skimpiest theoretical swimsuits, in order to award the prize to the most beautiful definition of them all. Instead, there will be a discussion of several issues relating to the values and conceptions of modern society. These issues relate centrally to what theorists have broadly identified as 'ideological issues'. In order to simplify the discussion, it might be helpful to identify two key themes of the discussion: the first concerns the links between formal ideological systems and informal common sense, and the second relates to the dilemmatic nature of modern common sense.

It will be assumed that the great political and philosophical systems of the modern world are not just the property of professional theoreticians.

Marx may have been a Hegelian philosopher by training, and he may have been a solitary figure in the British Museum as he wrote his unreadably complex manuscripts, but his effect upon the thought patterns of the twentieth century has been incalculable. However, our main emphasis is not upon the traditions of Marxism, but upon those of the liberal philosophy of the Enlightenment, in order to see how the concepts of the intellectual ideologists have become represented in modern everyday consciousness. Particular attention will be directed towards the notion of 'individualism', which is sometimes thought to characterize the values and philosophy of the capitalist world. Later chapters will observe how the great ideas of individualism have been transformed into everyday concepts, which possess dilemmatic qualities.

In examining this transformation from formal philosophy to everyday thinking, the analysis will be investigating similar sorts of problems to those which Serge Moscovici has identified as being central to social psychology (Moscovici, 1981, 1984a, 1984b). One important part of Moscovici's project is to investigate how the concepts of science have become represented into common sense. He himself has studied in detail the mass diffusion of psychoanalytic ideas in everyday thinking (Moscovici, 1976). It is part of his argument that modern common sense has become so dominated by socially shared representations of abstract scientific concepts that it is qualitatively different from the common sense of traditional societies.

Although Moscovici's theories of social representations concentrate upon the passage of concepts from scientific discourse to lay discourse, similar transformations can be observed with philosophy: notions can be observed to pass from formal ideological theories into the lived ideology of ordinary life. It can be expected that this passage will transform the concepts, just as scientific notions are altered in their social representation in everyday discourse. A further point needs to be made. The passage need not be unidirectional, going from intellectual discourse to mass discourse. The reverse journey is also made, as intellectuals take up the concepts of everyday life and embellish them in their theorizing. This can be observed in a number of modern intellectual activities. Perhaps most dramatically it occurred when theorists of race claimed to be using scientific procedures to confirm widespread notions about racial differences of superiority and inferiority (Billig, 1981). However, in the present work the emphasis is not upon the commonsensical origin of intellectual notions, which can be returned in a transformed state back to common sense and thereby be further transformed. Nevertheless one point must be stressed. The emphases of the present work should not be interpreted as implying that the process by which commonsensical ideas become transformed into intellectual theory is any less socially important than the reverse process. A more complete and ambitious work than the present might care to examine both passages of ideas in relation to each other.

A study of the way that intellectual ideology is transformed into everyday ideology need not of itself recognize the importance of the dilemmatic aspects of thinking. In fact, many of the conventional images of ideology assume that ideological thinking is non-dilemmatic. They tend to treat ideological systems as integrated systems of thinking, or, to use a current psychological term, as schemata *par excellence*. Therefore the passage from intellectual ideology to everyday ideology is often assumed to be one in which an elitely constructed consistency is imposed upon mass thinking, with the result that ideological consistency becomes socially diffused. Our approach, with its emphasis upon the dilemmatic aspects, questions this image, for it focuses upon the contrary elements of thinking.

As will be discussed below, these contrary elements can arise from different sources. They could be represented by the contradiction between possessing a theoretical ideology and at the same time living within a society whose everyday life seems to negate that ideology. Examples of this will be given, but these illustrations will not carry the main burden of the argument, which is to portray the contrary themes within ideology itself. In particular, it will be suggested that the liberal traditions of modern capitalist society contain their own contrary themes or unresolved theoretical tensions. Within the ideology of liberalism is a dialectic, which contains negative counter-themes and which gives rise to debates. These debates are not confined to the level of intellectual analysis; both themes and counter-themes have arisen from, and passed into, everyday consciousness. And, of course, this everyday consciousness provides the material for further intellectual debate.

In analysing the ideological representation of dilemmas in modern consciousness, we are not viewing individual thinkers as blindly following the dictates of ideological schemata. We see them thinking, but within the constraints of ideology and with the elements of ideology. Thus ideologies in everyday life should not be equated with the concealment, or prevention, of thought. Also, in a real sense ideologies shape what people actually do think about, and permit the possibility of thought.

Lived and intellectual ideology

In order to sustain the argument outlined in the preceding section, it is necessary to make a distinction between two meanings of ideology. There is first of all 'lived ideology', which refers to ideology as a society's way of life. This sort of ideology includes what passes for common sense within a society. On the other hand there is 'intellectual ideology', which is a system of political, religious or philosophical thinking and, as such, is very much the product of intellectuals or professional thinkers. There are, of course, some theorists who claim that the lived ideology constitutes the essence of the concept of 'ideology', whilst others says that the intellectual ideology is the prototypical example. For present purposes it is unnecessary to take sides in that dispute, but it is necessary to distinguish the sorts of phenomena which are denoted by these rival interpretations of the concept.

Lived ideology

The notion of an ideology as representing a society's way of life is to be found in Karl Mannheim's influential *Ideology and Utopia*. Mannheim characterized an ideology in the following way: 'Here we refer to the ideology of an age or of a concrete historico-social group, e.g. of a class, when we are concerned with the characteristics and composition of the total structure of the mind of this epoch or of this group' (1960: 49–50). Beliefs, values, cultural practices and so on are crucial components of the total mental structure. This conception comes close to equating the ideology of a society or epoch with its culture. Thompson has drawn attention to the similarity between this interpretation of ideology and the notion of culture. He writes that 'The broadest and most inclusive definition of ideology is one which makes it almost coterminous with culture' (1986: 66). He adds that investigators of ideology are typically interested in the relations between social beliefs and the operation of power in society, in a way that investigators of culture frequently are not. Despite this difference of emphasis, the concepts of culture and lived ideology are similar because both seek to describe the social patterning of everyday thinking. It might be said that ordinary people living in a particular society partake of the general cultural patterns of that society, and their thinking is shaped by these patterns. The word 'culture' could easily be substituted by 'ideology' in the previous sentence and the essence of Mannheim's conception would still be preserved.

Intellectual ideology

The notion of a lived ideology is very different from a view of ideology as an intellectual system of ideas. Here we are talking about ideology not as the everyday way of thinking of a particular group, but as a formalized philosophy. The French sociologist, Raymond Aron, used the term in this sense when he wrote that 'An ideology presupposes an apparently systematic formalization of facts, interpretations, desires and predictions' (1977: 309). According to this conception, the ideology of liberalism is not represented by the maxims, casual beliefs and informal values expressed by those who might be contemplating voting for a liberal party at a general election. It will be expressed by the great theorists of liberal philosophy such as Voltaire, Locke and Adam Smith: in other words, by those who have attempted to construct the ideas of liberalism into a systematic philosophy.

The distinction between lived and intellectual ideology is the difference between a formalized and a non-formalized consciousness. Lane made a similar distinction in his examination of the political consciousness of the American working man, when he talked of 'forensic' and 'latent' ideologies. Lane suggested that it was necessary to 'distinguish between the "forensic" ideologies of the conscious ideologist and the "latent" ideologies of the common man' (1960: 16). The ordinary working men of his study might not have possessed a formal system of political thinking, but nevertheless they partook of the political and cultural values, or latent ideology, of their society. Perhaps one of the most famous distinctions between lived and intellectual ideology is to be found in Lenin's essay 'What is to be done?' Lenin called upon middle-class intellectuals to develop the ideology of Marxism. He claimed that the working class would be unequal to the task. Workers only possessed a 'trade-union consciousness' and, as a result, they lacked the philosophical insight to construct a genuinely radical ideology. In other words, the working class could not transcend its lived ideology to produce the intellectual ideology, which would eventually transform the lived ideology.

The distinction between the two forms of ideology is crucial for posing the question whether the ideas of intellectual ideology can travel beyond the mythical ivy-covered walls of theory in order to enter into the hustle and bustle of ordinary life. Moscovici's theory of social representations rests upon a similar distinction between the ideas of science, formulated by an intellectual minority, and the more general common sense, into which the social representations of scientific concepts are translated. It will be suggested later than many of the grand notions of liberal philosophy have become transformed into everyday thinking. However, the present analysis is not intended merely to document the passage from intellectual to lived ideology. It is also intended to provide a social psychological commentary on the nature of ideology. This is possible because the present conception of ideology, whether lived or intellectual, departs from that of many theorists. The difference resides, above all, in the images of the thinker, or bearer of ideology, to emerge from those views which stress the dilemmatic aspects of ideology, as against those which assume the basic internal consistency of ideology.

According to most conceptions, ideology is seen as some sort of mould which patterns the thoughts of its bearers. Ideology is often seen to provide an internally consistent pattern, so that the thoughts, beliefs, values and so on fit together into the total mental structure. There is a similarity between this conception of ideology and the psychological notion of cognitive schemata, through which incoming stimuli are filtered. Accordingly, ideology is conceived to be some sort of giant, socially shared schema, through which the world is experienced. In the last chapter the ideas of the schema theorists in social psychology were criticized because they underestimated the importance of deliberative, or dilemmatic, thinking. So analogous criticisms can be applied to the respective notions of ideology – lived and intellectual – which suggest that the individual thinker is essentially an unthinking bearer of a present programme for thinking.

The assumption of internal consistency is most apparent in the notion of intellectual ideology. Aron's (1977) depiction of ideology suggests that the ideologist possesses some sort of grand theory, from which all manner of attitudinal positions and stances can be systematically derived. It is rather like a mathematical theory, which permits a wide number of propositions to be derived from a few axioms which are free from dilemmatic inconsistency. If the Marxist ideologist wants to know what stance to take on the latest world event, the basic themes of dialectical materialism must be computed to provide an answer. It is unthinkable to the ideologist that the all-encompassing ideology will have nothing to say on the matter (for descriptions of the way that ideologists use the ideology of Marxism to formulate such stances, see Almond, 1954; Newton, 1969). In this way the bearer of the ideology will appear to have an answer to all major questions. Critics of such ideological thinking often depict the bearer of ideology as an unthinking bigot, and such criticisms are expressed in social psychological theories of authoritarianism or dogmatism (Adorno et al., 1950; Rokeach, 1960; Altemeyer, 1981). These theories suggest that the bearer of intellectual ideologies has a closed mind, for all has been settled psychologically in advance. All contradictions are dismissed, or are explained away by the ideology. The cost of this consistency is a high degree of unreality and a brittle personality, which cannot abide ambiguity. Although this psychological characterization is undoubtedly an exaggeration (Billig, 1985), it does reinforce the image that an intellectual ideology provides the ideologist with an internally consistent system.

In the same way, the lived ideology is frequently depicted as possessing some sort of inner consistency. This notion can be traced back to Marx and Engels's (1970) discussion of ideology in *The German Ideology*. There they suggested that the dominant ideas of an epoch, and in particular the dominant ideas of capitalism, tend to depict society as a coherent whole. Contradictions are concealed by ideology. From this it is a short step to suggesting that those who live within an ideology possess thoughts, actions and values which form some sort of internally consistent pattern. This internal consistency hides from consciousness any notions which might contradict the ideological view. According to Mannheim, the mental structure of each epoch contained an 'inner unity' (1953: 76). Mannheim also suggested that each ideology can only provide a partial view of reality. It blots out views which may be discrepant to its inner unity, just as schema theorists, describing information processing at the level of the individual, suggest that schemata systematically distort the views of the individual.

The image of the thinker living within ideology is not a more flattering one than that provided by schema theorists in psychology. The image depicts a person whose mental structure is systematically biased and who helplessly, and unseeingly, conforms to the dictates of this structure. Such an image is apparent, for example, in the writings of Louis Althusser on ideology. It is a central part of Althusser's thesis that modern society does not command the acquiescence of its members by physical force alone. Modern capitalism has it ideological state apparatuses, which ensure that the members of the state pick up and abide by the socially correct values and beliefs. Althusser's images of the ideologically influenced citizenry suggest obedient and unthinking conformity. For example, in one of his most important discussions of ideology, Althusser illustrates his arguments by considering the religious believer as the bearer of the state's ideology. The religious person has not only a set of doctrinal beliefs, but also a set of associated behaviours: 'If he believes in God, he goes to Church to attend Mass, kneels, prays, confesses, does penance...and naturally repents and so on.' The citizen who has absorbed the socially approved ideology will 'have the corresponding attitudes, inscribed in ritual practices "according to the correct principles"' (Althusser, 1971: 167).

Althusser's believer is an obedient citizen, who is following prescribed rules of behaviour. In this respect the religious believer resembles the information processor, whose mind is continually following the cognitive rules of the schema. It is significant that one of the major theoretical examinations of schema theory, that of Schank and Abelson (1977), possesses an extended example to show how the ordinary person must follow social rules and must possess an internal schema if a meal is to be purchased, eaten and paid for in a restaurant. Both Althusser's citizen obeying the rules of ideology, and Schank and Abelson's hypothetical schema follower, are obediently engaging in social rituals in going to church or the restaurant. Both are unthinkingly following predetermined norms. There is a further parallel, in that the neither the ideology follower nor the schema follower are presumed to have an undistorted view of reality. Schema theorists assume that schemas simplify and thereby distort social reality (Billig, 1985). So also Althusser depicts his church-goer as unthinkingly accepting the unrealistically consistent consciousness which is provided by the ideological state apparatus (Gane, 1983).

The dilemmatic approach, by contrast, does not start with the assumption that there is an 'inner unity' to schemata or ideologies. By assuming that there are contrary themes, a different image of the thinker can emerge. The person is not necessarily pushed into an unthinking obedience, in which conformity to ritual has replaced deliberation. Ideology may produce such conformity, but it can also provide the dilemmatic elements which enable deliberation to occur. The person living within ideology need not be seen merely as a follower of rules or as a well-programmed machine. However, to uncover the dilemmatic aspects of ideology, it is necessary to look for the contrary themes of lived ideology. This means rejecting any assumption that the relations between lived and intellectual ideology are in any sense simple. It should not be assumed that the consistencies of theory are somehow imposed upon the schemata of everyday life, so that everyday life is a social representation of the consistent intellectual ideology, albeit in a baser, more conventional and essentially unthinking form. Instead it is necessary to consider the contradictory themes both between and within lived and intellectual ideology.

Conflicts between lived and intellectual ideologies

The very distinction between lived and intellectual ideology suggests one obvious source of an ideological dilemma. Ideologues and social theorists may face particular dilemmas because they simultaneously possess both sorts of ideology. Their thinking embraces both the great theory, constructed in the calm of the study and realized in its systematic completeness on paper, and the everyday beliefs which enable the theorists to go about the normal business of society. For instance, a revolutionary idealist might hold grand notions about how society should operate. These idealistic visions of the future will also be criticisms of the present state of society. Yet this idealist may have to conduct everyday activities and, in fact, may be quite well adjusted to many of the society's practices. Sometimes the head of the lived ideology and the heart of the utopian ideology may pull in different directions. And at all times, the possibility of dilemmas may be present.

Marx and Engels provide examples of intellectuals whose theories seem at odds with the details of their everyday lives. These great critics of bourgeois society lived eminently bourgeois lives themselves. Engels was a businessman and, in fact, was quite a good one. He was constantly offering financial advice to his less fortunate friend. Although reduced to straitened circumstances, the Marx family maintained a respectable domesticity. *The Communist Manifesto* may have sneered at the conventional family and its morality, but Karl Marx was always the concerned father and husband. Of course there was that business with the family maid, but thankfully with the help of kind Engels it was hushed up without a nasty scandal. Nor are such contradictions confined to the radical left. Today, there are right-wing theorists who wish to transform society into the utopia of Adam Smith's imagination. They hope to reduce the state's role to the absolute minimum, yet they formulate their theories from their offices in state-funded universities or from homes purchased with financial assistance from the state.

One further example will illustrate the tensions between the demands of intellectual theory and those of everyday life. David Hume's philosophy represented an exposition of radical scepticism, but his personal leanings were to genial conviviality. In the conclusion to the first book of *A Treatise of Human Nature* he described the dilemma of being a cold theorist with a warm inclination. He knew his scepticism, which doubted causality and religion, was out of sorts with the prevailing mood: 'I foresee on every side dispute, contradiction, anger, calumny and detraction. . .all the world conspires to oppose and contradict me' (1964, vol. I: 250). Not only were his philosophical ideas creating enemies, but also they were directly cutting him off from the life he wished to lead. He wrote about the 'philosophical melancholy' which attends intense philosophical doubt. Luckily, nature provides its own cure for such melancholy. The mind relaxes itself, and 'I dine, I play a game of backgammon, I converse, and am merry with my friends; and when, after three or four hours' amusement, I would return to these speculations, they appear so cold, and strained, and ridiculous, that I cannot find in my heart to enter them further' (p. 254). Despite the pleasant backgammon games, Hume recognized there still remained a conflict between his 'natural propensity' for philosophical reasoning and the 'animal spirits and passions' which drove him to an 'indolent belief in the general maxims of the world' (p. 254).

Whether or not Hume's philosophy could be called an ideology, he was describing in vivid form a conflict between intellectual ideas and the lived world. In Hume's case the conflict is presented as a dilemma in which a choice is to be made: he has to decide whether to sit at the study desk or the backgammon table. However, the problem is not merely one of a choice of which room to enter or which piece of furniture to sit upon. There are also the contrary elements of Hume's thinking, which can culminate in the painful choice each evening between serious solitude and cheerful company, but which possess wider dilemmatic quality. Hume's rationalism and his conservative respect for tradition were mingled, so that part of him could cling fiercely to the value of intellectual inquiry, whilst the other part urged him to reject the whole business of philosophy as ridiculous. Had his outlook been wholly rationalist, or had it been wholly based upon respect for traditional custom and the general maxims of the world, the nightly dilemma might not have arisen with such force. Nor might Hume have included in an overtly rationalist work of philosophy a passage which seems to mock the whole pretensions of sceptical philosophy in favour of the superior good sense of ordinary life.

Hume's image of the lived world was a social one: it was a world where people met and basically got on with one another. Like the ideological world described by Althusser, it is a world of unreflective routines, although for Hume, but not for Althusser, it is a world of good sense. In playing backgammon, probably with a glass in hand by a roaring fire, one is following the same sort of cognitive script which enables the customer to have a pleasant trip to a restaurant and which permitted the Marx family to enjoy their walks on Hampstead Heath. It is a script to be followed, rather than thought about. This image portrays ordinary life as being essentially undilemmatic. All would have been peace and backgammon had not Hume had his unfortunate propensity for melancholy philosophy. He would have been a happy, untroubled man following the scripts and maxims of everyday life.

In this image there is a clear disjunction between the thoughts of the theorist and the unthinking routines of everyday life. Dilemmas are not seen as properties of everyday living, but originate from thinking which is somehow external to ordinary life, or more precisely from the clash between the contemplative and the non-contemplative life. Yet this is a simplification. Ordinary life is not so routinely organized that it does not possess its dilemmas and more generally its dilemmatic qualities of thinking. Moreover, these dilemmas and dilemmatic thoughts are not untouched by the thinking of the theorist. Many of the great themes of ideology and philosophy have entered into the consciousness of epochs, thereby ensuring that the lived ideology has its own dilemmatic elements.

Individualism and its limitations

Dilemmas may arise from the possession of the two different ideologies: a lived ideology that adjusts one to mundane life, and an intellectual ideology that seeks to overturn everyday reality. However, ideological dilemmas may also arise within ideologies. The person who possesses only a lived ideology, or perhaps has an intellectual ideology which justifies present conditions, does not necessarily escape from ideological dilemmas to sit by the fireside. In outlining how dilemmas can arise within an ideology we shall be taking issue with the assumption, or at least with a simple interpretation of the assumption, that ideologies as mental structures possess an inner unity. This assumption suggests that an ideology, although it might contain a variety of beliefs, norms, representations and so on, will be based around a dominant theme or value. As regards modern capitalist society, a number of theorists have claimed that the dominating principle is that of 'individualism'. This assumption will be outlined, and then criticized because of its underestimation of the dilemmatic aspects of ideology.

The equation of individualism with capitalist ideology is meant to highlight the link between intellectual and lived ideology. Here, it might be thought, is the principle which dominated the liberal philosophy of the Enlightenment, and now is represented in the thinking of modern mass publics and their tendency to vote for politicians who praise the value of individual achievement. Abercrombie, who criticizes those who identify individualism as the ideology of capitalism, offers a useful definition of individualism: it is a 'set of social theories whose distinguishing feature is the insistence on the social priority of the individual *vis-à-vis* the State, the established Church, social classes...or other social groups' (1980: 56). The identification of this set of beliefs with capitalist ideology can be found in the writings of the Marxist critic Georg Lukacs. In *History and Class Consciousness* Lukacs referred to the 'individual' principle of bourgeois society. This principle dominated the economic, cultural, political and philosophical life of bourgeois society, and would, claimed Lukacs, be swept aside by the 'social' principle of the proletarian society.

Another example of the identification of individualism with the ideology of modern capitalism is provided by the social psychologist Edward Sampson. In a perceptive critique of individualist assumptions in psychological theory, Sampson suggests that 'a predominant theme that describes our cultural ethos is *self-contained individualism.*' Sampson characterizes this ethos as emphasizing 'individuality, in particular a kind of self-sufficiency that describes an extreme of the individualistic dimension' (1977: 769). Sampson points to the development of modern psychology as expressing and justifying this culture of self-contained individualism. Modern psychologists, he argues, take the goal of individual adjustment as their psychological ideal and, in consequence, they reinforce values derived from the individualist culture of which they themselves are a part.

There is no denying that the values of individual rights are strongly held in modern capitalist, democratic societies. No serious politician in the United States or Britain or France would declare him or herself to be opposed to individual freedom. Nor would any march behind a banner which proclaimed 'Down with individual rights.' Yet this does not mean that a value for individual freedom has itself an unopposed freedom in the modern world. In the previous chapter, it was argued that the maxims of common sense find themselves held in check by their antithetical rivals. Similarly, the noble themes of individualism, it will be suggested, find themselves opposed in modern ideology by counter-values that are just as high-minded. If the maxim of 'Too many cooks' curtailed the dangerously extremist tendencies of an unchecked 'Many hands make light work', so the philosophy of individualism needs its strictures against selfishness and lack of social responsibility. And who, likewise, would unashamedly declare themself in favour of 'selfish, social irresponsibility'?

It is not difficult to see why there might be a requirement for counter-values to the obvious values of individualism. The great values of the French Revolution can be taken in illustration. Freedom, equality and fraternity sound undeniably desirable to the modern ear (except for the masculinity evoked by the third term of the triad). When faced by absolutism, these values could be proclaimed with an unlimited enthusiasm, which suggested that all three would be perfectly attainable in reality once the crown had been removed from the tyrannical head. But once the crown, and indeed the head itself, had been removed, then not merely could values be proclaimed; dilemmas had also to be faced. Limitations to the great principles needed to be established, and these limitations, of course, needed to be just as principled as the principles which they limited.

If liberty were to be individual freedom, then it was necessary to establish why the individual should show loyalty to the state and social responsibility to fellow individuals. Liberty would result in anarchy lest some form of authority could be established. Nor should it be forgotten that the modern capitalist era may have freed individuals from feudal restrictions, but it has also seen the emergence of the state in its most powerful form.

In theory, equality may be the value of the modern democracy: all are theoretically equal in the eyes of the law and in the privacy of the ballot box. However, equality cannot get out of hand in a society whose commercial and cultural life seems to be so devoted to proving the productive reality of inequality. Every day there is evidence of success and failure: some businesses are proved to be more successful than others, some popular songs are greater hits than other less fortunate recordings, some football teams win more matches than their rivals, and some children pass more examinations. If there is equality in this cultural climate, it is not a straightforward equality; it is an equality which allows the successful to be more equal than the rest.

As for fraternity, this too needs its qualification. The message of individual freedom and equality seems to be a universal message. The rationality of the Enlightenment *philosophes* was a universal rationality, which knew no national boundaries. The value of freedom was not to stop at the foothills of the Pyrenees, nor was it presumed to get fatally seasick if crossed the Channel. The *philosophes* talked grandly of the rights of man, meaning all men regardless of nationality (but perhaps not regardless of gender). In this vision, national boundaries would collapse as all joined together to submit freely and individually to the universal authority of reason. Yet the world of individualism has not been a world which has seen the crumbling of nationality. Far from it; the governmental states, which have grown so powerful in the past two hundred years, have been national states demanding national allegiance from their freely individual and politically equal members. The fraternity cannot be universal when it is the fraternity of the fatherland or the mother country.

All this suggests that the major themes of individualism need to be considered in relation to their counter-themes. Nor should the dialectic between themes and counter-themes be interpreted as a conflict between philosophically derived notions and those existing in an older, pre-philosophical common sense. The major themes of the Enlightenment did not meet counter-themes because they confronted maxims of common sense, which warned in a traditional manner against the evils of selfishness or a failure to respect one's elders and betters. It is within the ideological traditions of liberalism itself that the counter-themes can be detected. As will be shown in later chapters, these themes and counter-themes are not confined to the printed volumes of the great thinkers, but are reproduced in everyday thinking in a way which gives it a dilemmatic quality.

Individualism and counter-themes

The obvious way to examine counter-themes in philosophy is by detailed exegesis. The work of an individual philosopher could be examined to show how dilemmas, which the thinker had believed to be successfully resolved, still continue to nag away. For example, one might take a liberal philosopher who attempted to square individual liberty with the responsiblity of the state, in order to demonstrate the underlying tension in the arguments. This would be a philosophical task. It is, of course, one that has been done many times, especially in relation to a thinker like Rousseau who, faced with the political reality of absolutism, could propound that the true freedom of the individual would be a socially conscious freedom. The ambiguities would become apparent once the Jacobins attempted to put this doctrine into practice with the aid of Monsieur Guillotin's invention. Later analysts can then examine the philosophical texts to point out the themes and counter-themes, which can be used both to criticize and to justify political authority. Chapter 5 will give a brief example of a continuing ideological dilemma in the writings of Durkheim: egalitarian and authoritarian themes continue to jostle dilemmatically despite Durkheim's claim to have effected an intellectual solution (Gane, 1988: 8–11).

Another way to demonstrate counter-themes is less philosophical and more social scientific. This is to set philosophy in its social and argumentative context. It can be assumed that the meaning of argumentative discourse must be understood in terms of its argumentative context: what is being justified by argument takes its sense from what is being criticized (Billig, 1987: chapter 4; 1988a, 1988b). Philosophy is above all argumentative discourse, and even the most self-contained of philosophical systems takes meaning from the fact that it is an argument against other possible philosophies. That being so, it is possible that a philosophy's counter-themes can be contained within its argumentative context. For example, the philosophy may take for granted values which *prima facie* seem to be attacked because it assumes that no one would seriously attack such values. Or it may leave opponents in debate to voice the counter-themes, tacitly assuming the reasonableness of the opponents whilst a particular point is pushed to its logical, or rather its rhetorical, conclusion.

Examples of both forms of philosophical counter-themes within liberalism can be briefly given. Geoffrey Hawthorn, in his book *Enlightenment and Despair*, discusses the differences between English and German individualism in the early nineteenth century. Unlike its German counterpart, English individualism seemed to be the more thoroughgoing, in that it was focused primarily upon individuals and their freedom to pursue their own ends. German individualism, by contrast, appeared to be more concerned with discussing the rights of the individual in relation to the rights of the state. Hawthorn argues that this difference must be understood in relation to the social context. If one just examines the philosophies in themselves, one might conclude that the English utilitarians were the more anti-statist. In fact, England possessed a comparatively secure political authority, which none of the English theorists would have dreamt of questioning. As Hawthorn said of Mill, he 'took his society for granted in a way that Continental intellectuals did not' (1987: 88). By contrast Germany, divided and weak, possessed no central political authority, and themes of authority, which the English could take for granted and therefore ignore, were uppermost in German writings. Therefore, to understand the ideological significance of the texts, it is necessary to go beyond the texts themselves.

The argumentative context can be all-important for examining ideological counter-themes. A philosophical treatise, which pushes a single principle as far as it can be pushed, may achieve great contemporary prominence, and so may be thought to express 'the spirit of the age'. However, the treatise may only represent one side of an argument. Moreover, the other side, which might be expressed with equal philosophical one-sidedness, may come from the same cultural or ideological tradition. Thus the 'spirit of the age' may be more accurately represented by the debate between the two adversaries rather by either party individually. For example, Edward Sampson has already been cited as suggesting that the individualism of psychology expresses the dominant ethos of capitalist culture. However, one should not forget the debates between psychologists and sociologists, and that the cultural tradition which has produced modern individualist psychology has also produced sociology. In fact, psychologists and sociologists may snipe at each other from across the corridors of the same educational institution, receiving their salary cheques from precisely the same source. In consequence, it seems an oversimplification to equate psychology with the dominant ethos, rather than to suggest that the dominant ethos is characterized by dilemmas about the role of the individual and the society.

A philosophical example can be given of the argumentative context of individualism. Theorists of individualism, like all philosophers, were engaged in debate, and their opponents were not necessarily representatives of opposing political ideologies. Some debates were debates between ideologies, but by no means all. When Marx attacked Mill, this was a debate between ideologies, as Marx explicitly wished to overthrow the society which Mill took for granted. However, when Walter Bagehot wrote *The English Constitution* as an indirect critique of Mill, it was to defend the society of which they were both notable parts. Bagehot's arguments, about the need of the state to seduce the hearts and minds of the masses, may have a passing resemblance to some of Marx and Engels's notions about the function of ideology, but there is no ideological resemblance. Bagehot fully approved of the constitution possessing its 'dignified part', to win the allegiance of the ill-educated and badly paid. His criticism of Mill was that, in constructing a philosophy and indeed a psychology based upon principles of individual interest, the great philosopher had forgotten social motives, which act as a conservative force for preserving tradition. Without taking into account these social motives, suggested Bagehot, one could not understand why the English have still clung to the symbols of monarchy whilst accepting a constitution whose effective aspects are in reality republican. The point is that the opposition between Mill and Bagehot was an opposition within an ideology, for politically they concurred more than they differed. Neither the abstract individualism of Mill nor the social conservatism of Bagehot can be taken as expressing 'the ideological spirit'. However, the debate between the two may catch better than does either singly an ideology which has not destroyed civil authority in favour of individual freedom, but which sets continual dilemmas regarding the competing claims of individual freedom and social authority.

It is not only in the debates between theorists that themes and counterthemes can be observed. They can also be clearly visible when theorists, not quite of the first rank, attempt the grand systematization to include all aspects of human knowledge. Unoriginal philosophers, lacking the innovatory obsession to develop a single theme, may attempt to synthesize all that there is. They may claim to resolve all contradictions in their systematizations, only to succeed in laying bare the terms of the contradictions, thereby revealing the dilemmatic quality of their own thinking. A good example is provided by the work of Destutt de Tracy, the Enlightenment *philosophe* who bequeathed to posterity the very word 'ideology'. De Tracy's *Élémens d'idéologie* was intended to provide the summation of all philosophical knowledge in a textbook to be used as the basis for advanced education in post-revolutionary France. Despite de Tracy's hopes, it is not difficult for the modern reader to detect contradictory themes within a work which proudly called itself 'ideology'.

Destutt de Tracy, like most Enlightenment *philosophes*, was an avowed champion of liberty. He declared in *Élémens* that the object of all intellectual inquiry was to satisfy the passion for liberty (vol. IV, p. 41). Volume V dealt with physiological knowledge, and in this volume the philosophical champion of human freedom became the materialist sceptic. De Tracy argued that all human thinking could be reduced to physiological movements which obeyed the physical laws of necessity. Human movements were just as obedient to these laws as any animal movements. Even the feeling of freedom was no more than a chimera, 'a sham liberty', produced by underlying changes in physiology (vol. V, p. 378). A more rigorous thinker than de Tracy might have attempted to reconcile these themes, subverting one to another. However, de Tracy, oblivious to contradiction, assumed that all elements of his rational ideology were equally true. In this, he reminds us that the French Enlightenment produced Voltaire and

La Mettrie, and that, at one and the same time, notions of individual freedom and the lack of freedom were being produced.

Nor was the contradiction between human freedom and physiological necessity the only contradiction in *Élémens*. De Tracy declared the essential equality of man, only to suggest that not all are created biologically equal: only some intelligences could be entrusted with the vote and be permitted to study 'ideology' to an advanced level. The others, unable to exercise freedom, needed to be directed by rational authority. Similarly, de Tracy described the basis of social life as the free exchange of goods between individuals. Yet at other stages he recognized the social divisions between the rich and the poor, suggesting that these divisions ensured that the poor, under the necessity of their poverty, were unable to bargain freely with the rich. As such, he was advocating a doctrine of free individual exchange whilst sympathizing with the unfree, who could only act under the compulsion of the cruel necessities of poverty. Freedom and necessity, equality and inequality, individualism and fraternity were limiting each other in this semantically original, but philosophically unoriginal, ideology (see Billig, 1982 for further details of the ideological contradictions of the French ideologists; see also Kennedy, 1978 and Head, 1985). And if these themes and counter-themes still seem to be grandly universal, upholding the global rationalism of the Enlightenment, the context should be remembered: the whole textbook was designed for a rigidly controlled curriculum of education within one country. For a time de Tracy himself was proud to serve the state in the Ministry of Education to oversee the creation of the national curriculum. In this way, the project of 'ideology' in its very existence took for granted the national state and its political authority.

These examples suggest that the ideological heritage is not a simple one. The intellectual ideology may not donate a series of solved problems to common sense. Instead, it may provide the conflicting themes of theoretical dilemmas to common sense, where dilemmas can be re-created and experienced in practical terms. Just as antithetical maxims represent the contrary themes of common sense, so ideology may be characterized by its dilemmatic qualities, which ensure that those living within the ideology cannot escape from the difficulties of dilemmas. The contrary themes of intellectual ideology can be represented in lived ideology, where, of course, they may be attached to the antithetical themes of older common sense. Murray Edelman (1977), in his analysis of the way that poverty is talked about today, suggests that the modern person possesses two contrary myths about poverty. On the one hand people share the myth that the poor are to blame for their own plight: themes of drunkenness, laziness and weakness of individual character figure largely in this mythology. It is a myth which concentrates upon the essential justice of the world (Lerner, 1977). If this myth is an individualist one, it is not the only myth used to describe poverty. There is another social myth, which expresses sympathy with the poor as helpless victims of an unjust society.

Survey analysis confirms that attitudes towards poverty and inequality are complex. Very few people believe that the world is just in a simple sense (Verba and Orren, 1986). Instead there is a tension in the discourse about poverty and equality between blame and sympathy (for example Furnham, 1982; Furnham and Lewis, 1986; Nilson, 1981). Contrary values are asserted, as the same people believe that the state should aid the poor and also that state aid is liable to undermine the moral worth of the poor (Golding and Middleton, 1982; Taylor-Gooby, 1983, 1985). These reactions might be thought to be a modern representation of the age-old dilemma between justice and mercy. Classical orators recognized in their controversies that there is much to be said on both sides of the dilemma: on the one hand it is good to show mercy, but on the other hand too much mercy will undermine justice. In the same way, the evidence from opinion surveys suggests that the modern public finds a similar simultaneous reasonableness in justice and mercy, believing that one must be merciful towards the poor, but on the other hand that too much mercy (in the shape of large welfare payments) will be unjust.

The point is not that the modern dilemmas and the modern discourse of dilemma can be seen to be a continuation of a much older dilemma. No doubt, in talking of poverty, people can bring to mind maxims and proverbs formulated long before the creation of the modern welfare state ('God helps those who help themselves'; 'Giving to the poor increases a man's store'). However, the modern form of the dilemma has been crucially shaped by ideology. The philosophy of individualism has not resolved the dilemma by vanquishing social mercy in the name of individual justice; instead, new force and discourse has been added to both of the dilemmatic horns. Therefore, in today's ordinary discourse one might expect to find the representation of Enlightenment philosophy in its dilemmatic, rather than systematized, aspect.

This representation can occur regardless of whether people are aware of the ideological traditions in which they are living. The traditions can even be structured semantically in the vocabulary used in everyday discourse. Today one might hear somebody justifying a decision to jettison family responsibilities with the words that they wish to 'maximize their chances of personal fulfilment'. Perhaps such a person envisages that their action is likely to attract criticism. Maybe they have already rehearsed the criticisms in their own internal deliberations, and have succeeded in dismissing the criticisms as being old-fashioned, even Victorian. Our deliberator and potential personal fulfiller may not be aware just how much their own justification seems to express the nineteenth-century philosophy of Benthamite utilitarianism. Even the vocabulary is Benthamite in a literal sense: the sentiment for personal fulfilment can be expressed without awareness that the very word 'maximization' was coined by Bentham himself. Unaware of our ideological and semantic heritage, we can still live within its tradition. In this way the currents of ideological history can quietly pass through our own thinking, in a way which ensures that our thinking is not purely our own. Moreover, the cross-currents and contrary tendencies of this history can continue to shape the contents of our thinking about the dilemmas of present ordinary life.

4
Teaching and Learning

Formal education has a dual ideological importance. It is often claimed to be the process by which ideology is transmitted, but it is also something that people have ideologies *of*. It is the latter issue that will concern us, namely people's conceptions of the educational process itself: of what education is, of how people learn, of how they should be taught, and to what ends. Conceptions of education are particularly appropriate for a general discussion of ideology. Education (in this context, formal schooling) is an important part of the larger process of becoming an adult member of society, and so ideologies of education necessarily include conceptions of human nature, of how we become what we are, of the relationship between individual and society, as well as prescriptions for the conduct of teaching and learning. Furthermore, education is organized and funded on a societal scale, and may be expected therefore to carry with it societal values about those things. In this chapter we shall demonstrate that the very process of education, quite apart from issues of what 'content' should be taught, is itself dilemmatic and ideological.

In *Hard Times*, Dickens provides us with a graphic parody of Victorian educational values:

> 'Bitzer,' said Thomas Gradgrind, 'Your definition of a horse.'
> 'Quadruped. Graminivorous. Forty teeth, namely twenty-four grinders, four eye-teeth, and twelve incisive. Sheds coat in the spring; in marshy countries sheds hoofs too. Hoofs hard, but requiring to be shod with iron. Age known by marks in mouth.' Thus (and much more) Bitzer.
> 'Now girl number twenty,' said Mr Gradgrind. 'You know what a horse is.'

Thomas Gradgrind's conception of what education is all about can be inferred from even so short an extract. It is based on an ideology of authoritative knowledge, of discipline and order, of the acquisition of received wisdom. Pupils respond when spoken to, and speak only to the teacher. It is all about filling the empty vessels of children's minds with 'facts': the cold transmission of ready-made bits of knowledge. But Bitzer's definition of a horse, while (presumably) accurate enough, would probably astonish a modern teacher. Pupils today are not expected to achieve understandings through the rote memorization of factual information. Bitzer may well have had no idea what he was talking about, what his parrot-learned words actually meant, why anyone would wish to possess such information, or what to do with it once they did.

The depersonalized 'girl number twenty' presumably had seen plenty of horses, knew they had four legs, and much else about them that Bitzer's list of characteristics would not mention – how they look and move and smell, and what people do with them. A modern teacher might well start with such everyday knowledge, and get pupils to cooperate in a project to find out more. This is not merely a different way of achieving the same ends. It is founded upon a different conception of education, of knowledge itself, of children and of what sorts of adult citizens the education system should be trying to foster: that is to say, a different ideology of education. At least, this is the general assumption, that we are dealing with different and contrasting ideologies. We shall argue that a single, dilemmatic ideology underlies them both.

How many ideologies?

Conventional treatments of educational ideology concern themselves with the issue of enumerating how many educational ideologies there are, and with listing their distinguishing characteristics. Each is defined as distinctly as possible from the others, with each possessing as much internal coherence as description allows. Indeed, as we have noted, theories of ideology are typically based on the assumptions that ideologies are internally consistent, that they are opposed to other consistent ideologies, and that these opposing ideologies are espoused by different people. So, in a discussion of the sociology of education, Meighan (1981) defines ideology as 'a broad but interlinked set of ideas and beliefs about the world which are held by a group of people and which those people demonstrate both in behaviour and conversation to various audiences' (p. 19). An educational ideology is therefore 'a coherent pattern' (p. 22) such that 'alternative patterns of ideas...coexist and compete for existence' (p. 155).

There are always at least two contrasting ideologies, and indeed, in treatments of education, two is the usual number. A conventional dichotomy is drawn between 'traditional' and 'progressive' education; other, roughly equivalent terms are sometimes employed, such as 'transmission-oriented' versus 'interpretational', 'authoritarian' versus 'child-centred' or 'democratic', and so on. In rough, graphic terms, transmissional teaching is the formal, lecturing sort: pupils sit in desks facing the teacher, who controls all talk and activity. The pupils are required to listen attentively, to 'read, mark, learn and inwardly digest' what is given. In contrast, child-centred education would typically be represented by classrooms where pupils are engaged in individual work, or in small cooperative groups, the classroom a hubbub of noise and activity as the teacher moves from group to group, supervising and facilitating each pupil's learning. Sometimes three, four or more ideologies have been distinguished (for example Williams, 1961; Cosin, 1972), and even as many as a dozen, though by the time that we are down to the criteria that define that many types of education, the term 'ideologies' has been replaced by 'teaching styles' (Bennett and Jordan, 1975).

From the theoretical perspective that we have outlined in the earlier chapters, the various depictions of educational ideology possess several interesting features. First, despite their presentation as ideologies of education, they clearly appeal to a set of issues whose currency is much wider than that of merely how to teach and learn. They are concerned with fundamental and instantly recognizable social and political issues, such as those of individual freedom of action versus authoritative constraint, and the conservatism of sticking to traditional ways and wisdom versus the encouragement of change, variability and the potential for new understandings. Educational ideologies are variants of more general ones.

Secondly, they are cast as opposites, alternatives, positions defined in contrast to other positions. This immediately suggests that they are not independently formulated ways of thinking about education, but rather the terms of a debate, positions extracted from a single dialogue. Each position is not formulated as an exercise in itself, as a self-contained schema or conception of the world, but rather defined point by point in contradiction to another position which must inevitably, therefore, belong to the same universe of discourse. It is important that we realize that it need not have been so. The argumentative, dialogical character of educational ideologies is not a necessary characteristic of the consistent schemata that, according to some theoretical perspectives, individuals carry around in their heads as they make sense of the world.

Thirdly, the values of each position are not mutually exclusive. Supporters of traditional, transmission-oriented teaching are unlikely in all contexts to insist that pupils must remain passive recipients of the received wisdom, that education is always one-way traffic, an unchanging reproduction of all that has gone before. Similarly, the advocates of child-centred, autonomous learning will not insist that children are taught nothing, that the acquisition of a largely ready-made culture of knowledge and understanding is not, in however child-centred a way it is achieved, an important goal of education. Similarly, on the larger scale, few would advocate the unconstrained liberty of individuals to please themselves, just as few would insist on the necessity for social constraints in all aspects of personal conduct. We are dealing with values from a common culture, recognizable and usable by advocates on either side of a debate.

The discussion of educational ideology which follows will begin by outlining briefly the modern 'progressive' approach, and then will proceed to examine how some modern teachers come to terms with its contradictions, both in how they think about it, and also in what they do in the classroom. Prompted by some remarks by the influential educational theorist Jerome Bruner, an advocate of such liberal approaches, we seek an origin for our educational dilemma in Plato's presentation in the *Meno* of a dialogue between Socrates and a slave boy. It is a passage rich in significance for our understanding of education, embodying all of the dilemmatic themes of child-centredness, of innate capacity, and of the exercise of authority that we shall first identify in modern teaching.

Teachers and teaching

Teachers do not have the luxury of being able to formulate and adhere to some theory or position on education, with only another theorist's arguments to question its validity. They have to accomplish the practical task of teaching, which requires getting the job done through whatever conceptions and methods work best, under practical constraints that include physical resources, numbers of pupils, nature of pupils, time constraints, set syllabuses and so on. But these practical considerations inevitably have ideological bases, which define what 'the job' actually is, how to do it, how to assess its outcomes, how to react to its successes and failures, how to talk and interact with pupils, how many can be taught or talked to at once. For example, in the traditional chalk-and-talk lecturing method, a large class size is not so great a practical *or* ideological problem as it is for a teacher who upholds the value of individual, child-centred learning.

Teachers' ideological conceptions tend not to be so neatly packaged and consistent as those posited by theorists of educational ideology; similarly, the practice of classroom teaching tends not to be a straightforward realization of some such coherent position. Rather, as we shall show, teachers may well hold views of teaching, of children, of the goals of educational practice and the explanations of educational failure, which theorists of ideology would locate in opposed camps. And so also will the practical activity of teaching reflect principles that are propounded by what are held to be opposed ideologies. Further, it is not unknown for teachers to be aware of such contradictions, to feel themselves involved in difficult choices and as having to make compromises.

We shall concentrate our analysis on a recognizably modern and widespread style of teaching which is of the 'progressive' sort. That is to say, it involves small-group, activity-oriented teaching, based on the view that pupils learn best through their own experiences. This is the 'child-centred pedagogy' that is associated with the psychological theories and research of Jean Piaget, with the principle of 'learning by doing', and with the enormously influential Plowden Report (1967), which has done much to shape the nature of British primary education since the 1960s (Valerie Walkerdine, 1984 provides a useful discussion of this approach and its limitations). It is explicitly opposed to the Gradgrind sort of pedagogy. In Piaget's words:

> Each time one prematurely teaches a child something he could have learned for himself, the child is kept from inventing it and consequently from understanding it completely. (1970: 715)

And, according to the Plowden Report:

> Piaget's explanations appear to most educationalists in this country to fit the observed facts of children's learning more satisfactorily than any other... Verbal explanation, in advance of understanding based on experience, may be an obstacle to learning. (paras 522 and 535)

Although the Report contained provisos and warnings against the mis-application of 'discovery learning', its general effect was to encourage teachers to take more of a back seat, to allow pupils to actively try things for themselves, to learn from their own experiences.

In fact, despite the obvious influence of these ideas on British educational thought and practice, it has become clear that a fundamental shift from transmission-oriented education to child-centred discovery learning has generally not taken place. Its implementation has at best been superficial or severely compromised, if not altogether illusory. Meighan (1981: 333) refers to 'the myth of the non-authoritarian primary school', and suggests that 'alternative forms of authoritarian schooling... are taken for radical non-authoritarian alternatives, and this gives rise to a variety of myths about educational practice' (p. 334). He cites a variety of research studies which support this conclusion (for example Richards, 1979; Berlak et al., 1975).

Indeed, theoretical and ideological opposition began in advance of any such research, from the moment the Plowden Report was published (for example Peters, 1969; Froome, 1970). It included some simple reassertions of principles that would have appealed to Mr Gradgrind: 'All knowledge consists of facts, and a step-by-step assimilation of those facts which are deemed desirable is the basis of learning' (Froome, 1970: 113). The invocation of knowledge which is 'deemed desirable' introduces an ideological dimension to the debate which was sometimes quite explicit. Marriott notes some instances:

> Kemball-Cook (1972), in an article critical of Plowden, argued that a relaxed approach to discipline is particularly unsuitable for boys; while girls in primary schools exhibit docility and eagerness to please, boys' toughness and aggression requires firmer handling. Similarly, the apparently ubiquitous abdication of teachers in primary schools was connected by such writers to impending or current economic difficulties; for example, Cox and Boyson (1975) argued that if the non-competitive ethos of progressive education was allowed to dominate our schools, the result would be a generation who would be unable to maintain current standards of living when opposed by overseas competitors. (1985: 34–5)

We seem to be faced with a quandary. Neither kind of education seems entirely satisfactory. The shift towards 'progressive' education was motivated by a deeply felt dissatisfaction with the nature and consequences of traditional chalk-and-talk teaching. The traditional methods, supported by the outmoded assumptions of innate ability and IQ testing, had given rise to the wholesale educational failure of large numbers of children, especially those of the working class. They were being left behind, falling off the back of the train as the teacher's single-track locomotive of educated thought and talk pushed on regardless, arriving at the final destination with only a few first-class passengers still aboard. The few who remained on the train, who matched the pace of the lesson, were evidence that the teaching was sufficient; the train itself was not to blame. Failure was due to pupils' lack of ability to learn. In the 'progressive' ideology, such a notion was untenable. The train was obviously faulty. Rote learning is not the same thing as achieving understanding. Pupils learn best and most deeply when actively involved and motivated in what they are doing, when relating ideas to their own experiences.

So what has gone wrong? Do we need perhaps to formulate another theory or ideology of education? Or is it simply that neither the traditional nor the progressive approach has been properly implemented, so that what we need to do is to have a more thorough bash at putting one or the other of them into practice? Or perhaps the answer is a compromise, a combination of the best of both worlds? If all we were dealing with were a couple of technical alternatives – ways of organizing classrooms, or topics to include in the curriculum – such a compromise solution might be a simple matter. But, as we have argued, we are dealing with much more fundamental oppositions, ideological ones that are part of much larger social and ideological debates than can be resolved merely by tinkering with what happens in the classroom.

It could be that the problem is solved already: that despite our difficulties in formulating an adequate theory of education, there is no dilemma when it comes to the practical business of teaching. Teachers simply get the job done; the compromises work. But of course, we are begging the question. By what criteria do we, the pupils or the teachers, the analysts or the society at large, judge education to be 'done' and to 'work'? Let us look more closely at what some teachers and pupils think and do.

The educational dilemma: what teachers say

We are in no position to offer any definitive or comprehensive survey of the thoughts and activities of teachers and pupils. However, it is possible to get a feel for the ways in which the sorts of ideological and practical dilemmas we have discussed are felt and acted on, and have a practical reality and relevance for those teachers and pupils that we and others have studied. We shall draw mainly upon a study of classroom education in which successive series of lessons with several classes of nine-year-olds were video-recorded, and the teachers and pupils interviewed about what they were doing (see Edwards and Mercer, 1987 for a fuller account). The teachers in this study were all identifiable as essentially 'progressive', as evidenced both in the way they taught in the classroom, and by comments in interview such as the following:

> Given sufficient time and resources I felt that the best learning experience is one where children work things out for themselves.

> I didn't want to tie them down to a heavily structured procedure because it might kill the possibility of children making their own observations and conclusions.

> In the practical work, where the children are much more interested, they will obviously acquire and retain more knowledge.

> The very meaning of the term [education] is not to input; it means to bring out.

In addition to these clear evocations of the Plowden ethos, the same teachers also expressed a variety of explanations of the fact that some pupils obviously succeed better than others. All of them offered explanations that appealed to innate intelligence. For example, in the words of one teacher (the last quoted above):

> They do better because they are more intelligent. . .you can't do anything about their IQ.

and on the importance of 'social conditions':

> Children from affluent families would. . .have books at home. They would be taken on educational trips. . .they achieve more at their level than children of a similar IQ with perhaps not such a good background.

and on more personal factors:

> You have to know which children in the class are. . .depressed or in trouble or distressed.

None of the teachers attributed educational failure to poor or inappropriate teaching.

So, while children are thought to learn through exploratory activity and experience, they fail not through the lack or inadequacy of it, but rather through being unintelligent, disadvantaged or beset by some personal or behavioural problem. These are notions that derive not from some single, coherent ideological position, as conventionally defined, but from conflicting theories of educational failure that are familiar in the literature. Teachers themselves are educated, of course, and will at some point in their training and in their wider reading have acquired at least a folk wisdom basis, and in many cases much more than this, in the social and behavioural sciences and in their orthodoxies, assumptions and established theory and findings with regard to education.

But from the viewpoint of educational ideologies, the doctrines of native intelligence and of experiential learning belong in opposed camps. And so also do the orthodoxies of psychology and of sociology. While Piagetian psychological approaches allow for pupil learning which is exploratory, self-motivated, creative and constructive of whatever understandings are achieved, sociological approaches (those of Durkheim, Parsons and so on) have typically stressed the transmissional nature of education, seeing it primarily as the socialization of pupils into an established system of educated thought, language and practice. To the extent that both the sociological and the psychological positions have any validity at all, and presumably they do, this places our teachers in a dilemma. There is socialization to be achieved, not only of the behavioural sort (disciplined conduct, respect for authority and so on) but also in terms of the more official curriculum: a pre-established body of knowledge, thought and skills to be taught. But these cannot be taught directly; the pupils have to learn it all for themselves. In fact, they cannot be 'taught' it at all, in the traditional sense. You cannot teach children what they cannot understand. In the words of one of our teachers, it cannot simply be 'input'; it has to be 'brought out'. But how can you 'bring out' of children what is not there? How do you get children to invent and discover for themselves precisely what the curriculum pre-ordains must be discovered?

It is a dilemma felt by the teachers themselves. In a junior school English teacher (in one of our own interviews), we find a clear awareness of competition between different educational philosophies:

> I think there's a place for both of these [progressive and transmissional philo-sophies of education]. I mean there are things that you've got to actually sit down and teach but you know lots of things...practically they do find out...I mean they do lots of creative work and writing stuff where they were using their own experience...but I think there's a place for both...I mean you know, there's a limit to how much to keep plugging it and how much you just wait for them and then they know it.

While this teacher hopes to resolve the dilemma by suggesting that there is a 'place for both', it would not appear to be a simple matter to define precisely what that place should be. Berlak et al. (1975) cite the following comments from a teacher caught in what is also an obviously *felt* dilemma (and they proceed to describe the compromises of constraint versus freedom of choice under which his pupils were allowed to work):

> I have yet to come to terms with myself about what a child should do in, for instance, mathematics. Certainly I feel that children should as far as possible follow their own interests and not be dictated to all the time, but then again...I feel pressure from...I don't really know how to explain it, but there's something inside you that you've developed over the years which says that children should do this...As yet I can't accept, for instance, that since I've been here I've been annoyed that some children in the fourth year haven't progressed as much as, say, some less able children in the second year in their maths, because they've

obviously been encouraged to get on with their own interests. But I still feel that I've somehow got to press them on with their mathematics. (1975: 91–2)

The dilemma felt by this mathematics teacher is, similarly, not simply a personal one, unique to his own perspectives and experience. He is pulled by the very values and criteria that we have located in the wider context of current educational ideology: the notion that some pupils are simply 'less able' than others, yet also learn from self-motivated activity and experience, but yet again have to achieve standards of 'progress' in the clearly predefined realm of 'mathematics' which, whatever the pupils might discover for themselves, the teacher knows already.

The educational dilemma: what teachers do

The most important arena in which this dilemma has to be worked out is not in what teachers say in interview, but in what they do in the classroom. Edwards and Mercer (1987) present a detailed study of the sorts of strategies that are adopted, through which teachers, apparently at least, manage to 'elicit' from pupils things that they did not already know. What frequently occurs is that teacher and pupils engage in an implicit collusion in which the solutions and answers appear to be elicited, while a close examination of what is happening reveals that the required information, suggestions, observations and conclusions are cued, selected or provided by the teacher. A simple illustration will suffice. In the following dialogue, the teacher is introducing to a group of nine-year-olds the concept of pendulums, concerning which they are about to embark upon some experimental investigations. She has begun by telling them a story of Galileo, and decides to elicit from the pupils the information that he used his pulse to time the swings of incense burners in church. (T is the teacher. Concurrent behaviour is recorded to the right. The diagonal slashes represent pauses; underlined words show vocal emphasis.)

T: Now he didn't have a watch/ but he <u>had</u> on <u>him</u> something that was a very good timekeeper that he could use to hand straight away/	T swinging her pendant.
	T snaps fingers on 'straight away', and looks invitingly at pupils as if posing a question or inviting a response.
You've* got it. I've* got it.	* T points.
<u>What</u> is it?// What could we use to count beats? What have <u>you</u> got?//	T beats hand on table slowly, looks around group of pupils, who smile and shrug.
You can feel it <u>here</u>.	T puts finger on her wrist pulse.
Pupils: Pulse.	(In near unison)
T: A pulse. Everybody see if you can find it.	All imitate T, feeling for their wrist pulses.

Through action and gesture the teacher manages to coax from the pupils the word she wanted. We may call this process one of 'cued elicitation'. The procedure was a pervasive one and was not restricted to such simple and obvious cases. It extended to the main activities, discoveries and conclusions of the lesson, all of which had been planned in advance. Before beginning the lessons on pendulums, the teacher had planned various features of them, including that the pupils should test *three* hypotheses about how to effect changes in a pendulum's period (the time taken for a pendulum to complete one swing). She had also determined *exactly what* these hypotheses should be, knew in advance that *only one* of the three variables (length of the string) should have any effect, and that the pupils should average their timings across *twenty swings* of the pendulum. All of these features (and others) were ostensibly elicited from the pupils during the lessons, as if it was the pupils themselves who were inventing and deciding upon them. So let us examine a somewhat less obvious elicitation, that of the decision to average twenty swings. (In the following transcript, simultaneous speech is bracketed together.)

T: Right/ now how many swings will she* have to do do you think// before she can work out for instance suppose she starts from here and she counts the swings and divides OK. Now we did five. Do you think that's a good number to do and divide by?

    * T referring to Sharon.

    T holding the pendulum bob out at an angle.

Lucy and Karen: Yes.
Jonathan: Yeh.
David: Yeh.

    Both nodding their heads.

    // (Pause, 3 seconds)

T: I don't know. ⎡ Why
David: ⎣ Ten Miss/ ten.
Antony: Six/ an even number six.
T: An even number/ makes it/ you reckon you can divide by six better than you can divide by five./
    Will it make any difference to the *accuracy*/ of what she's doing if she did a *larger*/ number of swings? For instance if she decided that if it was/ um/ five swings she was going to do/ right/ and then she divided by five/ but suppose she decided as you've just said on ten. Which one of those readings would be the more accurate?

    David shouts, interrupts T.

    T looking at Antony.

    T laughs, then Sharon laughs.
    T speaking slowly and clearly, with small pauses as indicated.

    T writes '5' on sheet of paper on table.

    T writes '10' next to '5'.
    T prods her pen back and forth from '5' to '10'.
    Pupils watch the pen.

Antony: Five.

    Antony points to the '5'.
    // (Pause, 3 seconds)

Antony: ⌈ Ten.
David: ⌊ Ten.

T: Why?

Antony: Because it cuts it down more.

T: Good boy. It cuts down/ what we call the margin of error doesn't it. It makes the error that much smaller. I think we could cut it down even smaller than ten.

Antony: Twenty.

T: Make the error   T continuing.

Antony: Hundred.

David: ⌈ Sixteen.
T: ⌊ Counting a hundred swings Antony we'd be here till the Christmas ⌈ holidays.   Antony smiles.
David: ⌊ sixteen.

Sharon: ⌈ Fifteen.
T: ⌊ Let's make it an easier number to ⌈ work with.
Antony: ⌊ Twenty. Twenty.

Various pupils: Yeh.

T: That would be all right wouldn't it? So if we *all* use twenty/ so we'll do   T writes down '20'.
twenty swings/ get the time/ divide by
twenty and we can use the calculator/   T picks up and shows calculator to
then we should get the time pretty   pupils.
accurately/ possibly in hundredths of
seconds. OK?   T looking round group, pupils' eyes
                    downcast and averted.

Lucy, Karen, Jonathan and David all appeared initially to be ready to accept five swings as a good number to use. Guided by a series of strategic pauses and prompts by the teacher, they eventually hit upon the required number – twenty. It is difficult to avoid the impression that the pupils were engaged in an exercise of trying to read all the cues, prompts and signals available from the teacher in an elaborate guessing game in which they had to work out, more by communicative astuteness than by the application of any scientific principle of measurement, what it was that the teacher was trying to get them to say. The advantages of this sort of teaching may well be considerable, for instance in terms of involving the pupils in an active pursuit of knowledge. But whatever the advantages, it is also clear that, despite the elicitation style of teaching, there is at least as much 'putting in' of knowledge going on here as 'bringing out'.

The communicative devices used by the teachers, through which curriculum knowledge was surreptitiously offered to pupils while overtly elicited from them, included the following:

1   Gestural cues and demonstrations while asking questions.
2   Generally controlling the flow of conversation – such as who is allowed to speak and when, and about what.
3   The use of silence to mark non-acceptance of a pupil's contribution (see pauses, and pupils' reactions to them, in the dialogue quoted above).
4   Ignoring or side-tracking unwelcome suggestions.
5   Taking up and encouraging welcome ones.
6   Introducing 'new' knowledge as if it were already known – and therefore not open to question.
7   Paraphrasing pupils' contributions so as to bring them closer to the teacher's intended meaning.
8   Over-interpreting observed events so as to make them seem to confirm what the teacher anticipated.
9   Summarizing what has been done or 'discovered', in a way that reconstructs and alters its meaning.

These and other features of classroom talk and education are discussed in some detail in Edwards and Mercer (1987). The point which concerns us here is their implication for educational ideology. To the extent that such findings have any generality at all (and they are indeed consistent with other research, such as Becker, 1968; A.D. Edwards and Furlong, 1969; Berlak et al., 1975), we are forced to the conclusion that the distinction between traditional, transmissional education on the one hand, and progressive, child-centred education on the other, is not so clear in practice as it may appear to be in theory. Both approaches involve a subordination of pupil to teacher, of personal discovery to the curriculum. Indeed, rather than stemming from two distinct and opposed ideological bases, they may well be alternative expressions of a single, though dilemmatic, ideology. That is the argument that we shall pursue.

Educational dilemmas and social values

The practical dilemma which we have identified hinges on the problem of how to 'bring out' of children what is not there to begin with, how to ensure that they 'discover' what they are meant to. It is this dilemma that gives rise to the variety of strategies we have outlined, through which the teacher manages to impose knowledge and understandings while appearing to elicit them. But this is a dilemma that rests upon a conflict of values and perspectives that are relevant to much wider issues than that of education alone – the contrasts between freedom and constraint, individual and society, growth from within (psychological development) and imposition from the outside (socialization). These are fundamental ideological oppositions, of the sort that are appealed to in general political debate and polemic. They may be invoked on either side of such a debate; 'freedom', and the contrasting necessity of 'social order', in one sense or another are claimed by both left and right.

Not only are these oppositions essential to many political debates, they are also basic features according to which we can distinguish a variety of theoretical positions and approaches taken within the social sciences. Behaviourism is a psychology of control and constraint, of imposition and socialization, explicitly set against the notions of voluntary action, personal growth, sense-making and self-determination (Wann, 1964; Skinner, 1971). Similarly, Dawe (1970) has identified two opposed currents of sociology, which can be distinguished in terms of their positions with regard to these issues of freedom and constraint, relations between individual and society, determination from within the individual or imposition from without:

> At every level, they are in conflict. They posit antithetical views of human nature, of society and the relationship between the social and the individual. The first asserts the paramount necessity, for societal and individual well-being, of external constraint...The key notion of the second is that of autonomous man, able to realize his full potential and to create a truly human social order only when freed from external constraint. Society is thus the creation of its members. (1970: 214)

It is clear that the 'two sociologies' are not merely alternative descriptions, but are ideologically opposed and prescriptive of human conduct, including notions of what is proper and necessary for our 'well-being'. For example, writers in the tradition which emphasizes the importance of social discipline and constraint can argue with reference to education that 'Society can survive only if there exists among its members a sufficient degree of homogeneity; education perpetuates and reinforces this homogeneity by fixing in the child, from the beginning, the essential similarities that collective life demands' (Durkheim, 1956).

In education, as in many other spheres of social life, these oppositions of freedom and constraint, of individual and society, of determination from within or from without, have to be worked out in practice as well as in theory. The point about them is that they are oppositions intrinsic to how we think of ourselves, oppositions in which each one of the pair is necessary to the meaning of the other, in which neither can survive alone. They do not belong to separate systems of thought. Society cannot socialize dogs, rhubarb or furniture into the requirements of mature human conduct, any more than an isolated individual can bootstrap herself or himself into a culture. In becoming twentieth-century citizens of Britain we have not merely realized a potentiality within us. The same thinkers and theorists (including us all) move freely from one side of an opposition to the other, as practical constraints or the requirements of argument demand. The same teachers who espouse the virtues of child-centred education, of learning by discovery and of the realization of innate potential also know in advance what will be discovered, prepare their lessons according to set books and syllabuses, and prepare their students for the knowledge that is to come. (The pendulums teacher even referred her nine-year-old pupils to aspects of the physics of pendulums that they would cover if, in perhaps eight years' time, they did the A-level syllabus upon which her own son was currently embarked.)

Education and the *Meno*

Educational theories and prescriptions which stress one side or the other of our opposite perspectives are likely to fall prey to the arguments and virtues of the other side. In an attempt to create an integrated account, the influential psychologist and educationalist Jerome Bruner draws upon the work of the Soviet theorist Lev Vygotsky:

> His basic view . . . was that conceptual learning was a collaborative enterprise involving an adult who enters into dialogue with the child in a fashion that provides the child with hints and props that allow him to begin a new climb, guiding the child in next steps before the child is capable of appreciating their significance on his own . . . The model is Socrates guiding the slave boy through geometry in the *Meno*. (Bruner, 1986: 132)

It is a modern, sophisticated view of education and of human development in general, one which gives an equal importance to the intrinsic activity of the child, and to the adult's role as carrier and representative of a ready-made culture in which the child is serving an apprenticeship. But it is not so modern that Bruner cannot trace it directly back to Plato. Indeed, the dialogue between Socrates and the slave boy is well known in the annals of educational history and philosophy, and is often cited as an early example of the modern, progressive sort of pedagogy. For example, Lawrence (1970: 26–30) cites it in an argument that Plato, rather than Rousseau, originated the notion that 'The function of the teacher is to help the learner to discover the truth for himself.' Similarly, Curtis and Boultwood (1965: 80) have it as a 'classic instance' of the doctrine, this time attributed to St Augustine, that we can only teach what is already implicitly known, that 'Teaching . . . is the activity of causing pupils to learn.' The *Meno* will repay a close examination, not only because its presentation as a dialogue invites comparison with the teacher–pupil conversations we have examined, but also because it is possible to discern within this famous and influential text the very issues and oppositions that have concerned us. Indeed, it becomes clear that it would not be difficult for a proponent of teacher-dominated pedagogy, or of the doctrine of the overriding importance of innate abilities, to present the same text as support. Gradgrind would have *The Republic* to draw upon too!

In a passage in the *Meno*, Plato provides an account of a dialogue about geometry between Socrates and a slave boy. Socrates was trying to convince Meno, the boy's master, of the reality of innate ideas, that concepts such as that of 'virtue' (*arete*) were not empirical, but depended upon being already present in the mind in a latent form, awaiting realization through experience. It was Socrates's belief that such innate ideas were memories (*anamnesis*) derived from the immortal soul's previous lives. Through dialogue with the slave boy, Socrates attempts to demonstrate to Meno that, despite an apparent initial ignorance of Pythagoras's theorem concerning the calculation of the areas of triangles and squares, the boy in fact knew the theorem all along, and simply needed to be questioned in order that this innate knowledge might be drawn from him. (The implication for Meno's benefit is that the same may also be true of the notion of 'virtue'.) In fact, Socrates was at pains to demonstrate that he *taught* the boy nothing. The slave boy dialogue is a peculiarly powerful and influential passage, in which we find the very themes of human nature, of knowledge and education, that we have identified in modern educational ideology.

Socrates asks Meno to 'Listen carefully then, and see whether it seems to you that he is learning from me or simply being reminded' (Plato, 1956: 130; the sequences of dialogue quoted below are taken from the translation by W.K.C. Guthrie). Let us also take up Socrates's invitation. In the following dialogue, he has drawn a square in the sand at his feet, and has established that the boy understands that it is a figure with four sides of equal length. Pointing to various parts of the diagram, Socrates establishes that the boy can calculate the square's area:

Socrates: Now if this side is two feet long, and this side the same, how many feet will the whole be? Put it this way. If it were two feet in this direction and only one in that, must not the area be two feet taken once?
Boy: Yes.
Socrates: But since it is two feet this way also, does it not become twice two feet?
Boy: Yes.
Socrates: And how many feet is twice two? Work it out and tell me.
Boy: Four.
(1956: 131)

Guthrie (1975), in a detailed account and discussion of this and other parts of Plato's philosophy, offers a distinctly progressive/Piagetian interpretation of the slave boy's achievements (of which more in a moment):

Mathematical knowledge cannot be handed over by a teacher like the chemical formula for water or the name of the first President of the United States. Each must comprehend it for himself, and when he does so...the surprising fact emerges that he discovers precisely what everyone else must discover. The boy does not say 'yes' or 'no' to please Socrates, but because he sees that it is the obvious answer. What shows him his errors, and the right answers, is not so much the questions as the diagrams themselves, and were he mathematically inclined he might, given time, draw the diagrams and deduce the truth from them, without an instructor. (1975: 255)

The 'surprising fact', that the boy comes to understand what everyone else does, is of course no surprise now to us. But let us examine this claim, that what the boy learns from experience is a realization of innate knowledge, and that Socrates does not teach but merely elicits.

The boy's contributions to the dialogue are clearly minimal, the first two being simple affirmations of propositions put to him by Socrates. If this were a transcript of natural dialogue that we are examining, we would probably assume that, preceding Socrates's 'Put it this way', the boy had paused, unable to answer the initial question. Indeed, several times in the dialogue Socrates has to rephrase and break down the problem into simple steps, as he does here. But in doing so, he asks recognizably 'leading questions', providing the answers within his own questions, with even the restricted choice between 'yes' and 'no' cued by the form of the question: 'must not the area be . . .', 'does it not become . . .'. Moreover, in breaking the problem down into a series of small steps, Socrates requires of the boy only that he performs small calculations; the boy's one substantive contribution is to work out what is twice two, a calculation he could easily have made without reference to geometry. If we conceive of the problem as constituted by the ordered series of steps rather than by its individual elements, it is difficult not to read the dialogue as essentially Socrates's thought rather than the boy's. In terms of the classroom discourse we have examined, what we have here is a piece of cued elicitation.

Let us examine, then, how Socrates proceeds to elicit from the boy Pythagoras's theorem. First, he establishes that the boy falsely assumes that a square of twice the area, that is eight square feet, will also have sides twice as long, that is four feet in length. As the dialogue proceeds, Socrates builds in steps a geometrical diagram of squares and rectangles to illustrate each step of the argument. He succeeds in eliciting the boy's acquiescence to the suggestion that 'Doubling the side [of a square] has given us not double but a fourfold figure.' Again, the boy's role in the dialogue is merely to confirm the propositions put to him by Socrates: 'Won't it be four times as big?' The sole exception is a minimal and tautological one, in which the boy is called upon to deny that 'four times' is the same as 'twice'.

Socrates's questions eventually reduce the boy to a state of confusion. He is brought to realize that a square with sides two feet long has an area of four square feet, and that a square of four feet long has an area of sixteen square feet. In pursuit of the sides of a figure of eight square feet, Socrates points out that they 'must be longer than two feet but shorter than four'; the boy appropriately suggests three feet, but is prompted to calculate that three squared gives nine. He despairs: 'It's no use, Socrates, I just don't know.' Socrates proceeds to enlighten the boy by drawing another diagram (shown here as Figure 1, constructed line by line in alphabetical order as the dialogue proceeds), in which ABCD represents the same area as

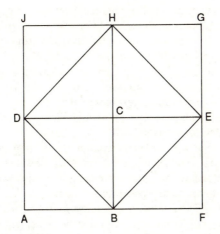

Figure 1   *Socrates's drawing*

before, i.e. four square feet. Socrates again exhorts Meno to 'Notice what, starting from this state of perplexity, he will discover by seeking the truth in company with me, though I simply ask him questions without teaching him.' Once more, 'in company with me' hardly does justice to Socrates's role in the discovery.

Socrates [*drawing in the diagonals*]: Now does this line going from corner to corner cut each of these squares in half?
Boy: Yes.
Socrates: And these are four equal lines enclosing this area [BEHD]?
Boy: They are.
Socrates: Now think. How big is this area?
Boy: I don't understand.
Socrates: Here are four squares. Has not each line cut off the inner half of each of them?
Boy: Yes.
Socrates: And how many such halves are there in this figure [BEHD]?
Boy: Four.
Socrates: And how many in this one [ABCD]?
Boy: Two.
Socrates: And what is the relation of four to two?
Boy: Double.
Socrates: How big is this figure then?
Boy: Eight feet.
Socrates: On what base?
Boy: This one.
Socrates: The line which goes from corner to corner of the square of four feet?
Boy: Yes.
Socrates: The technical name for it is 'diagonal'; so if we use that name, it is your personal opinion that the square on the diagonal of the original square is double its area.
Boy: That is so, Socrates.

Socrates goes on to conclude that, having been elicited by questions rather than through direct tuition, 'These opinions were somewhere in him. . . This knowledge will not come from teaching but from questioning. He will recover it for himself' (Plato, 1956: 138).

The dialogue of the *Meno* is in many ways unlike naturally recorded conversation; it is altogether too neatly ordered, and there are moments of implausibility in the boy's responses. It is, of course, whatever its historical origins, a quasi-dialogue written by Plato. Nevertheless, the role of Socrates bears comparison with that of the teachers in the sorts of 'discovery learning' we have been examining. He remains in control of the talk, governing the taking of turns at speaking, closing the boy's options even to an extent that we have not witnessed in schools, by merely inviting affirmations of ready-made propositions – the familiar 'leading questions' of the courtroom. The assumption implicit in Socrates's account of the process, that he will 'simply ask him questions without teaching him', is that questions do not carry information, that they may not inform and persuade, command and convince. Of course, this is a demonstrably false assumption, one unlikely to be made even by the pre-Socratic Sophists, the experts in rhetoric (Billig, 1987), let alone by modern scholars of language and communication. As one of the latter remarks, 'Questions will generally share the presuppositions of their assertive counterparts' (Levinson, 1983: 184).

Most strikingly, we find in the *Meno* an example, at least as clear as any we may find in school, of a contrast between the teachers' overtly expressed insistence that their pupils learn from experience, realizing an innate potential and learning for themselves rather than being 'taught', and the surreptitious way (via gesture or presupposition, for example) that the teacher implants knowledge and assumption, defines what is relevant and true, structures experience and assigns significance to it. The boy's conclusions were, like the principles of pendulums, established by Socrates and the teachers in advance of the 'lesson'. Their pre-existence was real enough, as Socrates claimed, but they existed not in the minds of the pupils but rather in those of the teachers – Socrates included.

The very term 'education' is a symbol combining contradictory themes. Its etymological derivation is a direct reflection of Socrates's conception of the process. It comes from the Latin *e-ducare*, which means, as many modern teachers are aware, to 'lead out'; this implies a process in which the teacher's role is rather like that of Socrates in the dialogue, drawing out of pupils that which is already latent and awaiting realization. But our discussion of educational ideology forces us to re-examine the word and its implications. The notion of 'leading out' is just that; the 'duc' of 'education' is the same as that of 'duke' and of 'Il Duce' (the title adopted by Mussolini), denoting leadership in the sense of power and command. It is no mere coincidence that Socrates's dialogue was with a slave boy.

Our examination of much less domineering sorts of 'elicitation' forces us to note that what is apparently elicited is often surreptitiously introduced, by gesture, assumption or implication, by the teacher. The knowledge attributed by Socrates to the slave boy was in fact constructed for him in the discourse itself, the boy serving merely as a compliant participant in an exposition dominated by Socrates. If the boy was 'educated' in the process, then it was at least as much a process from the outside in (induction) as from the inside out (e-ducation). What Socrates and Plato offer us is not so much a demonstration of the reality of innate ideas, as a somewhat unreal piece of surreptitious tuition.

In fact, the slave boy section of the *Meno*, despite the special significance that educators have attached to it, is a rather untypical example of a Socratic dialogue. The usual form of the Socratic dialogues is different in both respects that we have emphasized; they are typically dialogues between social equals, and they are also typically dialogues about contentious issues (such as the nature of virtue or of justice) rather than about problems for which there is a unique and demonstrably correct answer. In the *Protagoras*, for example, Socrates and Protagoras deliberately swap roles of questioner and answerer. The interchange with the slave boy is very different. Like Gradgrind's 'girl number twenty', the boy has no name, and must do as he is bidden. He also must answer the questions put to him, and does so briefly, and does not question or answer back. But if we take the *Meno* as a whole, rather than just the slave dialogue section of it, we can see that it is not really so exceptional. The true dialogue was not with the slave at all, but with Meno, his master. The boy was not invited to participate with Meno and Socrates in the discussion of 'virtue'. The slave dialogue is merely an interlude in that discussion, a demonstration performed on the boy by Socrates to convince Meno of the validity of an argument concerning innate ideas. The real issue was not geometry but the innate idea of virtue – a genuinely contentious issue. The dialogue with Meno continues before and after that with the boy, and even during it, as in the quotation above when Socrates pauses to make sure that Meno appreciates the significance of the demonstration. The slave boy is called in like a medical exhibit in a lecture on psychiatry or anatomy.

It is a peculiar fact, then, that it is the untypical slave boy dialogue rather than those between Socrates and Meno or Protagoras (or any of the others) that has appealed to liberal educators as embodying principles of pedagogy. Perhaps this is merely because the slave was a child, and education is generally conceived to be a process oriented to children. But surely the other features of that untypical case are also important: power and the pre-existence of knowledge. The teacher is in control, the child cooperatively subjugated, the agenda closed and determined by the teacher, the learning process defined as one in which the pupil attains an understanding already attained by the teacher. Absent are the qualities of open argument and debate, of true negotiation of issues and understandings, that we find in Socrates's real dialogues.

The notions of innate knowledge, and of education as drawing out (or 'bringing out') from pupils the capacities and cleverness which they possess already within them, are clearly reflected in modern educational theories. Indeed, they are a cultural heritage, an ideology of education that we have inherited from Plato. In the *Thaetetus* he calls it 'mental midwifery', and in keeping with the metaphor the modern word 'concept' has the same root as 'conceive', in the sense of 'become pregnant with'. It derives from the Socratic dialogical method of drawing out meanings – the 'maieutic' (midwifery) method, with Socrates the midwife, and the pupil giving birth to ideas that were latent within. More recent variants of the nativist doctrine include the arguments by the linguists Chomsky and Fodor for the necessity of postulating an innate knowledge of language. (How, Fodor asks in an argument reminiscent of the *Meno*, can one learn a new concept unless one can already hypothesize it?) But the dual, oppositional character of the educational process was present even in Plato's treatment. R.S. Peters puts it nicely:

> When Socrates described himself as a midwife in the service of truth he used a brilliant image to illustrate this dual aspect of a teacher's concern. He must care both about the principles of his discipline and about his pupil's viewpoint on the world which he is being led to explore. Both forms of concern are obligatory. Respect for persons must not be pursued with a cavalier disregard for standards. (1966: 59)

The twin pillars of educational philosophy most clearly espoused by the teachers in our study were variants on the theme: an assumption of innate intelligence as the prime factor in pupils' learning problems and abilities; and the principle of 'e-ducare', of leading or drawing out, helping pupils to learn for themselves, to realize their intellectual potential through their own activity and experience. The slave boy's knowledge of geometry was elicited, on Plato's and Socrates's accounts, merely through 'questioning' and by confronting the boy with the properties of squares and triangles. We find articulated and embodied in the *Meno* the foundations of both poles of our ideological oppositions: discovery learning versus transmissional teaching, the realization of personal potential versus the exercise of social power and determination. We even have the denial by Socrates that any such control is being exercised. It is a set of oppositions and pretences that recur not only in modern education, but in many other contexts of our social and political life.

The hidden dimension of the slave boy dialogue – indoctrination, as opposed to elicitation – is in fact quite explicit elsewhere in Plato's writing. Indeed, his major treatments of education are to be found not in the *Meno* (in which Socrates ostensibly teaches nothing), but rather in the *Republic* and the *Laws*. Here the major recommendations concern the ends, rather than the means, of education. And the ends are clearly predetermined and heavily imbued with ideological values – the rearing of children so that they become good citizens, virtuous and dutiful, each to their allotted place in the creation of the ideal state. It is no open-ended creative process; the midwife has a clear, socially defined conception of the required offspring's character: 'Education is the process of drawing and guiding children towards that principle which is pronounced right by the law and confirmed as truly right by the experience of the oldest and the most just' (*The Laws*, book 2, para. 659). Indeed, steps should be taken to prevent any possibility of unpredicted or open-ended outcomes. While toddlers would be encouraged to play, this must be carefully constrained in middle childhood, for fear of rearing innovators: 'Children who make innovations in their games, when they grow up to be men, will be different from the last generation of children and, being different, will desire a different sort of life, and under the influence of this desire will invent other institutions and laws' (*The Laws*, book 7, para. 797). Marvellous, we might now think, just what we want children to be. But from Plato this was a dire warning, consistent with his recommendations for editing, restricting and bowdlerizing children's literature. Indeed, it was the very rationale for starting the educational process in early childhood, that it is then that our nature is at its most malleable: 'For it is then that it is best moulded and takes the impression that one wishes to stamp upon it' (*The Republic*, book 2, para. 377).

So, the very process of child-centred elicitation, of conceptual midwifery so keenly espoused by the liberal educationists, contains also the predetermined curriculum, the character training, social values and constraints of the opposed camp. They originate in Plato's philosophy as parts of a single ideology. They come together in the pursuit of clear social goals, the creation of a highly structured, determined and just society, the realization of the natural virtue and goodness that are founded upon the careful midwifery of reason and understanding. As with all such ideological positions, what is socially arbitrary is offered as something natural.

The notion that education is as much a process of in-duction as of e-ducation brings us back to Jerome Bruner, whose invocation of the *Meno* prompted our examination of it. According to Bruner, education is best conceived as an induction of pupils into culture, with culture itself conceived as a 'forum' within which shared meanings are defined and negotiated. It is a revised version of the 'progressive' ideology of education, contrasted with the older 'transmissional' sorts of pedagogy, but with the introduction of a communicative induction into culture in place of the all-discovering, self-fulfilling child:

It follows from this view of culture as a forum that induction into the culture through education, if it is to prepare the young for life as lived, should also partake of the spirit of a forum, of negotiation, of the re-creating of meaning. But this conclusion runs counter to traditions of pedagogy that derive from another time, another interpretation of culture, another conception of authority – one that looked at the process of education as a *transmission* of knowledge and values. (Bruner, 1986: 123)

Bruner's vision is an attractive and perhaps even an achievable one, but it is not much like what happens in schools; indeed, it is not much like what happens in the *Meno*, at least not in the slave boy section of it. If anything, it has more in common with Socrates's dialogues with the Sophists. What Bruner refers to as the older conception of 'authority' is not so easily dispensed with. It merely reappears in disguised form, as it did for Socrates. The same ideological oppositions are revisited; the contrasting values of creation and reduplication, of individual self-determination, and the reproduction of the established order. And in the absence of fundamental social changes in the nature of our culture and politics, in the underlying origins of our ideology, it is unlikely that the theorists and the practitioners of education will be able to avoid merely, at the ideological level, shifting from one foot to the other.

5
Expertise and Equality

The behaviour of the teachers discussed in the previous chapter is a reflection of the contemporary dilemma between authority and expertise. In a strictly stratified society, in which the charisma of authority can be recognized for its own sake, the dilemma does not arise: authorities can behave in an uninhibitedly authoritarian way. However, in a society imbued with democratic norms, the position of an authority is not so straightforward. The norms of democracy are fundamentally egalitarian. They suggest that each person is to be respected as having opinions valuable enough to have an equal say in the destiny of the country. It is taken for granted that it is desirable to be democratic: the term 'undemocratic' is a criticism, likely to be levelled against high-handed authority. The contrast between the desirability of being democratic and the desirability of being authoritarian is expressed even in psychological theory. The classic work in the psychology of prejudice, *The Authoritarian Personality*, rested upon a contrast between those persons who were presumed to possess 'democratic personalities' and their psychological opposites 'the authoritarian personalities' (Adorno et al., 1950). There was no doubt in the psychologists' minds about which was the more desirable type. The democratic types were the healthy ones, and it was the authoritarians who were the neurotic, distorted bigots with irrational cravings for authoritarian chains of command.

The teachers, in their behaviour, showed how authority can be restricted and, most importantly, can restrict itself in a democratic society. Within the classroom the teacher is the constituted authority with direct power over the pupils. Yet this authority is not maintained in an authoritarian manner. Instead the teacher becomes the *primus inter pares*, and uses democratic semantics: 'we' discover things together, rather than 'I', the authority, tell 'you' the already discovered facts. It is as if the teacher and the pupil have set sail together on a voyage of discovery. Having left the port, the teacher has come down from the ship's bridge and has discarded the old-fashioned uniform with its golden epaulettes of command. Now, teacher and crew are gathered on the ship's deck, discussing freely where to head for. Yet, authority has not been totally abandoned. For all the discussion, the passage has already been charted. The teacher still possesses the navigational maps, the compass and the power to ring the ship's bell. Even on the deck the teacher must direct the crew, and thereby the ship, but must do so without appearing too directive. These modern teachers, standing among their crew, cannot exercise their authority with the certainty of a Captain Ahab. Nor would they wish to.

The teachers, in not demanding deference, are behaving in a way which is general in modern society and which has ideological roots. Edward Shils has connected the decline of deferential behaviour to the rise of modern democracy: 'The egalitarian tendencies of contemporary Western societies have not only witnessed the attenuation and restriction of deference, they have seen it assimilated into the pattern of intercourse among equals' (1975: 289). Nevertheless, matters are not quite so simple. If the members of society were in actuality equals, then an egalitarian pattern of intercourse would fit happily into the pattern of reality: teachers and pupils would be genuinely embarked upon that exciting voyage of discovery. On the other hand, an egalitarian pattern within an inegalitarian social structure is fraught with dilemmatic aspects.

Modern society may have produced the democratic values which ensure that Captain Ahab is an outdated figure. Yet it has also produced modern authorities in profusion (Johnson, 1972). Each aspect of society has its authorities, or experts, whose authority has been duly accredited by requisite, duly constituted authorities. No longer is it possible for anyone with minimum literacy and maximum confidence to enter a classroom as a teacher. Examinations must be passed and official certificates must have been issued. The very process of examination is intrinsically authoritarian; the official authorities question the supplicant and, if the answers are sufficiently correct, authorized certification can be issued (Rueschemeyer, 1983).

Ideologically produced dilemmatic thinking arises when two valued themes of an ideology conflict, and these dilemmatic elements can spill over into a full-scale dilemma, when a choice has to be made. A conflict between the valued aspirations of an ideology and the reality of the society need not, of itself, produce an ideological dilemma. For example, there might hardly be a problem if all members of modern society consensually agreed that it was a shame that authority had to be exercised on occasion and that full assimilation of equalitarian tendencies was self-evidently desirable. Everyone would then be looking forward to the day when authority could be eliminated. However, as will be seen, matters are not this simple, because respect for authority has not been totally dismissed. Authorities are expected to be respected and to behave in a way that can be respected. Social norms may criticize the concept of authority, but they also justify the same concept. The *British Social Attitudes* report of 1986 revealed overwhelming support for the idea that it was important for schools to teach fifteen-year-olds 'respect for authority'. Less than 4 per cent of the respondents believed respect for authority to be unimportant. An even lower percentage dismissed the importance of 'discipline and orderliness' (Jowell, Witherspoon and Brook, 1986: 233).

This chapter concentrates upon the authority of the expert. At first glance the concept of 'expertise' seems to resolve the dilemma between equality and authority; however, as will be seen, it only re-creates the dilemma in new forms. It will be suggested that modern relations between experts, and between experts and non-experts, are characterized by ambivalence rather than by the egalitarianism described by Shils. Although the democratic norms may have been assimilated into patterns of intercourse, they have not driven out all authoritarian tendencies. Patterns of discourse and behaviour are marked by what Wetherell, Stiven and Potter (1987) have called 'unequal egalitarianism', or perhaps a 'non-authoritarian authoritarianism'. In this pattern the modern expert does not have Captain Ahab's commanding manner. Instead the expert is like a large individual caught up in a throng of smaller persons. The giant attempts to look inconspicuous by bending at the knees and hunching the shoulders. Trying hard not to step on tiny toes, the giant nevertheless tries to move the throng gently in the desired direction. One push too hard and the Lilliputians will turn in fury upon our Gulliver. One push to few and they will blame him for not sharing the vision provided by his extra height. The hunched-shouldered authority must proceed warily.

The hunched-shouldered authority

Two examples will be given of the discourse of experts, and in these the tension between authority and equality will be found. Both examples look at expertise in a group setting, and there is a similarity between both sets of expertise. In each case, the experts are authorities on children with difficulties. In both instances, there is no question that the experts are dedicated professionals, caring for the children and the anxieties of their parents. Moreover, these professionals have to cooperate amongst themselves and are well aware that the good of the children will be jeopardized by any professional jealousies between different specialisms. Cooperation and care must guide their activities. As expert authorities, who care and cooperate, they unthinkingly and uncynically hunch their shoulders, so as to prevent onlookers being blinded by the flash of an official epaulette.

The first example is taken from a study by Mehan (1983) of the language used in decision-making committees. Mehan was particularly interested in the language of professional experts, who worked in 'school appraisal teams' deciding how to classify school children with special educational needs. He noted how the definitions imposed by the professionals in their diagnosis of the 'problem' determined the decisions about where the children would be sent. The language of the professional authorities, whether medical or psychological, was grounded in expertise. They presented their official reports in a specialized format, using technical terms. Most of the professionals had only a slight contact with the child whose case was being discussed. Those with first-hand knowledge, such as parents and classroom teachers, spoke in a less professional way at the institutional meetings. Their reports lacked the expert vocabulary and the fluency of the professionals. The experts would typically present their fluent reports without interruption, whereas the non-experts suffered frequent interruption. And, of course, the less authoritative discourse was associated with lower prestige in the institutional setting.

The example concerns the way that one professional, a psychologist, called upon a classroom teacher to speak to the committee: 'Kate, would you like to share with us?' (Mehan, 1983: 197). In fact, Mehan does not discuss in any detail this invitation, being more interested in the patterns of the reports themselves. The words of the psychologist chairperson constitute the sort of speech act commonly studied by conversation analysts. The words can be seen as a successful conversational gambit to achieve the plan of eliciting discourse from the classroom teacher (Hobbs and Evans, 1980). One might note that the plan is executed with politeness. This is to be predicted, for it has been claimed that successful conversation is marked by a 'politeness maxim' which is part of a more general 'cooperative principle' (Grice, 1975; Bach and Harnish, 1979; McLaughlin, 1984).

If one examines the specific character of this conversational plan and the nature of the politeness it embodies, one can see the influence of ideology. According to Althusser (1971), ideology 'interpellates' or 'hails' the subject. The discourse of the psychologist chairperson hails and interpellates another. Not only is the other called upon to perform discursively, but also the other is hailed by name, Kate. The chairperson did not glance brusquely around the table and merely call out 'Mrs X' in a tone which commanded words from the classroom teacher and silent attention from everyone else. Instead the chairperson's words and syntax are not those of confident command; there is a linguistic hesitancy. The form is that of a question, phrased with delicacy to avoid offence. And the offence would have been that of imperious command. The first name is used (an intimacy which may not have been reciprocated, but the norms of equalization would not have forbidden the reciprocation). The first name conveys a friendliness, as if the professional and Kate were friends. The relationship of friendship is, of course, one of equality, at least in theory, in the way that the relationship between high-status expert and lower-status semi-expert is not. Instead of a command there is an invitation, as if one friend is inviting another. The impression of equality is emphasized by the choice of words to describe what Kate is being invited to do. She is not invited to give her report to be assessed by expert decision-makers. She is not even invited to give anything, for that would imply that others were taking. Instead, she is invited to 'share'. What could be more egalitarian than sharing with friends? The language is that of free and equal exchange without any hint of a competition. And so the authority metaphorically hunches its shoulders and draws itself inwards in a way that only makes sense against a background of ideological assumptions about the nature of persons and how they should conduct their business.

The second example is a British one, and it is taken from a research project which examined the workings of a child development centre (for more details see Middleton and Mackinlay, 1987). The centre is a unit attached to a hospital, and is of a type which has been promoted in a number of government reports on service provision for the mentally and physically handicapped (Court Report, 1976; Warnock Report, 1978; for critical assessment of multiprofessional practice see Tomlinson, 1981 and Gliedman and Roth, 1980). Instead of being staffed by a particular specialized type of expert, this type of centre is multidisciplinary and comprises a broad range of professionals. There are paediatricians, nurses, physiotherapists, educational and clinical psychologists, social workers, health visitors, nursery nurses and so on. All have an immense commitment to the unit in which they work, and they represent a group of specialists who are determined to sink professional rivalries and inequalities. The ethos is that the interests of the children should come first; and that all the experts, whatever their different specialist backgrounds, should combine to work towards common goals. It is an ethos which expresses democratic aspirations and opposes the authoritarianism of rank.

In this second example, the interviewer is talking to the nursery nurse in the centre's general office. Normally, the nursery nurse is of low status in the context of a children's hospital. She – and the ascription of gender is appropriate – is barely an expert in a world of highly trained and prestigiously accredited experts. She is telling the interviewer how much she enjoys working at the unit. She feels part of a team; the others, especially the physiotherapists, do not think themselves all-important. In the unit, she explains, no one thinks themselves superior: 'We all do everybody else's job and we all take advice from each other.' They work 'so much as a team', without any consciousness of status. In fact, she explains, they are all friends as well as colleagues. It was only people outside the unit who looked down upon the position of nursery nurse. At this point, the speech therapist enters the room to ask politely, 'Excuse me, have we got any medicine cups?' So polite is the phrasing that the nursery nurse interprets the interrogative as a question rather than a command. Thus she replies that there might be some in the drugs cupboard, but the pharmacy stores provide them. This is not the response that the speech therapist was wishing for: her conversational plan has not succeeded. She states: 'I want it now, though.' The nursery nurse responds by obediently searching for the cup. However, the switch from the democratic interrogative of the first person plural ('have we?') to the command of the first person singular ('I want') has been too abrupt. It has conveyed an unintended authoritarianism. The speech therapist starts to parody her own words: 'I want it *now*' she says, in the humorously exaggerated tone of a sergeant-major. In so doing she distances her own command from the sort of authoritarian, military command which would have been unacceptable.

The tones of command had to be inhibited, for they would have been inappropriate in the egalitarian atmosphere of the unit. The tones have been transformed into humorous parody, but the command has not been negated. The nursery nurse searches for the cup and is pleased to find one for her colleague and friend. The order is obeyed so long as the commander denies that an order is an order. Like the teachers discussed in the previous chapter, the speech therapist has not negated authority as such. No one wants democracy to go that far. At another point the nursery nurse, in talking about the equality of the centre, claims that she does the same sort of work as the sister: 'I run the clinics, I do exactly the same as sister.' However, the equality is not entirely devoid of inequality: 'The difference between us is that she has the responsibility, she carries the can.' And so the nursery nurse is prepared to accept the authority of the sister, the most dominant figure in the day-to-day running of the centre, just as she accepts a reasonable order which politely parodies authoritarianism. But her acceptance cannot be taken for granted. Delicate semantics and syntax are required to express the unequal egalitarianism.

Expertise and equality

Many social scientists analyse relationships and conversations in terms of 'negotiation', with the implication that, as people react to each other, they are negotiating their respective statuses, roles, identities and so on. The two examples given in the previous section would be well suited to such an analysis. They suggest that in relationships between experts of different status, there is a continual negotiation of the limits of expert authority. If the expert is too direct in giving orders, there may be a reaction. On the other hand, if commands are phrased too hesitantly as questions, the questioner may elicit in response a factual answer rather than a compliant action. The conversation in the child development centre showed such a negotiation, as the speech therapist oscillated between question, command and parody of command in order to strike the right balance. One might say that the two conversationalists were negotiating the appropriate tone of the conversations and thereby negotiating their respective roles and identities. Similarly the psychologist chairperson in the first example needed to negotiate her identity as an authority, but a friendly one.

An important factor is omitted if one concentrates entirely upon the negotiations between the individual participants in these everyday dramas. This is the ideological factor. The dilemmas involved in these interpersonal negotiations represent more than the problems of the individual personalities involved. Similarly, they represent more than the tensions of the organizations involved. They are representations of a basic ideological dilemma. The values which the participants wish to respect, and to be seen to respect, are central ideological values. The interpersonal representations of these ideological dilemmas do not result in the ideological dilemmas being negotiated to a satisfactory conclusion and thereby disappearing from everyday life. In fact, the reverse is the case. Because the ideological dilemma persists at a deeper level, the interpersonal dilemmas of equality and expert authority are never fully resolved, but continue to reconstitute themselves in varying forms.

The basic dilemma of democracy and authority was well expressed by Durkheim in his essay 'Individuals and the intellectuals', first published in 1898 (full text in Lukes, 1969, to which page numbers refer in the following). This essay was a defence of the philosophy of rational liberalism, and his immediate opponents were the traditional conservatives who were supporting the prosecution of Alfred Dreyfus. Durkheim was writing at the height of the controversy surrounding the conviction of Dreyfus, a Jew and French army officer, on a charge of treason. Although there had been abundant evidence of the Captain's innocence, Dreyfus was convicted in an atmosphere of violent anti-semitism. Irrational respect for traditional authorities, opposition to the progress of modern democracy and xenophobia were all intermingled in the conservatism of Dreyfus's opponents. Their stance in its political outlines resembled that which Adorno et al. (1950) claimed much later to characterize the 'authoritarian personality'. In criticizing the anti-Dreyfusards Durkheim may have been criticizing traditional authoritarianism, but he was no anarchist, wishing to abolish all authority. The problem was to substitute a rational authority for an irrational one.

Durkheim's article discusses a basic problem for a democratic society: if democracy produces a multiplicity of opposing opinions, how is a harmonious society possible? In posing the question, Durkheim was raising the issue whether a democracy can be harmonious society if it recognizes that all opinions are necessarily equally valid:

> It will be said, if all opinions are free, by what miracle will they then be harmonious? If they are formed without knowledge of one another and without having to take account of one another, how can they fail to be incoherent? Intellectual and moral anarchy would then be the inevitable consequence of liberalism. (p. 24)

Durkheim was concerned to argue that liberalism did not lead to intellectual anarchy. Not all opinions were to be regarded equally. He suggested that liberalism 'does not sanction unlimited right to incompetence', for expert knowledge should be respected:

> Concerning a question on which I cannot pronounce with expert knowledge, my intellectual independence suffers no loss if I follow a more competent opinion. The collaboration of scientists is only possible thanks to this mutual deference. (p. 24)

Traditional deference might be irrational, but the equality of liberalism still needed a modern, rational deference. For this the role of the rational expert was of importance. At first glance, liberal individualism seems to conflict with rational authority, for a philosophy based on freedom of opinion would seem to lead to anarchy rather than to rational authority. However, Durkheim suggested that if individualism is not interpreted in terms of unlimited self-interest, and its social basis is recognized, then 'All these apparent contradictions vanish as if by magic' (p. 23). In other words, there will be no basic ideological dilemma to trouble the rational dreams of the liberal.

Durkheim was representing the same dream which gives force to the aspirations of the members of the child development centre, and indeed to countless other professional groups. The members of the group see themselves battling enlightenedly against the irrationality of those who revere status for its own sake. The egalitarian impulse, which attacks irrational defence, seeks to institute a deference based upon reason and respect for expertise. The psychologist in the unit talked about the way that status differences were reduced by recognizing the expertise of all members of the unit: 'If one allows others to be expert, then there isn't a tension. . . . the tension doesn't arise if you say "I have reached the limit here; I need your help."' Moreover, as Durkheim suggested, the recognition of expertise depends upon some common feeling. The members of the child development centre stressed their feeling of cooperation and group loyalty. The psychologist went on to add: 'The answer to a child's problems and help for a child's problems lies in two people working together and arriving at a solution that neither of them would have arrived at separately.'

The ethos of the group was that cooperation was rational because it produced desirable results. The approach was a problem-solving one. According to one member of the team, describing the history of the unit, 'Problem-oriented record-keeping was very useful in actually helping to eliminate petty rivalries, because we focused our attention on what we were going to do for the child, rather than what was going on within the team.' In other words, deference to status and the self-interest of status were intrinsically irrational because they hindered the solution of problems. All attention should be directed to the problems themselves and not to the irrelevancies of status. One member, referring to professional jealousies in the early days of the unit, commented that 'The thing that most impressed me was that those sort of feelings only lasted a very brief period. . . we quickly focused our attention on the children and the family rather than on the workings of the unit.'

Cooperation, based upon a common recognition of specialist expertise, encouraged the free expression of expert opinion, which jointly would lead to rational solutions of problems. Putting rationality first and recognizing that all opinions should be equally respected, so long as they were expert, would lead to progress over the old, inefficient and irrational concerns with authority. Moreover, a cohesive group would be created out of this rational individualism, just as Durkheim had envisaged that liberalism as a philosophy, or ideology, would lead to a rationally coherent society. There is one further point. The members of the centre, in describing their rational, egalitarian philosophy, stressed the harmony of the group and how their philosophy, so obvious and so commonsensical, had resolved the sorts of conflicts which are common elsewhere. To paraphrase Durkheim, it seemed that apparent, and very real, contradictions had vanished as if by magic.

This is the image of an applied philosophy, or ideology, which has conquered the problem of dilemmas: all has been harmoniously resolved under the benevolent direction of rational good sense. Yet, the dilemmas between equality and authority are not so easily, even magically, disposed of. Later, some of the dilemmas of the child development centre will be discussed. For the present, the dilemmas in theory can be seen. As Durkheim was seeking to reconcile opposing values, so they were separating themselves on his very pages. Durkheim raised the obvious question: if the expert opinion is to be respected, is not this an intrinsic threat to democracy, for the opinions of experts are to be given greater credence than those of non-experts? In answer, Durkheim suggested that respect for expertise only concerned technical issues, for which expertise was relevant. There was a whole range of civic issues which needed no special expertise. Casting his eye upon the Dreyfus case, Durkheim commented: 'In order to know whether a court of justice can be allowed to condemn an accused man without having heard his defence, there is no need for any special expertise. It is a problem of practical morality concerning which every man of good sense is competent and about which no one ought to be indifferent' (p. 25).

However, the separation between technical and civic issues is not so straightforward. Durkheim seemed ambivalent about whether the rational experts, when pronouncing upon the great civic and moral issues of the day, were actually just as equal as the mass. The purpose of his essay was to defend the Dreyfusard stance of liberal intellectuals. Why was it, he asked, that so many intellectuals had taken that stance? It was their 'professional activities' which had led them to criticize the official proceedings: 'Accustomed by the practice of scientific method to reserve judgement when they are not fully aware of the facts, it is natural that they give in less readily to the enthusiasms of the crowd and to the prestige of authority' (p. 25). In other words the expert, quite 'naturally', had a more rational way of thinking than the non-expert. Thus expert, and particularly scientifically expert, opinions on the great civic issues would be more rationally based that the irrationally authoritarian opinions of the masses.

All at once, as if by magic, the basic dilemma has reappeared, like a jack-in-the-box rudely bursting open its lid. Durkheim's grand jack-in-the-box is the sort of art work which is preserved in museums, which to this day are still regularly visited by academic tourists. However, in everyday life people are carrying around with themselves much smaller jack-in-the-boxes, designed along similar lines to Durkheim's but mass produced and incorporating modern features. As will be seen the members of the child development centre have not in practice resolved the dilemmas of ideological theory. Moreover, they carry a particularly difficult modern feature in their dilemmatic jack-in-the-boxes. The distinction between the authority of technical expertise and the democratic respect for the opinions of other people becomes even harder to draw (or to negotiate) when the expertise is not merely an expertise about scientific procedures or the operation of machinery. When the expert is an expert about people – other people – there are a whole range of problems to trouble the democratic spirit.

The expert in human relations

Durkheim's solution to the dilemma between democratic equality and expert authority suggests a boundary is being put around the scope of expertise. In certain matters the rational authority of expertise is relevant, but in others matters everyone has the capacity, indeed the obligation, to be rational. The solution suggests that there could be a harmonious and non-dilemmatic parallel development of equal personal relations and rational expertise. In fact, according to Durkheim's analysis, the growth of modern liberalism demands such a parallel development. There is evidence that, since Durkheim's day, something like this has occurred, for the equalization of intercourse, of which Shils wrote, has coincided with the modern growth of the professionalization of expertise. Although processes may be parallel in their development, this does not mean that they are necessarily harmonious, or that their separate functions enable ideological dilemmas to be resolved as if by magic.

The decline of deference raises questions about how the expert is to be treated. Perhaps the delineation, implied by Durkheim, has been translated into everyday practice, so that there is respect for the knowledge of the expert but not necessarily for the person of the expert. The comments of the psychologist chairperson could be interpreted in the light of such a distinction. The chairperson introduces the non-expert in friendly terms, but the way that the experts react to the report of the non-expert indicates a lack of respect. As Mehan (1983) shows, there is no deferential and silent respect paid to the non-expert's report. Yet, the lack of technical equality is not matched by a lack of personal equality. The chairperson's comments emphasize the equality of intercourse, as one individual to another within the democratically equal society. In fact, one might predict that in these circumstances there will be a correlation between the equality of chairperson's introductory remarks and the inequality of the treatment of the introduced report. It is precisely those whose expertise is deemed unequal who must be reassured that personally they are just as valuable as anyone else.

This prediction need not be based upon an observation of behaviour in committees, but can be derived from knowledge about how a skilled chairperson should act: the humblest person in the gathering should be put at their ease and not be made to feel slighted. Herein lies a paradox. The equalization of intercourse under these circumstances is itself a part of rational expertise. It is the expert professional who will act in this way. Thus the very enactment of equalization – the democratically polite tones of 'shall we share' – belongs to the rational authority, and inequality, of expertise. Similarly the liberal teacher, who enables the class to feel that they have jointly just discovered what they had been intended to learn, is exercising the specialized skills of modern pedagogy.

This implies a distinction between the expert as a figure and the content of expert's knowledge, the possession of which confers expertise. The equalization of interpersonal relations suggests that the expert should not be respected as a figure, or even as a possessor of expertise. It is the expertise which should be respected. In this regard, the modern growth of expertise has seen a semantic change in the concept of 'expert'. No longer does it imply experience of a personal kind. In *Troilus and Criseyde* Chaucer used the phrase 'expert in love' to describe someone who had experienced the emotion of love: he was not referring to some medieval sexologist, equipped with duly accredited certification and no debarring scandal to their name. The semantic shift seems to imply the notion that expertise is separable from the personal characteristics of the expert. The modern concept of 'expert system' would appear to reinforce such a separation, for the expertise is presumed to lie within a systematic body of information which is potentially available to all, including computing machinery, who wish to acquire it.

The delineation between the expertise, to which respect must be paid, and the expert individual, who is ordinarily equal, cannot be easily maintained, as the paradox of the friendly expert shows. The idea that expertise is separable from the expert may be readily accepted by the general public (Dreyfus and Dreyfus, 1986), but it does not accord with the actual practice of expertise. Schon (1983) has shown that all too often experts are not applying a fully determined and systematized body of knowledge. Instead, experts frequently improvise their way through novel situations, engaging in a 'conversation' with the situation. Modern expertise possesses a further feature, which blurs a simple distinction between the person and the expertise: so many experts are experts at human relations, and thus their expertise relates to the qualities of the person rather than the system.

The experts in the child development centre, like the modern professional teacher, have to be experts at handling others. Nor is this peculiar to the examples chosen; it is a characteristic of a wide variety of professions. Johnson (1972: 58–9) has suggested that the higher the prestige of a profession the less technical expertise is shown: 'Those professions which are "client-based" and diagnostically oriented provide services in which the element of non-technical interpersonal skills is most important.' Foremost amongst such high-status, 'client-based' professions is the legal profession, where an ability to deal with people counts for more than an encyclopaedic knowledge of the legal texts. To use current psychological phraseology, such experts have to show 'social skills'. Indeed, psychologists offering such training sometimes imply that the acquisition of social skills is a moral requirement for anyone who must conduct smooth and effective relationships with their fellows (Soucie, 1979).

The ambivalence in the position of the modern expert can be seen in the figure of the doctor. Merton has introduced the concept of 'sociological ambivalence' in his suggestion that social roles typically contain an ambivalent aspect. Each role contains more than a simple role prescription. It will include subordinate role prescriptions, which are often the opposite of the dominant prescriptions. Merton discusses in detail the role of the doctor. The dominant role prescription is to be objective and scientifically neutral. However, if the doctor's behaviour were the result of only following the norms of strict medical expertise, the doctor would be a poor doctor. It is a part of the role of the doctor that the doctor should be something other than a doctor. There is the requirement that the doctor should also be a friend. As a respondent noted in a recent study of general practitioners: 'We're not general practitioners, we're family doctors, which means you're a family friend' (Horobin, 1983: 97). However, the doctor is neither really nor merely a friend, but must act as if a friend. The friendly face which greets the patient in the surgery must convey that the doctor and patient might be friends, if only they did not have to meet in such a formal setting. But, of course, that is usually the only way that they have occasion to meet. In this way, the good doctor must employ a manner which oscillates between the impersonality of the medical authority and the easy equality of the friend. Because the easy equality is itself a necessary part of the unequal professional expertise, the equality cannot be total, but is itself a variety of unequal egalitarianism.

The notion that the expert must be an expert in relating to people is expressed in a popular guidebook for nurses, entitled *Interpersonal Relations* (Burton, 1979). The author stresses that, over and above the specific skills which a nurse must acquire, the nurse must become 'an expert in human relations'. Perhaps the average nurse might be daunted by the prospect, continues the author, but 'A nurse is responsible for improving human relations by making a patient feel at home in the hospital or comfortable with his illness wherever he is' (p. 129). The book gives a series of examples showing how the proficient nurse is such a human relations expert.

The concept of an expert in human relations is an ambivalent one, especially if expertise is intrinsically marked by inequality and human relations are seen to be characterized in their present form by signs of equalization. Certainly the 'expert in human relations' is not envisaged as an 'expert system', but as someone who is experienced in dealing with people and who is equipped with all the necessary social skills. If all people have experiences of 'human relations', then the expert has ordinary skills but to an extraordinary degree. The expert in 'human relations' does not allow personal feelings to cloud the ordinariness which must be shown in an extraordinary way. For example, the ordinary person might answer back sharply when criticized, but the nursing expert in human relations should avoid reacting in this way (Burton, 1979: 201). The nurse should be like a friendly hostess, 'responsible for making strangers comfortable in her hospital home' (pp. 140–1). The analogy of hosts and guests suggests the equality of friendship, but the visits are not reciprocated, for it is the patient who is always the guest of the nurse. Above all, the expert in human relations must show the ordinary touch whose expert accomplishment is so different from the acquired expertise necessary for running complex equipment or bandaging bloodied limbs: 'What a patient requires is a genuine interest in his total welfare, a sincere desire to make him comfortable, and a nurse's perceptive ability – the ability to put herself into his bedroom slippers' (p. 136).

The demand for the expert to be friendly – to be a hostess – is one which Merton (1976) recognized to be charged with ambivalence. If the expert is too friendly the claim to expertise is endangered, whereas too much technical expertise threatens the friendliness. The human relations expert is the expert with the expertise to balance the competing claims of equality and authority, and to do so in an authoritatively friendly manner. Above all there is nothing secret in this. The guidebook for nurses is not revealing secrets. In fact, its banality stems from its lack of secret information to impart to the trainee in human relations. The experts, whether doctors, lawyers, chairpersons or physiotherapists, are aware of the dangers of appearing too imperious in their expertise or, conversely, of allowing friendliness to cloud professionalism. They must be ready to deny that they are being high and mighty (a denial which must seem strange to the respected figures of former ages). Yet, on the other hand, they cannot allow that anyone can do their jobs, for then they cease to be experts.

If the expertise is perceived as being too ordinary, then the claim can be made that anyone can be an expert in human relations. Counsellors and psychotherapists have faced the problem of lay helpers, lacking the necessary certification, but offering human relations guidance (Durlak, 1979;

Nietzel and Fisher, 1981). These lay helpers are sometimes called 'para-professionals', a grand term which accords them enough expertise, if not to be the equal of the full professional, at least to put them above the totally ordinary unprofessional member of the public. Thus the paraprofessional is seen to possess human relations expertise which is a cut above the person haphazardly advising strangers in railways carriages or bars. Even the paraprofessional must follow the professional in stressing that their expertise in human relations is not so ordinary as to be possessed by completely ordinary people. By definition the expert is an expert, and the very choice of term 'expert in human relations' is designed to enhance the respectful distance between ordinary person and professional.

Experts and non-experts

There is one point that cannot be stressed too strongly. The friendly smiles of the expert, produced so expertly and divorced from genuine friendship, are not to be confused with hypocrisy. There may be some experts who are hypocrites. In bad faith, such hypocrites may knowingly flash their smiles whilst plotting to manipulate with cynicism. It is possible that the chairperson, who delicately introduces the classroom teacher at the case conference meeting, has quite explicitly decided to 'turn on the charm' for some ulterior purpose. However, for every ill-intentioned schemer, there are many more for whom the friendly style will be accepted unquestioningly as the proper form of behaviour. Moreover, donor and recipient of the smile may agree with this social propriety. The teacher who has been introduced might well feel slighted unless the chairperson has conveyed a gesture of friendly equality, and this mutually recognized code of reciprocity is very different from hypocrisy. As Mannheim in *Ideology and Utopia* pointed our, deliberate deceit does occur, but it is nowhere near as frequent, or as theoretically interesting, as the well-intentioned operation of ideology.

The significance of the polite intercourse between the chairperson and the teacher should not be confined to interpersonal relations. The attempt to convey friendliness should not be boiled down merely to a strategem of etiquette between two persons, or be seen only as a form of 'impression management' by which one actor presents their self to another. There are ideological dimensions at work in between the management of individual images. The experts are not merely conveying 'friendliness' because they want others to think well of them as individuals, although doubtlessly they want this as well. They are also following what may broadly be termed a philosophy of friendliness. They genuinely believe that the forms of discourse which represent the equality of friendship, rather than the stiffness of authority, are beneficial to the world. The liberal teacher's prime motive is not based upon a wish to be liked by the class, or even by fellow professionals: it derives from a firm belief, whose efficacy is tested daily in the classroom, that education should be pursued in a friendly, egalitarian spirit. Similarly, the nursing guide stresses that the nursing will bring more benefit to the patients, if nurses 'get along' with patients, fellow nurses and all the other professionals in the hospital. The general practitioner who is friendly may be a nicer person than the unfriendly doctor, but that is beside the point: it is the friendly doctor who is the more expert doctor. Thus the friendly intercourse of egalitarianism is not considered merely more congenial than an authoritarian mode, but it is seen as being more effective. Because it works and solves the problems, which must be solved, it is the more rational form. In consequence the experts, whose friendly smiles might appear superficial when compared with smiles of genuine friendship, are not being hypocritical, for they believe their conduct to be correct and rational. Moreover, they have good grounds for believing that the recipients of the signs of friendliness demand this extra display of expertise.

The execution of such expertise is not without its problems. The liberal and egalitarian motivations, which might attack the old-fashioned displays of inequality, nevertheless have to be expressed within a social world, which is not itself perfectly liberal or egalitarian. As will be seen, there is a tension between egalitarian and inegalitarian, liberal and authoritarian forces in the practice of expertise. This tension ensures that it is too simple to hope that contradictions will vanish magically with the application of well-intentioned liberalism. Further examples drawn from the personnel of the child development centre will show how liberal motives can result in illiberal consequences and how the practice of professional egalitarianism can bring into play new inequalities. These examples illustrate the dialectic between equality and authoritarianism in two interrelated directions: first, the relations between different experts; and secondly, the relations between the experts and the non-experts.

Relations between experts
The child development centre illustrates on a tiny scale one aspect of Durkheim's vision of a modern rational society. If such a society were to be attainable it must possess moral coherence and could not be based upon the coincidence of individual interests. Similarly the centre was based upon a moral philosophy of interdependence, in which loyalty to the group and its aspirations was paramount. The members strongly identified with the collectivity, and it was only through the collectivity that they sought to pursue their individual goals. In establishing the group, according to one member, 'The big thing to learn was that your job did not come before everyone else's.' Responsibility was shared, in a way that demanded that the group be cohesive. As the sister said, 'People take on responsibility beyond any strict definition of what they are trained to do in order to make

sure that a problem is acted upon when it crops up.' Loyalty and identification were thus transposed from their professional speciality to the unit, as members sought to think of themselves not primarily as 'psychologists', 'physiotherapists' or 'nurses' but as members of a team with a common goal.

Here was a process that social psychologists could describe in terms of the creation of group identification (Tajfel, 1981; Taylor and Moghaddam, 1987; Turner, 1987). In this case, the group possessed the rationalist objective of 'getting the job done' and breaking down unhelpful barriers of status between group members. However, the desire for group commonality, despite its egalitarian philosophy, created its own illiberal, authoritarian demands. If the group were to function cohesively, dissent and egoism could not be tolerated. To use the language of Durkheim, individualism could only be expressed through the collectivity. In practice this entailed that a 'party line' had to be insisted upon. According to the sister, 'If people have come to work here and do not fit into our way of going about things and if they try to kick against it. . .they either modify their ways or leave.' The psychologist specifically linked the authority of the group to its egalitarian philosophy. In this egalitarianism not all views were equal, only those that were egalitarian: 'If someone came to join the unit and found it difficult to accept the idea that we all have equal rights to suggest ideas for what to do next, then they either had to change their approach or leave.' The friendliness of the group could only be maintained if there were an illiberal determination to get rid of the unsatis-factorily inegalitarian.

Experts and non-experts

There is social psychological evidence that the creation of strong group ties affects the way that group members view non-group members (Tajfel, 1981; Turner, 1987). As ties between ingroup members become stronger, so there is a corresponding distancing from outgroups (Pepitone and Kleiner, 1957; Sherif, 1966). Certainly within the unit, the creation of group cohesiveness can be seen in terms of the creation of group isolation. The members viewed themselves as battling against entrenched orthodoxies and interests within the hospital. At the same time there was an unplanned distancing from the general public and, in particular, from families of the patients. The members of the centre were acutely aware of this distance and they sought to combat it. The particular form of this distancing cannot be explained in terms of general social psychological theorizing about intergroup relations and the universal properties of ingroups and outgroups, whatever their nature. Instead, it derives from the ideological dilemma of the liberal expert, who simultaneously accepts and rejects authority.

The expert may seek to serve the interests of the non-expert (the member of the public), but in so doing the expert is faced with the issue identified by Durkheim: the non-expert has no unlimited right to incompetence. Yet on the other hand, the expert has no unlimited right to dismiss contemptuously the views of the non-expert, however uninformed they might be. A party line might be achievable within the group, but it cannot be imposed over the general public which the experts seek to serve. The liberal aim of rational cooperation was expressed. The social worker at another child development centre claimed that 'Our aim is to foster an alliance between the team and the families.' Again there is the rhetoric of rational egalitarianism, as both parties work together towards a common end. Yet the alliance cannot be an egalitarian one, for the view of the expert must somehow impose its rational authority. The social worker continued: 'You have to get the parents on your side if you are going to be able to do anything useful.' The parents were going to have to come over to the side of the experts. This was not seen as an alliance to be formed upon a middle ground. In recognition of the pressure that expert authority can place on non-experts in these sorts of situation, there have been calls to 'democratize' therapeutic intervention and to 'empower' parents in their contact with professionals (Wolfendale, 1986; Cochran, 1986). The professional, of course, faces a dilemma: the more that 'consumer rights' are afforded, the more the experts are in danger of giving away their authority.

There is evidence from other studies that the dialogue between experts and members of the public is not an equal one based upon rational persuasion. The experts of the medical profession will impose their views, or schemata, upon the very different ones held by the patients; whilst the patients may accede in the face of rhetorical pressure, they do not actually change their own schemata (Tannen and Wallat, 1986). The unity of the group increases the pressure on the parent. Instead of being faced by a single expert, whose advice might be checked by a second opinion, the parent is faced by a united phalanx of experts. From the nursery nurse to the paediatrician, all are agreed upon a single diagnosis and recommended course of action. As the sister said: 'In getting together and discussing the child's problems we are able to give the mums and their families the same advice from everybody and not conflicting advice from all different professionals. We look at all the different points of view and come up with some agreement of how best we can all help the child.' Again the rationality is impeccable. Who would want conflict? And who could deny the value of different professionals cooperating to produce the most helpful advice? And yet the power of the 'mums', and of their outlook, is reduced as expertise is strengthened through unity and rational cooperation. Sometimes the 'mums' are not even considered equal enough to enter the dialogue. The prognosis for their children may be so dispiriting that they are not considered ready to accept all the information. The team possesses human relations expertise, which enables judgements to be made.

This expertise, which must use kindness and sensitivity in 'winning over' the 'mums', emphasizes the gap between the experts and the non-experts. And the more sensitivity which is shown, the more the inequality is emphasized, because the sensitivity is itself part of the expertise which separates the expert from the recipient of expertise.

The unit's tension between equality and authority can be crudely summarized: the greater the equality within the group, the more the authority of the group was strengthened in relation to the non-experts. Thus equality within the group seemed to enhance inequality between the group and non-experts, and therefore the egalitarian motivations of the group had an inegalitarian effect. The unit's members were aware of the problem, and they recognized that their attempts to lessen the gap between experts and non-experts involved accepting the inequalities between experts. One of the psychologists was discussing how the families tended to be overawed by the higher-status professionals. This higher status, in turn, prevents the expert from gaining the trust which is so necessary if there is to be a successful alliance. In consequence, it is the lower-status nurses who are assigned the task of winning over the families: 'The nursing staff are the most accessible because people. . .have a concept of nurses as nurturant and caring. So they are not threatening or at least not daunting like other therapists might be, the psychologists for example. This gives us a way in.' This comment expresses an awareness that, in order for the unit to deal best with the children and their families, it was necessary to accept the philosophy of status, which the group saw as hindering those ends. In this sense, the rational liberalism was coming up against the illiberal presumptions of the society. As a result, the unit was caught between either accepting and working with the authoritarian presumptions, or failing to establish the rational authority of its expertise. Either way, equalization could not banish authority.

What should be emphasized is that the members of the unit were aware of these dilemmas, and talked of them openly with the interviewer. They knew from daily experience that the contradictions did not vanish as if by magic, but that the work of their own unit, of which they were fiercely proud, threw up fresh problems. In winning over the 'mums', they might have to cajole, or even conceal information. This was something which was done with reluctance. They might have to acknowledge the status which in their own relations they wished to eradicate. Above all they knew that expertise could exert unfair authority over the inexpert and the powerlessly confused. Yet they knew also that they could only help the families and their handicapped children if the expert view were the *primus* amongst the *pares* of other views. We should not dismiss this dedicated group of professionals as being cynics who manipulate the weak in order to further their own professional interests. Nor should we patronize them as being unthinking optimists, blindly driven by a set of principles and oblivious to all dilemmatic difficulties. Instead, these are experts who know from daily experience that the general principles, which sound so rationally obvious in theory, do not in practice resolve all difficulties. Like so many other modern experts in other fields, they are aware of the dilemmas of expertise: they talk about them, argue about them and continue to search for that magic solution which will, once and for all, rationally exorcize the ghost of Captain Ahab.

6
Health and Illness

Illness is often thought of as if it were only a matter of physiological change or decline, having a matter-of-factness beyond dispute. However, this is clearly not the case. The dividing line between sickness and health is one that has been drawn and redrawn many times over the years, both in relation to changes in the symptoms which people present and in the way that doctors define disease. This ambiguity in definition is equally apparent in the way that different cultures treat the same bodily signs; in some countries diarrhoea and scrofula are matters for medical assistance, in others the conditions are part of life's everyday burdens. Illness, therefore, is subject to social definition, and so are the patients who suffer it. This is as true of people who have physical conditions as it is of those who are described as mentally ill. Students of social science are well used to explanations of psychiatric conditions which view them as being maintained through social definitions and labelling. At the same time these explanations challenge the epistemology of medical thinking which locates this illness 'inside the heads' of those involved. In this chapter we shall not be discussing mental illness but instead be taking the opportunity to explore the ideological character of being physically ill, and the dilemmas which can arise through the sharpening of contradictory demands implicit in people's bodily and social conditions. Illness – or better still, 'being ill' – is also ideological in the sense in which other topics in this book are subject to that term. The sick are subject to a social discourse which locates them in society, which gives them rights and obligations out of which their capacities and opportunities in other spheres of life are expanded or, more often, curtailed. While ideologies attaching to illness are not limited to the sick, the experience of the contradictions implicit within these ideas is not equally available to all. It is when people fall ill that these ideological contradictions are experienced by them in ways which, as healthy individuals, they could not have fully anticipated beforehand.

While it is believed by some that 'you make yourself ill with worry' or that fretting over illness is largely a function of 'mind over matter', there is something incontrovertible about kidney failure or influenza which belies attempts to 'psychologize' illness away. As we shall see, there is an unavoidable conjunction of thinking and being in all talk of dealing with illness; just as some speak of the power of right thinking over the body's health, so in the past others have believed that a body brought under the rule of a healthy regimen is the basis for soundness of mind (Turner, 1984). This relationship of body and mind is something that runs, like an underground channel, beneath the structures of so much of modern thinking about illness and health. While it is hidden from view by the edifice of medical technology, which separates out the body in order to subject it to treatment, it is revealed in the case of illnesses where medicine has been less successful, the prime example today being cancer. Then there are appeals to a different sort of treatment, a 'holistic approach' in which the attitudes and feelings of the patient are summoned as a resource to combat disease. These competing views about illness make for an interesting examination of problems in their application, and of the dilemmas which arise for medical practitioners of each persuasion. These, however, are very much questions of expertise and of practice, to which we have given attention in the previous chapter. They arise, not only because there are doctors on the one hand and patients on the other, but also because of the competing demands upon ourselves which are juxtaposed when we are prey to sickness and disease. Examining these demands goes some way towards understanding the different shapes that contradictions take in everyday experience, and towards revealing the ideological basis of the beliefs which are there even in the world of unreflecting healthiness.

Before doing this we need to set some boundaries to our discussion: first by comparing illness to some other areas of experience, and then by asking ourselves whether illness can, in fact, be taken 'all of a piece'. Being ill is clearly not like going to school, except in as much as both are, for some, conditions to be suffered. While there are competing views as to the value of different kinds of knowledge, or even of 'how much' knowledge, there appears to be universal agreement that pain and disease are unwelcome and unwanted. Perhaps we should qualify this and say that pain and disease that lead to death or to permanent injury are unwanted. For there are notable exceptions in which some pain and temporary disease are either sought or thought fitting and appropriate. There is a strong body of opinion that pain, as part of natural childbirth, is preferable to the anaesthesia of drugs; in wartime there are testimonies that soldiers envied colleagues who left the battlefield with slight but incapacitating wounds; and who has not felt the reassurance of a bad (but tolerable) headache or other symptom which confirms the wisdom of having stayed in bed rather than going to work that day?

These exceptions are cited, if really necessary, to show that illness in general is not a thing about which many people are divided. There are few 'pros' and an overwhelming majority of 'antis'. We should expect, therefore, that when people are ill they will reveal a wholehearted dislike of their situation and a wish to be well again. In the experience of illness there should appear a unity of belief and purpose which challenges the argument that there is a dilemmatic aspect to our everyday lives. This idea of a unitary set of beliefs surrounding illness is consistent with the view that ideologies surmount distinct fields of people's experience or topics in social science. There would then be an ideology of medicine (or of education) which made sensible the problems lying within that area alone. The problem with this view is that it leaves each field of social life as separate in experience, so that the very issues in everyday thinking which are double-edged in their implications would simply not arise. It is because people must continue to act in a world of inter-penetrating values and practices, stemming from various life fields, that the consequences of taking one line of action rather than another is of particular significance. If it were not so, if people lived in a world of relative standpoints, then their perspectives would be prescribed and their thinking across contexts effectively dislocated. As this has been stated already: 'In effect, social action is not really constituted by opposition or unities of discrete groupings of people, but by a *praxis* which expresses a multiplicity of relations at any one time' (Radley, 1979: 86).

With regard to illness, this means that we should expect any ideology of the sick person or of the illness situation to draw upon and to have implications for other areas of social life. As will be demonstrated later on, the appreciation of good health depends, in no small way, upon an understanding of what it means to be a sick person. The world of illness provides a repertoire of constructs which can be employed in setting out our attitudes to other matters of social significance. Sontag (1979) provides useful examples in her references to Hitler's description of the Jews producing 'a racial tuberculosis among nations', and to John Adams's diary entry in 1771 when he wrote: 'The Body of the People seem to be worn out by struggling, and Venality, Servility and Prostitution eat and spread like a Cancer' (p. 80). Of course, the specialized application of medical knowledge gives rise to an informed position with regard to how ill people should act and should be treated in return. There is a danger, however, in describing medical thinking as ideological in this regard, if by this is meant that it sets out a unified 'forensic' system separate from the 'latent' ideology of its patients (see chapter 3 for a discussion of forensic and latent ideology).

There is, however, another reason why we should not regard illness and health as worlds separated by distinct ideologies; this has to do with the fact that, when ill, people still partake of the world of health. This is obvious in the case of minor and temporary afflictions where they can still live their lives largely as normal, but it is equally true of those chronic and often serious conditions with which people must live for much of the time. This not merely provides a tension within their experience, but actually gives form to the way in which they conceptualize matters of health and of illness.

Illness in a world of health

> 'This is not the season of the year for a business boom, of course, we admit that, but a season of the year for doing no business at all, that does not exist, Mr Samsa, must not exist.'
>
> 'But sir,' cried Gregor, beside himself and in his agitation forgetting everything else, 'I'm just going to open the door this very minute. A slight illness, an attack of giddiness, has kept me from getting up. I'm still lying in bed. But I feel all right again. I'm getting out of bed now. Just give me a moment or two longer! I'm not quite so well as I thought. But I'm all right, really.'
> (Franz Kafka, *Metamorphosis*)

This quotation from Kafka's story of the man who woke up to find himself transformed into a giant beetle consists of an exchange between the victim, Gregor, and the chief clerk of the firm where he works. It is, in allegorical form, an illustration of the discourse between the worlds of health and of illness. It is no mere accident that society's agent is represented by a man of business. For most people in Western culture being ill means not being able to work, so that what defines their condition is not so much a bodily condition but an incapacity. To be healthy is to be 'fit for' social duties; to be ill is to be unable to satisfy them. Determining which of these situations one is in is often fraught with uncertainty, as is revealed by Gregor's own claims to fitness. It would appear that he is very much in two minds as to whether he is well or ill, fit or unfit; even in the totality of his metamorphosis there remains the need to be a fully functioning member of society, to be 'all right, really'. Is this situation in any way peculiar for being drawn from a fictional setting? We think not. A moment's reflection on many people's part will soon recover instances of times when they have struggled on when under the second signs of illness, or when they or others have returned to work before being completely recovered. This is so much part of one's general expectation of active life and social duty that this surface inconsistency has quite a normal ring to it. Indeed, there are credits and benefits to be gained, not from denying illness completely, but from conducting oneself in such a way that one's actions both hide and reveal the shape of the illness one is labouring under. Service beyond the call of duty, and courage, are made of such things. Yet this is a balance that has to be properly gauged. Drag yourself to work when obviously ill and you are a fool; lie abed for days after a fever has passed and you risk being called a malingerer.

This issue can be explored further by reference to real examples, in this case drawn from a study more fully reported by Radley (1988). This is what two men, typical of several, said concerning their life after cardiac surgery for severe coronary disease:

> I think they have made me as well as I possibly might be. No, I'm not ill, I don't feel as if I am anyway, I'm as well as I am going to be, possibly, and if I'm as well as I'm going to be I feel that I'm well.

> I don't consider I've got an illness now. Even before...I tended to pop another tablet in my mouth and carry on...I suppose it might gradually get better, but if it doesn't it won't make any difference.

While the second quotation has about it a surface quality of unexceptional matter-of-factness, it is the expression of a viewpoint which appears consistent because the speaker is able to allocate the exceptions to his health to a special part of his life or, as in many cases like this, to a special part of his body. 'It's only my heart' said one patient in the same situation. This attitude arises during illness so that there is a separation, in experience, of aspects of the body from the individual as a member of society. At all times individuals know that they *have* a body and yet *are* their bodies; during health the latter is coextensive with social life. There is a body for working, for resting, for loving through which people are free to participate in the world of activity. However, in illness the body which is injured or sick, in being withdrawn from social life, becomes one to which one becomes subject. In these times, the difference between these two conditions must be resolved as best people can, often through the maximization of what they can do freely and the minimization of what they are forced to limit themselves to do. This attitude of 'normalization' (Davis, 1963) appears unitary because it makes exceptions and locates these at a different level from the significance of social life. Let us illustrate this further, and then go on to show how this attitude depends upon a set of assumptions which are at variance with those other views which the person expresses.

A man awaiting cardiac surgery, who was particularly concerned to 'work quite normally', said:

> I'm not worried about it or anything like that. I'm in professional hands like. When you've got something wrong with your car you take it to the professionals don't you?

In this quotation the problem of illness is reduced to a malfunctioning part of the body which awaits correction by expert medical practitioners. Another patient said:

> I don't feel ill. I don't feel ill at all...right up until Christmas I've led an active life, slowed down knowing my limitations, but again we come back to the same answer...something has got to be done about it. I'm hoping that I shall be even better than I was before.

Both of the above examples express a confidence in the retention of active life through the correction of what is held to be a temporary disorder. In the balance between the freedom of social participation and the constraint of the body, there is expressed the belief that the latter is but a minor term in the equation. On the face of it this is an understandable attempt to keep things in perspective, to cope with a stressful episode by maintaining a consistent attitude of overall good health in spite of an exceptional symptom. However, there is implicit in all of these statements an attitude which is at variance with the impression fostered of being 'all right, really'. There is an acceptance of the doctor's authority to indicate the extent of the healthiness of the body and to describe the boundaries of sickness. This then provides a certification, as it were, of the person's health 'with the exception of...'. It is as if an ex-patient of a mental hospital were to attempt to prove his/her sanity by reference to a discharge note which s/he carried. In the affirmation of health, even where people retain their social engagements, they are obliged to make use of the constraints of the body in order to define their sense of well-being. If an attitude of 'good health' were merely defined by the absence of illness, then there would be very few people expressing a healthy outlook or defining themselves as such today. For most people have something 'wrong' with them most of the time. Health and illness are not, therefore, discrete states from which one moves in a unitary fashion, but are interdependent terms in experience. This specific feature has been anticipated in our general thesis that ideological thought is dialectical (see chapter 3) and signals a need, at this point, for us to examine this issue more closely.

When, like other descriptions of psychological life, health and illness are abstracted from real settings they become opposing terms or poles of a particular construct. However, the apparent equality of the terms is misleading, for where health describes for much (or most) of people's lives a background condition, the default state of our existence, illness signifies a break or discontinuity in that state. Whereas health is normally assumed, enjoyed yet defined only with difficulty, illness is figured in experience, foregrounded as an exception of the rule, suffered and given both physiological and social form. In the words of the science of linguistics, 'healthy' is the 'unmarked pole' and 'unhealthy' is the 'marked pole' of this dimension (Greenberg, 1966). We do not talk about people being 'un-ill'. It follows from this analysis not that ideological thinking is determined by language, but that the values which are placed upon the poles of health and illness are indicative of social forms of which language is an expressive mode. For a person who is chronically ill, health ceases to be a background condition, illness becomes the default state of being, and in extreme cases periods of relief from pain can become figured against that background of suffering.

The remarks made above are also suited to occasions where illness is less threatening. Being 'all right, really' is the norm for most people's condition, the attitude which is expressed even from the sickbed as those concerned look forward to picking up soon their everyday duties. The inconsistency to which we have drawn attention, on the surface so mundane as to pass without comment, is a requisite outcome of the condition of people as embodied beings, as those who freely use, yet are limited by, their mortal frame. Note, however, that this inconsistency is not necessarily one between 'body' on the one hand and 'social obligations' on the other. When one is ill in bed with a fever it is likely that the limitations of one's body are experienced as opposing all attempts to live normally. Where, as in the examples cited above or in the case of a broken leg, people are able to locate the illness or injury within a bodily part, then the balance is struck across the dimension of body versus person. Individuals are both free and constrained bodily, just as they are both in their attempts to carry out their social duties.

Illness sets limitations and, sometimes, offers opportunities. From the standpoint of health, a day off work, ill, can seem quite appealing. From the standpoint of illness, that very freedom from social obligations can be transformed into constraint. As one heart patient said:

> My idea of heaven is sitting around all day doing nothing. No it's not. My idea of heaven is being free to sit around all day and do nothing; but being forced to sit around all day and do nothing, that's hell.

In this case being 'forced to sit around' refers to social constraints, not bodily ones. Freedom and constraint become reversed in experience when one's body is limited (but still able) and opportunity for action denied. Then, as Herzlich (1973) pointed out, rather than being something outside oneself, illness is identified with the person and health appears the province of other people, of society. What has been described as a basic inconsistency in the apprehension of general good health becomes highlighted in attempts to keep illness a small part of life. For chronic illness, when people are varyingly healthier or sicker, places them in situations in which this ambiguity is then repeatedly brought to the fore.

The opposition of health and illness

In the previous section it was argued that assertions of good health rest upon a fundamental inconsistency, and that this has its origin in the relationships of health to illness, and of 'being embodied' to 'having a body'. In the middle of health we are in sickness. However, in the world of everyday minor illnesses, such things need not be experienced by those concerned as presenting them with dilemmas. As pointed out, there is no dilemma about whether to be ill or healthy, though difficult choices might arise in the context of striking the balance between the two. When a person has a symptom, there might be difficult decisions to be made about whether to go to the doctor or whether to take a day off work. These may be complicated by the costs and benefits to one's family from taking different courses of action which, while throwing up difficult choices, are not in themselves ideological dilemmas. The inconsistencies in thinking to which attention has been drawn are things of which people are generally unaware, if only because the logic of 'good health' achieves such a comfortable fit with 'malfunctioning body part'. Dilemmas, as the term is used in this book, are experienced by people in situations in which they must see things from opposing standpoints, so that there is an awareness of the consequences of one line of action for the other, and of their incompatibility for the person concerned. To experience a dilemma is to live out an opposition, so that one is divided upon it in the failure to achieve a resolution.

For the person who has been sick for some time, health and illness cease to be external relations but become two poles of experience, two parts of oneself. There is a part that struggles against illness and a part which, emerging alongside the disability, establishes its own claim upon the individual concerned. There may be, for a while, a struggle to keep back this other side, born of the illness. One man said first, concerning his heart condition:

> I don't know an awful lot because I've chosen not to know. I want to know the positive things. I don't like looking on the black side. I know there's a black side but I think that can work against you. That's a bit of a contradiction from what I've said before, because you just want to know everything. It's 'Catch-22', you can't win.

'Wanting to know everything' is an aspect of what we have referred to already as the inevitability of having to gauge health in terms of sickness. It also points to the fact that how people learn about sickness is not only from doctors, but from their experience with their own sick bodies which stands in marked contrast to the beliefs which they form as healthy individuals. The patient quoted above then continued:

> I used to think of it as a battle. I used to think if I walk up the hill I'd see if I could do it. I suppose, if you like, you dare yourself to have another heart attack. I've walked along and I've been saying (you are chuntering to yourself, you try not to move your lips...) 'Go on then, if you are going to come, come now.' I always say, 'I ain't going to have another heart attack.'

Here, in this quotation, is an example of a dilemma which embraces both the person's thinking and his bodily conduct. There is no mere choice to be made here; what is raised instead is the question of how to bear one's condition. The opposition of health and illness is no longer restricted to the alternatives 'body or society' ('me or others'), for the person is both the sick and the healthy, the challenger and the challenged and, in the event of a heart attack being provoked, the victor and the victim. As an example of dialectical thinking it reveals how an attempt can be made to define one's health by pursuing illness to its limits. By locating the degree of bodily constraint – even if it is as great as a heart attack – the person is then able to redress that balance as an agent, as a free social individual.

The claim of the healthy world upon that of the sick gives rise not only to dilemmas which can be articulated, as in the foregoing example, but also to contradictions which lie, as it were, between the spheres of thought and action. The opposition of health and illness expressed in words or acts is the form of 'either–or' with which we are most familiar in discussions of choice or of dilemma. In certain circumstances, the healthy and the sick aspects to which we have drawn attention are not things of which the person is equally aware, if only because they are divided between two or more people. It has been shown that, for some male heart patients, their struggle against their illness is parallel to their strained relationship with their wives (Radley and Green, 1986). In each case, the men's opposition to illness was a vacillation of fight and collapse in the context of a relationship of unequal effort with their spouses. Those husbands who most wanted to dominate the illness, dominated their wives; those husbands who felt resigned in the face of coronary disease relied upon wives who carried heavier burdens. And yet, the men who sought to dominate were prey to fears and to sudden collapses; the men who were resigned attempted, from that position, to reassert control in fits of resentment. There were, on occasions, discontinuities between the men's attitudes to illness and their styles of conduct which marked these couples out as particularly subject to strain. In these cases, unable to conceptualize the contradiction in which they participated, these men (and their wives) together suffered a dilemma which they were unable to put effectively into words. It was a mark of these people most troubled by illness that the ambiguities in their beliefs were both individual and interpersonal, so that the opposing features of their problem were not equally available to consciousness, and were not on the same plane. Dilemmas of this kind are not only 'of the mind', causing conceptual confusion, but embrace the whole person in an ontological problem manifested within bodily conduct as well (Bateson, 1971).

This section has developed, through example, the forms of ambiguity which are part of the situation of illness. Initially, in the discussion of 'general good health', this took the form of illness as exceptional, as something which is discriminated against the background of overall well-being. Illness, in this mode, acts as a marker. Is it by accident, we wonder, that when asked in passing 'How are you?' one replies 'Oh, not so bad' or 'Can't complain' more often than '100 per cent fit' or 'At the peak of health'? The latter terms are more often reserved for occasions in which one's health is actually in question! It is not that people do not wish to tempt fate with inflated claims, but that without any evidence to the contrary their assertions of good health remain somewhat empty. To take up the situation of one person being clearly ill – for example, with a streaming cold – the question 'How are you?' might elicit the response 'Awful, I feel like I'm dying.' This means that the same state of health may be described in different ways, depending upon the context of the description. To switch the emphasis between health and illness is not to be devious, even if it appears inconsistent, for these switches are predicated upon knowledge shared by the different people involved in the exchange. This is an issue which will be confronted again in chapter 8, when we discuss the semantics of gender.

Although the sore throat or the broken arm remain tangible matters, they are not the basis for dilemmatic thinking. This term we reserved for the opposition of health and illness in experience, the division of their competing claims in consciousness. And finally, it was only with ambiguity premised upon different planes that we spoke of contradiction. Each of these is a different form of the balance of health versus illness, which has its oppositional form in an ideology which is shared by the healthy as well as the ill. We are dealing with a social and not an individual phenomenon, and so we need to examine how others in society think of illness and articulate a rationale for dealing with its consequences.

The problem of curing and caring

> But in the same moment as he found himself on the floor, rocking with suppressed eagerness to move, not far from his mother, indeed just in front of her, she, who had seemed so completely crushed, sprang all at once to her feet, her arms and fingers outspread, cried: 'Help, for God's sake, help!' bent her head down as if to see Gregor better, yet on the contrary kept backing senselessly away. (Kafka, *Metamorphosis*)

There is little, if any, disagreement that illness calls for curing and that the patient requires caring on the part of those whose job it is to help. In Western society the task of curing illness is recognized to be a duty of doctors, while the task of caring is something which comes 'naturally' to the person's family and friends. As has been seen in the previous chapter, this division is, of course, an oversimplification because people also require doctors to show compassion in their manner, while relatives and friends are expected to cooperate in effecting a speedy cure.

There is a balance to be struck, too, between these positions as they are expressed in the efforts of those who help the sick person. In as much as there is a discrepancy between what doctors diagnose and what the patient can achieve, then problems of reconciling these differences can result. As one wife put it:

> Well obviously anything to do with your heart is of major importance but the fact that he's not changed, the fact that he's still doing his job, still running about, still doing what he wants, sort of is on one side and then you've got the other swing of the pendulum, what the specialist is saying, how serious it is, and I can't bring these two things together.

This quotation reveals an awareness of different standpoints rather than a contradiction in thinking. And yet it indicates the competing demands of the body and social obligation which point up the inconsistencies in attitudes to patients' illnesses which we have previously outlined. In the case of this quotation, it is not an attempt at resolution of bodily restraint and social freedom which is called for, but a setting of social limitation (that is, the diagnosis) against the perceived freedom of bodily action.

This problem of curing and caring is particularly marked when people are chronically ill, when the obligations to 'look after oneself' at the same time as attempting to fulfil social obligations can produce contradictions of the kind which we have described previously, embracing not only the patient but the spouse as well. The wife of one heart patient expressed the problem this way:

> He'll probably some days be doing too much and I say 'Look, don't do all that, just do a bit, it you feel tired sit down.' 'I'm all right.' This is what I get. 'Just leave me alone, I'm all right', and that's what I get. So now I tend to think to myself 'Oh, get on with it, it's you that's going to come out the worse.'

Why is it that the good intentions of this wife should come to grief in this way? It is simply because she is married to an intransigent husband? If we accept that these are contradictions in the outlook of patients and that these embrace their relationships with others, then it is clear that these competing features are also to be found in the attitudes of the healthy towards the sick. What we have termed 'striking the balance' between health and sickness is also part and parcel of the views of medical practitioners. Despite its emphasis upon a technologically produced cure, the medicine with which we are most familiar in the West nevertheless still stresses the need for patients to make an effort in their own recovery. Failure to do this may be labelled 'invalidism', and excessive zeal to be well 'denial'.

Our point is that the dilemmatic aspects of thought during illness are there in the attitudes of the healthy towards the ill. While they may only become apparent during times of illness they are there to be seen among curers and carers as well as among the afflicted. For example, Voysey (1975) describes the ideologies of parents of handicapped children through which ideas they attempt to render their situation as sensible and their actions as being morally acceptable to others. Finding and establishing one's place again in the everyday world demands what is often sensed by other people as a form of 'double-think'. The mother of a Down's syndrome child said 'At least she's got her health', while the parent of a spina bifida child expressed the view that 'I should be thankful she's not mentally retarded' (p. 199). In each case, the status of the child's *avowed* health is qualified by the *implicit* knowledge of her actual impairment. For this kind of claim to be successful in the everyday life of the families concerned depends not upon other people being either 'fooled' or wholly persuaded by this argument. On the contrary, the roles of the parents and of the child are established through other people's awareness of the burden under which they operate. Only if the parents communicate their total belief in their assertions of their child's health (that is, that things are all right, *really*) are others likely to comment upon the inconsistency between the parents' claims and the evidence of the child's presentation. Then, at that point, people are likely to say 'They have to say that, don't they?'

The balance between health and illness is struck between the individual and society, between people as separate and sick versus people as belonging and healthy. In certain circumstances individuals are unequivocally the former – when ill with fever or racked with pain. But, more often than not, sick people must present themselves in the terms dictated by a world which exacts penalties for the privileges which they are actually obliged to ask for. They must appear as well as possible in order to gain the acceptance by others of their limitations; to do otherwise is to risk sanction or exclusion. Nevertheless, this acceptance is limited by the healthy persons' demands that the sick, though appearing as well as possible, should not claim for themselves those rights which full health bestows. Goffman (1963) has made this point in relation to the stigmatized, and we can extend his argument to the sick in general, particularly those with chronic conditions. Paradoxically, of course, the more successful the sick are in hiding their illness from others, the less care or understanding they will receive. The price of successfully implementing strategies of duplicity in order to attain acceptance is to experience the loneliness of increased isolation at those times when one's illness becomes acute and disabling.

What were previously described as forms of contradiction in thinking about illness can be seen to have their basis, not in some natural division of the body as experienced by individuals, but in an ideology of health and illness which is essentially social. Indeed, the dominant aspect of the opposition of these two conditions is health, and it is in those terms that the sick – in as much as they believe themselves basically healthy – establish what they ought to do and think. One of the consequences of this – which we have already seen in the duality of oppositional thinking – is that it places upon sick people the burden 'not to overdo it' while at the same time making sure that they 'make an effort' and 'put a brave face on things'. The question of good adjustment – which has entered the research literature through the efforts of social and behavioural scientists working on its behalf – is one that reinforces the dilemma by insisting on helping the patient to deal with the problems of being ill. The 'good adjuster' is the person who can trim his or her life in order to steer between the Scylla of bodily constraints and the Charybdis of unyielding social institutions. Such trimming or coping can become a 'real' problem for the patient, made ever more tangible by the attempts of other people to help the person concerned to carry it out more effectively. Where other members of the family also become engaged in making these adjustments, then they too are subject to an ideology which claims, if not good health, then normality in the face of illness or injury. Examples of this kind of adjustment have been given by Davis (1963) in his study of the families of child polio victims, describing the moral demands upon them to espouse normality in recognition of difference, to enter into an ideology containing contradiction. This is illustrated in his description of the experience of a handicapped child and her mother:

> Seven year old Polly Manning, for example, decided to enter a contest sponsored by a magazine issued for handicapped children by a local welfare society. The contest asked the children to submit a name for the magazine. When Polly told her mother her first choice – 'The Crippled Children's Book' – Mrs Manning replied, 'Well, that's right long. They said they wanted a short happy name, and that doesn't sound too happy.' Polly then suggested 'Cheer'. With her mother's approval, this was the name she submitted. (1963: 140)

How acutely such contradictions are experienced, how tangible they become for those who must hold these views, depends in large measure upon competing claims to 'strike the balance' in different ways. Where families of the sick have made adjustments in order to stress the quality of their home life (care) as a means towards good health (cure), they may yet find themselves in conflict with medical practitioners who stress the management of the illness over the patients' desire to come to terms with their condition. As pointed out already, it is not simply that there is a clash of two different though internally consistent ideologies; there is instead the exacerbation of a contradiction which runs through both lay and medical thinking and practice. This is revealed in the advance of medical expertise which creates further demands upon how people should conduct themselves under or after treatment. Medical practice enters into lay ideology most obviously when it touches people's lives directly. As one man said after heart surgery which had failed to relieve his symptoms:

> I think it would be an insult and an abuse to what's been done, and an insult to the surgeon that did it, not to do things – just carry on as normal.

Turning back to the first quotation from *Metamorphosis* given earlier in this chapter, we can say, figuratively, that adjustments which ameliorate the difficulties of sickness and disability are always threatened by the world of health in the form of the chief clerk pounding at the door.

The ideology of good health

So far we have made a case for illness raising ideological inconsistencies, oppositions or contradictions. These conditions were distinguished in order to show that, experientially, they are not the same, either in their availability to consciousness or in their functional form (Wilden, 1980). However, if being ill leads to such inconsistencies, does this imply that health, freedom from dis-ease, is a condition of consistency of thought and action? In addressing this question we have to bear in mind that notions of sick and healthy people are not constants, but can be seen, through historical analysis, to be changing social constructions (Herzlich and Pierret, 1985). What we think of today as being ill is neither a historical nor even a cultural universal so that, when we speak of the inconsistencies or contradictions which illness reveals, these are embedded in the matrix of other social values, beliefs and institutions. Not least, there have been changes in the scope of medical knowledge which have shaped the way in which people think of themselves as potential patients, as individuals who need to regulate their lives in the terms of the new medical order (Armstrong, 1983). These days, health is becoming less and less a passive backcloth to life and more an aspect to be worked upon and directed. There is a new health consciousness which has given rise to changes in a number of areas of people's lives – jogging and diet, to name but two. The tracksuit and the yogurt pot are the new symbols of health, in addition to the apple that once, taken daily, somehow kept the doctor away.

The new ideology of health achieves its aim not through an understanding of any science of health, but through a focus upon features believed to cause particular diseases. This means that our understanding of healthy living is derived from an inversion of what we know of illness: knowledge gained, as it were, by using a mirror to look back over one's shoulder. This way of proceeding has the effect of extending to everybody the moral obligations hitherto reserved for the sick. This means that ideological positions are established on the basis of 'What is unhealthy must be bad' and, therefore 'What is (by inference) healthy must be good.' The logic of this position is strained, however, when one examines the advice given to people who may have a type A behaviour pattern or hard-driving personality, argued to be a risk factor in coronary disease (type B people are those whose acceptance of life constraints avoids this issue):

> Whether you are a dentist, attorney, architect, physician or business executive, your secretary at first may not willingly cooperate in this showdown. . .if she cannot live with a type B office, she should be dismissed! (Friedman and Rosenman, 1974: 208)

and in order to cut down interruptions,

> Each caller may be told in splendidly courteous language that you are presently in conference. . .if. . .the caller is insulted, then he is probably a bit sick himself with type A behavior pattern. (1974: 210)

The problem which is inherent in these recommendations – particularly for fired secretaries phoning around for new jobs! – is the attempt to control health as if it were merely the obverse of illness as we know it, leaving social conditions untouched as they stress the merits of personal change. In its wider form – applied to people generally – the contradiction of much health consciousness lies in its dictum that people stay healthy by constantly patrolling the borders with illness. They are free to be healthy only in as much as they submit to the controls which increasingly regulate how they use their bodies. While guilt has long been recognized as a source of stress, if not physical illness, there is as yet little awareness of the effects of guilt upon those who will feel that they have not lived up to the norms of 'good health'. In a consumer society, in which health consciousness is transformed into a 'health craze', the season in which 'no business is done' becomes (paradoxically) also the season in which 'health is not striven for' – neither season, of course, being allowed to exist.

These remarks are intended to show that the inconsistencies and contradictions which mark illness are not limited to that experience, but are part of the world of health which surrounds it. They apply to us as carers for the sick and as carers for our own potentially sick bodies. Without wishing to be tendentious, we may compare this situation to that of peasants ('the sick') who are oppressed by a bourgeois majority ('the healthy'): for the former their existence is a 'duality which has established itself in their innermost being' (Freire, 1972: 24). Their dilemma lies in their being both oppressed *and* oppressor in outlook, in viewing themselves from their own position and yet within the terms of others who dictate their condition. For the peasants, there is the chance that, through education or revolution, this situation might change; for the sick, and for us all as mortal beings who must eventually fail, that resolution can never come, though the duality must always be endured.

It is not surprising, perhaps, that where those who are healthy apprehend these inconsistencies they try to overlay them. A few years ago there was a report of officials in an English town who acted upon requests from a man's neighbours that he should close his curtains while dialysing at home. Another seaside town was reported to be dissuading handicapped people from coming to stay in 'too large' a number. Illness brings out in others not only a need for care and cure, but also the dual response of compassion and avoidance, relating to a condition of the body which, in the extreme of death, evokes both awe and revulsion at the same time. The relationship of health to illness does not stand alone, but generates further conflicts in people's dealings with the ill and with the healthy. Illness takes on a metaphorical status in the ways in which we use it to describe either particular groupings, sections of society or even historical epochs (Sontag, 1979). The contradictions of illness are always in terms drawn from social life; illness does not enter into society as a separate phenomenon, but has its meaning in terms of the relation of the individual to society. It both structures and is shaped by social affairs. Writing today, at a time when the awareness of AIDS as a threat is now general, one of the striking things about public response is the need of so many people, not only to believe in its ease of transmission, but in its resistance to cure. We cannot, at present, cite evidence on this point. Nevertheless, it suggests that in our dealings with various groupings in society the AIDS virus serves as a way of making both distinctions between certain kinds of people and moral judgements about them. The world of health is not a neutral world; nor, in its relationship with illness, does it stand on an equal footing.

Underlying all the dilemmas and all the comments of the heart patients has been the opposition between freedom and necessity. We have seen individuals struggling with the demands of being simultaneously free and unfree or, to be more precise, with the demands of viewing themselves as being free and unfree. In their comments they make use of images of the person which are not culturally universal, but which possess their own ideological history. These are images which see the person as being both an agent with free choice and an object which is determined by a bodily materialism. Such images preoccupy the thinking of those individuals forced by illness to think about their lives. Yet these people do not create these images themselves, nor do they create the contradictory themes of individual freedom and material necessity. As was discussed in chapter 3, both images figure strongly in the philosophy of the Enlightenment. In this respect the examples of the present chapter show again that the course of ideological history can be detected in the dilemmas of everyday life.

At first sight, there might appear to be a convenient division of labour between the two contrary images of the free agent and the determined body. The individual is free so long as bodily constraint does not intervene. Similarly the individual is constrained when the body forbids the exercise of freedom. This conceptual division of labour would identify the state of health with freedom and the state of illness with bodily necessity. However, the examples of this chapter demonstrate, again and again, the superficiality of such an identification. Within the so-called freedom of health there are constraints, and within illness there are freedoms. Since both illness and health are social states, there are social freedoms and constraints to complicate matters. Moreover, the individuals themselves are aware of the dilemmas. For instance, there was the patient who was aware of the philosophical dilemmas of his own precarious existence; he chose not to know about the inevitability of his body, but knew he had chosen not to want this knowledge. The choices exercised and not exercised set up further constraints and freedoms for the individual's family. The awareness of such dilemmas, like the states of health and illness themselves, are not merely an individual matter. The terms in which we think about these things are grounded both in particular social relations and, more generally, within ideological practices for controlling health and sickness.

7

Prejudice and Tolerance

> You'd think at our ages we wouldn't be colour prejudiced because we've been
> to school with them. But we're not really. Things have happened. Just silly
> things happen, and it turns us against them.

This is a fifteen-year-old girl speaking, living in the West Midlands of
England. Wendy and her friend had been expressing their support for the
unambiguously racist political party, the National Front. They had been
justifying this support with tales about the violence of West Indians, the
shortages of jobs caused by immigration, and the differentness of Asians.
In outlining these tales, Wendy and her friend had been displaying the
signs which psychologists normally associate with prejudice. They were
advocating discrimination against non-whites, for both believed that non-
whites should be expelled from Britain. Both made free use of stereotypes,
as they described West Indians and Asians in simple terms. No doubt a
standard attitude questionnaire might have been given, and these supporters
of the National Front would have provided the answers which psychologists
would have little trouble in defining as prejudiced.

It is not difficult to view prejudice in a comparatively undilemmatic way,
which assumes that the unprejudiced are liberal, healthy and egalitarian,
whereas the prejudiced are the repositories of the very opposite values. The
classic psychological approach to prejudice, *The Authoritarian Personality*
by Adorno et al. (1950), tends to view prejudice in such a relatively
straightforward manner. The prejudiced person was seen as psychologically
unhealthy, and a bundle of complexes, as compared with the tolerant individual. Whereas the unprejudiced person could cope with the ambiguities and
the equalities of modern life, the prejudiced individual hankers after rigidly
authoritarian structures. If the unprejudiced person stands for freedom, the
prejudiced person, like Wendy, is drawn toward the politics of totalitarianism. However, as previous chapters have suggested, such an image may
be too simple, for equality and authority, illness and health, and freedom
and necessity are not so easily separated. Modern celebrations of equality
have not eradicated authority. Even a celebration of health does not dispel
the spectre of illness. Similarly, as this chapter will argue, prejudice is not
undilemmatically straightforward; there is a dialectic of prejudice. If there
is a dialectic of equality which includes authority, and one of health which
includes illness, the dialectic of prejudice is even more dramatic in its
revelation of the dark side of the ideological tradition of the Enlightenment.

The dilemmatic aspects of prejudice will be explored by looking at one
aspect of the topic which has tended to be ignored by psychologists: the

meaning of 'prejudice' itself. Most psychologists study prejudice by examining the images which people have of other groups or by looking at people's reactions to other group members. In so doing they avoid studying the meaning of prejudice itself. It needs to be recognized that prejudice is not merely a technical concept to be found in the writings of psychologists, but a concept used in everyday discourse, as the comments of Wendy illustrate. It is not a simple concept, and her usage indicates ambivalence. She was accepting the moral evaluation attached to the notion of 'prejudice': that it is wrong to be prejudiced, just as it is assumed to be wrong to be undemocratic or tyrannical or to encourage illness. If she did not accept this moral theme, there would be little point in her denial that she was 'really' prejudiced. Yet at the same time she was expressing – and, what is most important, she realized that she was expressing – views which might be considered to be prejudiced.

As will be suggested, the very concept of 'prejudice' is one that expresses Enlightenment ideals. Therefore, a paradox is evident in Wendy's comments. The ideological themes of the Enlightenment are to be found in the discourse of this supporter of a racist, fascist political party. Moreover, as can be seen in Wendy's comment, the Enlightenment theme of 'prejudice' is not to be found in a separate compartment from the racist themes. It is not the case that at one point she and her friends use the vocabulary of the Enlightenment to the interviewer, whilst at another time darker themes of an older discourse surface, rather as if she has one vocabulary for the classroom and another for the playground. On the contrary, the notion of prejudice appears just at the point when she appears to be expressing her most unenlightened views. Moreover, it is part of this expression. Her semantics, when talking of her support for a fascist party, reveal her as a product of Enlightenment philosophy. Yet at the same time she is expressing views which *prima facie* contradict every dream of tolerance and which lead to the unenlightened irrationality of fascism. Moreover, she is hinting at 'things' – whether personal events in her life or broader trends of society – which are overwhelming the notion of 'tolerance' and making it impracticable. These things are not destroying the value of tolerance as an ideal: after all, she herself, as she is careful to stress, is not prejudiced 'really'. This simultaneous affirmation and contradiction of 'prejudice' suggests the presence of a dilemma of ideological proportions, as the young woman wrestles with the heritage and realities of her society.

Enlightenment and nationalism

Hans-Georg Gadamer, the hermeneutic philosopher, has pointed out that the modern meaning of the word 'prejudice' was formed by the liberal Enlightenment: 'Historical analysis shows that it is not until the Enlightenment that the concept of prejudice acquires the negative aspect we are familiar with' (1979: 240). The very term 'prejudice' denotes the evils of irrationality, which enlightened people should try to eradicate from their thinking. This meaning was expressed quite plainly in that great project of the French Enlightenment, Diderot's *Encyclopédie*. The entry on prejudice, written by that assiduous contributor to the *Encyclopédie*, Louis de Jaucourt, made clear that prejudice was the enemy of rationality. The entry starts with the definition of prejudice as 'false judgement which the mind holds on the nature of things, after insufficient exercise of the intellectual faculties; this unfortunate fruit of ignorance forestalls the intellect, blinds it and holds it captive' (Diderot, 1966: 284). Bishop Berkeley suggested that 'Prejudices are notions or opinions which the mind entertains without knowing the grounds or reasons of them and which are assented to without examination' (1872: 99). As will be seen, this sort of conception of prejudice is also to be found in Voltaire. At root all these views of prejudice rest upon psychological assumptions about the way the mind might best, or most rationally, gather and judge information. Prejudices are said to arise when the gathering of information, or the judging of it, are said to be insufficiently rational.

As part of a psychological account about the operation of mind, these conceptions of prejudice could refer to judgements on any topic. The eighteenth-century *philosophes*, when they spoke of prejudice, tended to have traditional theology in their argumentative sights. They were not particularly referring to race or ethnic prejudice. This sense was to become prominent in the twentieth century, and was the meaning most naturally used by the young girl in the comments quoted at the beginning of this chapter. Of course, before the twentieth century there are examples of writers using 'prejudice' in a way which seems thoroughly modern because of an allusion to racial or ethnic factors. For example Hazlitt, in his essay 'Prejudice' written in 1830, refers to the prejudice by which a black man was formerly 'thought to forfeit his title to belong to the species' because early travellers unthinkingly exaggerated the importance of skin colour (1934: 317). Walter Bagehot, writing about Scottish philosophy in general and Adam Smith in particular, mentioned that 'Scotch writers', who were unsuccessful in England, 'were apt to impute their discredit to English prejudice' (1965a: 84).

However, neither Bagehot nor Hazlitt were using 'prejudice' in a prototypical sense; they were employing a general term to describe a particular phenomenon which they wished to mention. In the twentieth century, the term has acquired a specific meaning in addition to its general condemnation of irrationality. This meaning makes modern speakers, when the term is used, think generally of the sorts of thing which Hazlitt and Bagehot were specifically describing. Today, 'prejudice' refers particularly to irrational feelings or attitudes which are held against social groups. When social scientists write books about prejudice, they primarily have in mind these sorts of intergroup prejudices. Thus Gordon Allport's classic work *The Nature of Prejudice* was an analysis of racial and national prejudices. Not only were the psychological and social roots of such prejudices examined, but there was an overall moral evaluation: such prejudices were to be eradicated in the name of tolerant rationality. Social psychologists frequently define prejudice in a way that suggests that the essence of the concept is to be found in racial and national attitudes. For example Harding et al., in their contribution to the *Handbook of Social Psychology*, state that 'by *prejudice* we mean an ethnic attitude in which the reaction tendencies are predominantly negative' (1969: 1022). The same sort of definition is to be found in popularly used textbooks of social psychology. For instance, Perlman and Cozby (1983: 417) define prejudice 'as a negative attitude towards members of socially defined groups'. Forsyth (1987: 614) has the following entry for 'prejudice' in the glossary of his textbook: 'An attitude toward an ethnic, racial or other social group.' In all these works, there is an assumption of obvious morality: prejudice is not merely to be analysed psychologically, it is also to be condemned.

The emphasis in the concept of 'prejudice' may have changed from Diderot to modern social psychology, but a similar underlying ideological tradition can be detected. Gordon Allport's *The Nature of Prejudice* was no radical tract, which flew in the face of basic ideological assumptions. In fact, it continually suggested that prejudice abrogated the values of liberalism, on which American and other democratic societies were founded. Similar themes were evident in Gunnar Myrdal's great prewar study of anti-black discrimination in the United States. Myrdal called his study *An American Dilemma*. According to Myrdal's analysis, the dilemma was not one that arose within what he termed the American creed. The dilemma had occurred because America had allowed to develop practices and beliefs which contradicted the basic creed and its values of freedom and equality. The practical problem was how to excise these unnatural excrescences in order that the creed of democracy might function as it ought.

In this way, the study of prejudice has often led to an affirmation of liberalism and the hope that a liberal practice may follow from a liberal theory. Other psychological studies have drawn attention to the antithesis between education and prejudice. Evidence has been produced to suggest that hostile attitudes towards minority groups are more likely to be expressed by the poorly educated (Selznick and Steinberg, 1969; Schonbach, 1981; see Bagley and Verma, 1979 and Altemeyer, 1981 for reviews). The temptation is to conclude that if the teachers were to make an extra effort, and if the politicians were to provide the classrooms with sufficient chalks, blackboards and instructional computers, then, at last, 'prejudice' could be eliminated from our society. Through the goodwill of teachers, politicians and, of course, enlightenedly educated parents, the prejudiced would have been educated out of their prejudices. An era of educated tolerance would then await our children and our children's children.

It might be predicted that a decline in national or racial prejudice would be attendant upon the growth in international economic arrangements, occurring during the age of capitalism. This was certainly the prediction made by Marx and Engels in the last century. In *The Communist Manifesto* they wrote of the shrinking of the modern world: 'In place of the old local and national seclusion and self-sufficiency, we have intercourse in every direction, universal interdependence of nations.' All this interdependence had an ideological consequence, according to Marx and Engels, for 'National one-sidedness and narrow mindedness become more and more impossible' (p. 39). One might say that national interdependence has produced the situation where national one-sidedness is now seen as the prototypical prejudice, and thereby the enemy of liberal rationalism, and earnest social scientists try to dispel its haunting spectre.

The philosophy of the Enlightenment would seem to be well suited to provide the mottoes for an ideology of modern internationalism. 'Liberty, equality and fraternity' will allow the air traveller to pass, without let or hindrance, from air terminal to air terminal. The inward-looking prejudices of isolated regions become insupportable when all humankind can equally and freely join together in admiration of the same film stars. Above all, traditional suspicions, bred of centuries of cultural isolation, have collapsed in the face of opportunities for untrammelled commerce. Enlightened economic institutions feel free to trade within their international brotherhood, and national airlines will take their representatives equally to their international destinations.

However, it is far too simple to describe the modern age as being one in which national interdependence has triumphed over national feeling. The creation of national states, with their national economies, has coincided with this supposedly international era. Modern life is full of examples which illustrate the simultaneous lack of national seclusion and the reality of nationalism. For example, air travel ensures that all countries are within easy reach of each other and the traveller may pass conveniently from hemisphere to hemisphere, arriving at an airport which differs little from that of embarkation. If air travel symbolizes the international culture, which has put its speedy girdle around the earth, then it also illustrates the visibility of contemporary nationalism. The aeroplane will, as likely as not, be adorned with national symbols; the modern traveller must carry more documents and emblems of nationality than ever did Marx in his various emigratory wanderings. Thus the reality of the nation state, and the seriousness with which its boundaries are treated, have become more evident during the period of growing internationalism.

Yet the twentieth century has not witnessed the unchallenged supremacy of Enlightenment ideals, even within Europe, the birthplace of liberal philosophy. If enlightened ideals seem to aspire to the destruction of old boundaries, then philosophies proposing new boundaries have been developed. Racial doctrines have claimed that the brotherhood and equality of mankind are illusory, as is freedom from biological inevitability. Nor have the racist doctrines represented simply a retreat from the Enlightenment into a medieval darkness. The racial ideas of the late nineteenth century and the twentieth century have often been expressed with the outward paraphernalia of scientific biology. Fascism has not been an anachronistic replay of the barbarities of earlier times, but it is peculiar to the twentieth century. Its ambitions for mass mobilization, the quasi-biological images of its ideology and the scientific precision of its massacres are all products of the modern age (see for example O'Sullivan, 1983 for a discussion of the essential modernity of fascist ideology).

However, the present concern is not with fascism, or with overt doctrines of race. In the modern world, states which define citizenship in terms of racial categories are in a minority. Nazi Germany and the South Africa of today enshrine racial doctrines in their constitutions, and in so doing overtly transgress basic democratic principles. There can be no equality and freedom to vote, or brotherhood (let alone sisterhood) of citizenry, where supposed biological criteria are used to divide the citizen from the non-citizen. Such states need fully fledged racial doctrines to justify their discriminations. By contrast, in the majority of Western states democratic rights are not allotted on the basis of an inegalitarian pseudo-biology. Yet in these nations, the universalistic dreams of the Enlightenment cannot be allowed to run unchecked. These nations are still nations: they need laws to divide the citizen from the foreigner, and they need cultural symbols to emphasize their national uniqueness.

It may be true that modern political discourse, in a country such as Britain, has become 'deracialized', but this does not mean that it is not predicated upon distinctions, often implicitly racial, between 'us' and 'them', between British and foreigners (Reeves, 1983). An ambivalence is to be expected between the universalism of Enlightenment themes and the particularism of national ones, with the latter needing to avoid the taint of 'prejudice' as defined by the former. Indeed, an ambivalence may always have been present, in order to enable a document such as the American constitution to declare the freedom and equality of all men in an age of legal slavery. Today, the situation is further complicated by the movements of populations in the modern world. In order to meet economic needs, large numbers of people have moved from poorer regions to more industrialized ones. National boundaries have, of course, provided little barrier to these movements of populations during times of economic growth, when the industrial countries have lacked the necessary labour force.

Since the Second World War, most European countries have recruited large numbers of workers from their former colonial possessions, and from the poorer regions of Europe itself. The result of this internationally 'free market' of labour has been the growth of populations occupying an ambivalent position. 'They', the foreigners, often with darker skin colour, have become part of the 'us', and as such are both 'them' and 'us'. The ambivalence of this position becomes emphasized when recession follows growth, and immigration laws are passed to prevent more of 'them' coming from afar lest 'our' national, and democratically national, way of life is threatened. The resulting laws might not define citizenship racially in the manner of Nazi Germany, but they emphasize the values of national particularity, with racial undertones a quiet, but persistent, subtheme (Barker, 1981; Miles and Phizacklea, 1985; Layton-Henry, 1985).

The language of the young girl, quoted at the beginning of the chapter, was full of the division between 'us' and 'them'. This is a division which, as she herself recognized, should disappear if the enlightened opposition to 'prejudice' were the sole guiding principle. Her language emphasized the ideological dilemma she faced when talking of classmates of a darker coloured skin. 'They' were like 'us', but unalike: 'our' neighbours, yet felt to be different; 'our' workmates, yet competitors for scarce jobs. Perhaps 'they' would have become just like 'us', but 'things' happen. Yet again, 'things' do not always happen. Immediately after the interview, conducted at school, this young supporter of a racist party, and of compelling all of 'them' to leave 'our country', was to be seen walking arm in arm with a young Asian girl, chatting and laughing in easy friendship.

Ambivalence and racial discourse

There is considerable evidence that nowadays people in the West generally do not speak about race in an unambiguous way. The evidence comes from studies which have conducted attitudinal surveys and from those which have analysed the patterns of actual speech. For example, American investigators of white attitudes towards blacks have talked of 'modern' or 'symbolic' racism (McConahay, 1986; McConahay and Hough, 1976; McConahay, 1981, 1982; McConahay, Hardee and Batts, 1981; Kinder and Sears, 1981; Jacobson, 1985). The results from these surveys suggest that the 'modern', or 'symbolic', racist is unlikely to hold attitudes which outrightly demean black people as being racially inferior. Name-calling and racial insults are avoided by the modern racists, who nevertheless express strong opposition to moves to advance the position of blacks within American society. This opposition is typically justified in terms of traditional values, and, in particular, in terms of values of equality and fairness. The modern racist believes that black people are 'getting more than they deserve' and are receiving unfairly generous, and thereby unequal, privileges. In this way, the crude sentiments of 'rednecked' racism are avoided, in an attitudinal pattern which claims for itself a degree of reasonableness (see also the studies on racial ambivalence by Katz, Wackenhut and Hass, 1986).

Investigators such as McConahay and Sears claim that this outwardly 'reasonable' expression of racism is basically a modern, post-1960s development. Nevertheless, there is evidence to suggest that the difference between old-fashioned rednecked racism and 'modern racism' may be exaggerated. This is a point made by Weigel and Howes (1985), who have compared the items on older and modern surveys of racial attitudes, and have found that there is not such a great qualitative difference between the two. Billig (1982, 1985) has re-examined some of the responses of the classicly bigoted persons in Adorno et al.'s *The Authoritarian Personality* (1950). These authoritarians, who supposedly showed a predilection for unambiguously hostile views against minorities, nevertheless hedged and qualified their views with a veneer of reasonableness. As Adorno noted in *The Authoritarian Personality*, even bigoted authoritarians were aware of the social norm against being prejudiced, or at least against appearing to be prejudiced. Perhaps the most striking evidence that the older rednecks were never completely uninhibited in their prejudices comes from Myrdal's *An American Dilemma* (1944). Researching at a time when racial discrimination was practised both *de jure* and *de facto* throughout the south of the United States, Mydral found that even whites who defended the discriminatory laws of their states displayed an indirectness in talking about blacks. Words were picked with care, and there was, above all, a desire to appear unprejudiced: 'When talking about the Negro problem, everybody – not only the intellectual liberals – is thus anxious to locate race prejudice outside himself' (p. 37).

Similar patterns have been noted by modern researchers who have examined ordinary discourse of race in a number of different settings. Wetherell and Potter (1986) and McFadyen and Wetherell (1986) have looked at the way in which middle-class New Zealanders talk about Maoris. Their respondents did not cling to a single, monolithically unfavourable stereotype (or 'prototype') of 'the Maori', in the way that the old-fashionedly prejudiced person supposedly did. Instead, ostensibly liberal respondents managed to introduce innuendoes and to cast aspersions in the most polite and outwardly 'reasonable' ways. Similar patterns have been said to characterize the way in which white Britons talk about non-whites living in Britain: the crudities of National Front propaganda are avoided, but 'they', despite the good qualities of some of 'them', are held to be different from 'us' and would, on the whole, be better off back in 'their' own countries (see Dummett, 1973 for an excellent portrayal of white British attitudes; see also Billig, 1986a; Cochrane and Billig, 1984).

Van Dijk (1984) has given an extremely detailed and fascinating analysis of comments made in interviews by working-class Dutch people about immigrants to Holland. Van Dijk points to the complex ways in which the interviewees expressed their views. On the whole, they had unfavourable things to say about immigrants, but rarely did the respondents present wholly unfavourable views. Delicate elisions, qualifications and shifts of topic were normal. Often questions which were aimed at eliciting negative attitudes did not produce direct answers. Van Dijk (1984: 65) offers the example of an interviewee who was asked whether he had ever had an unpleasant experience with blacks. He replied:

> I have nothing against foreigners.
> But their attitude, their aggression is scaring.
> We are no longer free here. You have to be careful.

Just as Myrdal noted in the prewar deep south of the United States, there is a reluctance to plunge into a denunciation of the other. There is a denial of prejudice ('I have nothing against foreigners'). As in the comments of the young British girl at the beginning of the chapter, there is implication that things have occurred beyond the control of the 'unprejudiced' speaker: 'their' attitudes and 'their' aggression are the cause of the views, rather than any biases within the speaker. Moreover, these 'causes' have destroyed one of the values of the Enlightenment: 'we' are no longer free, 'they' are the enemies of freedom.

One of the aspects of racial discourse which van Dijk notes is the way that contrary themes are introduced, often with a connecting 'but'. The interviewee has nothing against foreigners, but.... There is, according to van Dijk, a give-and-take in the exchanges between interviewer and interviewee, paralleling a give-and-take between positive and negative comments about immigrants: 'The interviewee agrees with or accepts some positive point of the interviewer (and thereby shows cooperation and tolerance) but at the same time wants to express his/her own negative experiences or evaluations' (1984: 148–9). Van Dijk refers to this as 'an "on the one hand" and "on the other hand" strategy of opinion formulation' (p. 152). In van Dijk's analysis, there is a tendency to view this strategy in terms of the interpersonal moves of a conversation, in which a prejudiced, working-class interviewee wishes to impress a tolerant, middle-class interviewer. Van Dijk suggests that there is a contradiction between expressing racist views openly and conforming to the norms of polite conversation. Speakers will wish to present themselves in a favourable light, and will, in consequence, avoid the unalloyed expression of their racist views. In consequence, the goals of self-expression and self-presentation 'may sometimes conflict: a direct or "honest" expression of the beliefs or the opinions from the speaker's situation model may lead to a negative social evaluation of the speaker by the hearer' (p. 117).

Although it may be the case that some interviewees might hedge their 'true' views in this situation, the ambivalence of their remarks cannot be solely attributed to the conflict between attitude and impression management.

One must ask why respondents assumed that the utterance of racist comments would make such a bad impression. Evidence suggests that the respondents were not paying lip-service to norms of politeness, which were foreign to themselves but which they knew the interviewer held. Instead, these were norms which they themselves shared. Just like the girl quoted earlier, there was a recognition of the moral inappropriateness of being 'prejudiced'. In a public opinion survey in Britain, Airey (1984) reports that the majority of the population believed that there was substantial prejudice against Asians and West Indians. Yet most respondents believed that other people were more prejudiced than themselves. Prejudice might be perceived as being consensual, but it was not recognized as being socially acceptable. In other words, racial prejudice was not something to admit of the self, even if people believed that it was widespread; prejudice was, as Myrdal noted, to be located outside the self.

This is also revealed in studies which catch respondents talking relaxedly amongst themselves rather than in formal tones to an interviewer. One does not find that the two-handed strategy disappears, to be replaced by uninhibited racism. Billig (1986b) has found the same style in the discourse of middle-class British young members of the Conservative Party. Not only did they talk about non-whites living in Britain in this ambivalent, two-sided style, but the same type of formulations were expressed by senior members of the party when they talked about South Africa. Naturally, as upright members of the community, they abhorred apartheid, but, of course, South Africa has been a good friend to the free world. . . . In this context the 'but' qualifies, and thereby renders innocuous, the declaration against racism. (For further examples of this style from right-wing political figures see Barker, 1981; Gordon and Klug, 1986; Reeves, 1983; Seidel, in press.)

According to Billig (1982 and 1986b) it is necessary to understand this sort of discourse in its rhetorical context. The two-handedness of the 'on the one hand, on the other hand' formulation is a form of prolepsis, which is aimed to deflect potential criticism in advance. Having stated an opposition to racism or to prejudice, the way is then opened for an expression of racist and prejudiced views. One might say that this rhetorical device is a signal indicating the existence of dilemmatic thought, or of an ideological pattern which is itself two-sided, rather than possessing the narrow one-sidedness by which Marx and Engels characterized traditional nationalism. Two contrary themes are expressed simultaneously, but not necessarily with equal force, in this ideology. To use the terminology of discourse analysis, it could be said that two contrary 'linguistic repertoires' are being used within the same two-handed statement (for a discussion of linguistic repertoires see Potter and Litton, 1985; Potter and Wetherell, 1987). The availability of such contrary repertoires indicates a divide within prevailing ideology.

It should not be thought that van Dijk ignores this pattern of ideology, by suggesting that the expressions of tolerance belong to the realm of interpersonal impression management, whilst those of racism are genuinely ideological. His own analyses of ideology take into account such complex factors (van Dijk, 1986, 1987), and, of course, in discourse there may be situational factors encouraging the expression of a particular theme at a particular time. What should not be overlooked is the ideological aspects of conversational themes. In this respect the denials of prejudice, and the recognition of the social inappropriateness of prejudice, are not conversational gambits devoid of ideological content. They can be bearers of ideological traditions and can indicate the possibility that the values of the Enlightenment are deeply engrained even in the norms of polite conversation. It is not merely the case that working-class respondents feel inhibited in the presence of middle-class interviewers and so conceal their 'true' feeling: if there is concealment, then it too has a social significance and reality in itself. The young British girl at the beginning of the chapter was not being overawed by a 'respectable' social scientist. She, like many of the other respondents described by Cochrane and Billig (1984), was taking animated part in a discussion group of peers. In her comment about 'prejudice' she was expressing a quandary which she personally understood and felt. It was even an issue, she said, that she had discussed with her own father. Similarly, the young and older Conservatives made their two-handed remarks in the social security of knowing they were amongst 'their own'. Even in such a relaxed company, surrounded by like-minded companions, the delicate two-handed phrasing is apparent. Perhaps one should say not 'even in such company' but 'especially in such company': the values of the Enlightenment, shared by one and all, can be reaffirmed, yet in a way that serves to emphasize their limitation.

Prejudice and reasonableness

The notion of 'prejudice' has been a central concept in social psychology, as Samelson (1978, 1986) has made clear in his historical accounts of the development of modern research in the topic. Although social psychologists have offered many different definitions of the term 'prejudice', most have sought to preserve, at least in a refined form, the ordinary meanings of the term. In consequence, the social psychological definitions are broadly consonant with the use by the young girl who denied that she was really colour prejudiced. As has been mentioned, a number of definitions actually specify that prejudice refers to attitudes towards ethnic groups. Most definitions also include the idea that prejudices are irrational, or wrongly formed, attitudes. For example, Allport in *The Nature of Prejudice* defined 'prejudice' as 'thinking ill of others without sufficient warrant', and he stressed that prejudices, unlike unprejudiced beliefs, are especially resistant to change in the face of relevant evidence. Aronson in *The Social Animal* defines 'prejudice' as 'a hostile or negative attitude toward a distinguishable group based on generalizations derived from faulty or incomplete information' (1976: 174).

The term 'prejudice', therefore, refers not only to the contents of the belief but also to the way in which it is formed. Some authors, including Allport, have stressed that emotional factors may play an important part in producing the unsound judgements of prejudice. He refers to the 'feeling-tone', or emotional antipathy, which often accompanies prejudice. On the other hand much modern social psychology, under the influence of the general cognitive movement in psychology, has tended to concentrate upon the unsoundness of the judgemental processes, rather than upon the 'feeling-tones' (Hamilton, 1979, 1981; Hamilton and Trolier, 1986; Tajfel, 1969, 1981, 1982; see Billig, 1985, 1987 for criticisms of the cognitive approach to prejudice). Despite the lack of attention to the 'feeling-tones', modern cognitive theory continues to associate 'prejudice' with a deficiency in judgement which leads to erroneous conclusions, especially about social groups. In this way, the very notion of 'prejudice' raises psychological problems about the holding of erroneous and irrational beliefs. For example Bethlehem, in his textbook on the topic of prejudice, takes a cognitive perspective. He suggests that 'the fundamental problem of prejudice, from the point of view of the cognitive psychologist, is to explain how it comes about that people make judgements and apparently believe things, or act as though they believe them, in the absence of adequate evidence' (1985: 2).

It is not only modern, professional psychologists who have linked 'prejudice' to psychological questions of thinking. The same theme is apparent in Enlightenment discussions of 'prejudice'. Voltaire in his *Philosophical Dictionary* included an entry for 'prejudice'. The entry starts with the statement that 'Prejudice is an opinion without judgement' (p. 351) Diderot's *Encyclopédie* is more detailed than Voltaire in enumerating the sorts of judgemental errors which lead to prejudices. In a discussion, which would fit well in the pages of a modern account of the biases of 'cognitive heuristics', the author of the entry gives a number of examples, especially where believers latch on to positive facts and ignore the negative ones. Religious prejudice will be strengthened if a person escapes from a shipwreck after having uttered a hasty prayer, believing that a miracle has occurred, but forgetting about all those poor souls, who have drowned despite imprecations. Similarly, the author talked about prejudices arising from overgeneralization, because people tend to deduce general laws from single facts. Neither Voltaire nor the author in the *Encyclopédie* linked 'prejudice' specifically to the possession of antipathetic judgements. Their prime target was unenlightened religious belief rather than attitudes *against* any groups or individuals.

There is a parallel between the prejudices which bothered the Enlightenment philosophers and those which bother modern social psychologists. In both cases there is a tendency to see respect for authority as an example of prejudice. Voltaire writes thus of respect for authority: 'It is through prejudice that you will respect a man dressed in certain clothes, walking gravely, and talking at the same time' (p. 351). This is not so different from those modern accounts which have linked the holding of prejudices with the personality characteristic of authoritarianism (Adorno et al., 1950; Altemeyer, 1981; Forbes, 1986). The theory of authoritarianism suggests that prejudiced people possess weak characters, which cannot face the realities of the world but are driven by the irrationalities of their psyche. They seek to compensate for their own inner deficiencies by seeking supposedly strong figures to venerate, as well as 'inferior' figures to dislike. In this way, these theories suggest that respect for the grave authority is as much part of the syndrome of prejudice as is the antipathy to racial outgroups.

Moscovici (1976) has suggested that psychological ideas, originating as technical theories, often become diffused into popular consciousness. Certainly it is true that 'prejudice' is not the conceptual property of the specialist intellectual, whether Enlightenment philosopher or modern psychologist. The term is well understood, and frequently used in everyday talk. Moreover, in everyday talk the term retains its psychological implication. The comments by the young girl at the beginning of this chapter suggest a naive psychology. She declares that she is not 'prejudiced'. In this way she denies that there is any psychological or irrational cause of her beliefs. Instead it is external events – the things that happen – which give rise to the beliefs. She suggests that the beliefs are not really prejudiced, for, lacking an internal psychological cause, they reflect the external world, not the internal psychology of the believer. Similarly, Myrdal's comment on the racist southerners shows the care with which they sought to locate the source of their beliefs outside their selves, and thereby to present themselves and their beliefs as rational. Van Dijk's respondents similarly denied their own 'prejudices', and thereby they were denying that there was anything wrong, psychologically or morally, with their selves. (For discussions of the effects of intergroup attitudes upon the attribution of causes see Pettigrew, 1979; Hewstone and Brown, 1986; for further discussions of the denial of prejudice see Billig, 1988c; Potter and Wetherell, 1988.)

The tag 'I'm not prejudiced but. . .' indicates this dissociation from the irrationalities of 'prejudice'. Hewitt and Stokes (1975) have described this linguistic move as 'credentialling': the speaker wishes to avoid being branded negatively and, in the case of prejudice, as being someone who harbours unreasonable antipathies. In this way, speakers can present themselves and their views as being reasonable, determined by the facts that happen in the world rather than by irrational feelings. Beyond the issue of self-presentation, there is an argumentative or rhetorical dimension. If views are to be presented as being rational and unprejudiced, then they must be seen to be justified, or at least to be justifiable. Thus the complaints which follow the 'but' in 'I'm not prejudiced but. . .' must appear as arguments, for which reasons are expected to be given.

Van Dijk noted that many of his respondents, who voiced complaints about immigrants, did so in two ways. They told stories about events which may or may not have happened to themselves, or they formulated their views in terms of abstract generalizations. Both these forms convey the image of reasonableness: the story implies that the expressed belief is based upon external happenings, and the abstract generalization further distances the psychological feelings of the speaker from the expressed conclusion. Both forms were apparent in the discussion groups of Cochrane and Billig (1984). Wendy, the young girl quoted previously, used both forms freely to justify why she felt that non-whites should be expelled from Britain. Wendy's stories included personal events, involving violent fights between gangs of whites and blacks. Her boyfriend had been picked on by black gangs, and 'They chased my boyfriend's brother with a metal bar.' There had been trouble at the local disco: 'I don't suppose you believe this, but there was one with a shotgun last night – a coloured with a shotgun.' And someone had been seriously hurt: 'There was one boy, he was unconscious, just lying on the floor and people just trampling all over him.' Then there were generalizations about immigration and unemployment: 'You can't go into a factory, it's just all Indians.' Her friend, Tracy, agreed vigorously: 'It's getting us to resent 'em more and more.' The syntax tells its own psychological story: 'we' are not resenting 'them' of our own accord, but something, and more often than not 'them' themselves, are getting 'us' to do the resenting.

This general style of discourse allows, even demands, that sympathy should be shown to the targets of the stories and generalizations. 'Best friends' might be produced to show that the speaker has no personal prejudices. Nor is there necessarily any hypocrisy in this. Wendy, herself, was clearly friendly with non-white girls in her class. In articulating her National Front view that all non-whites should be expelled, she commented

> I'm not being colour prejudiced, you know. I've got friends, who I would like to stay in this country. But if it was either get 'em all out, or keep the odd ones here and keep 'em all in, I'd rather get 'em all out.

The style is to express reluctance: hard choices, conflicting with non-prejudiced feelings, are being forced upon 'us' from outside. Wendy even spoke about having had a 'half-caste' boyfriend. She had been called names by other white girls. It hadn't been right, all that name-calling. But it happens. She was asked whether she would think of having a non-white boyfriend in the future. Her answer was two-sided. First, there were her feelings: 'I suppose I might, you know, if I met somebody who I really liked.' But then, external to her, were the things that might happen: 'But, then it's gonna cause that much trouble that I think I'd say no. Because, you know, my parents are going to resent me.' The feelings of her parents were converted into one of the facts of the world. In this way her discourse could still claim to be based upon the rhetoric of fact, and not upon that of prejudice, but nevertheless it could still incorporate prejudices uncritically. The parallel is with those politicians who introduced legislation to restrict non-white immigration, not allegedly because they themselves harboured any prejudices, but because regrettable facts had to be faced, and because others, notably their prejudiced constituents, demanded it (for examples see Reeves, 1983). In this sort of discourse there is a denial of freedom. Things are happening – to make 'us' resent 'them', to make 'us' legislate against 'them' – which force on 'us' a necessity, beneath which 'we' must necessarily bend. 'We' have to do things, feel things, even say things which we would not choose to do, feel and say if we were free from the yoke of necessary things. In this way the discourse employs a style which simultaneously deplores, denies and protects prejudice.

The symbol of irrational prejudice

In the modern discourse of 'race', contradictory themes are apparent. Wendy, like many of the adolescents observed by Cochrane and Billig (1984), and in common with the respondents of van Dijk (1984), simultaneously expressed views which seemed to be ever contradicting themselves. Complaints against 'immigrants' or 'foreigners' would be made, only to be followed by concessions. Blame would be mingled with sympathy, as tolerant themes follow upon those of prejudice. Seldom in the discussion groups of Cochrane and Billig would there be direct confrontation between those who only voiced tolerant sentiments and those who clung to unalloyed prejudice. More common were discussions in which all shared the contrary themes, and all chipped in with remarks which added the 'but...' qualifications to previous assertions. Nor did it matter whether it was the same or a different speaker who had made the previous statement which seemed in need of qualification. The members of the discussion group would argue with their own assertions just as much as they did with those of others, whose contrary assertions they largely shared in any case.

This form of agreement by disagreement occurred when all shared the contrary themes of 'reasonable prejudice'. Nevertheless, this form of discourse must be prepared to argue with those who express 'unreasonable prejudice'. If one of the themes of reasonable prejudice is a rejection of 'prejudice', then it needs a symbol of unreasonable 'prejudice' from which to distance itself and with which to argue, in order to prove its own unprejudiced reasonableness. Those who deny their own prejudice need, implicitly or explicitly, to envisage a boundary between their own unprejudiced selves and the prejudiced bigot. In other words, the reasonable discourse of prejudice needs its unreasonably prejudiced Other.

Wendy's comments, and those of her friend Tracy, made it clear that there were certain sorts of activities of which they did not approve. Wendy mentioned name-calling of the sort which she had suffered when she had dated a non-white. Tracy said that her sister went out with a half-caste boy: 'She gets called all sorts of names, which aren't very nice. I wouldn't repeat them, I don't think it is fair.' In the same way, she said that 'If a Jamaican boy comes up and puts his arm around you, then you get called names – you're "wog-bait", that's what they call you. It isn't fair, is it?' Nor was it 'fair' for gangs of white boys to search out and beat up young Jamaicans. All this could be conceded. In fact, it needed to be conceded, if there were to be such a thing as 'prejudice' located outside of the self.

These young girls were not inventing the forms and themes of their discourse. Despite the talk of personal experiences of discos and boyfriends, the basic forms are discernible in the discourse of respectable politicians. Like Wendy and her friend, modern politicians need to deny prejudice, and thereby they need the symbol of prejudiced behaviour from which to distance themselves. The notion of a boundary becomes evident in their discourse, when it is perceived that one of their number has transgressed the codes of reasonable discourse. For example, in 1986 a Conservative MP was widely reported as having referred to West Indians as 'bone idle and lazy'. Fellow party members instantly recognized this as a piece of unreasonably prejudiced name-calling. In attacking the transgression, they could defend their own contrary reasonableness with a qualifying 'but...':

> Mr Teddy Taylor, joint secretary of the Conservative backbench home affairs committee, said: 'I have always been regarded as being on the right wing of the Conservative Party and one who wants strict immigration control. But I think this kind of bone-headed racial abuse is uncalled for because many of the problems facing West Indians are a direct result of the way we brought them into this country. (*Guardian*, 2 September 1986)

One should note how this condemnation of name-calling includes a lay psychological diagnosis of the name-caller. The person who utters abuse is 'bone-headed', and thereby fails to show the intellect of rational judgement. Yet the condemnation of prejudice, and the sympathy for the problems of West Indians, do not rest unqualified. They accompany the call for 'strict' immigration control. In this way a politely respectable elision between 'race' and 'immigration' is effected, so that 'immigration', not 'race', can be talked about. The resulting discussion of 'strict control' is then about such reasonable matters as the facts of 'overpopulation', 'numbers' and the movements of population. In such discourse there need be no explicit mention of 'race' or anything else, which overtly smacks of the language of prejudice. Instead there is ostensibly little more than the language of fact and number.

There is no better symbol of prejudice than the outwardly racist political parties, such as the National Front. The identification of their unambiguous racism allows the denial of prejudice from the reasonably prejudiced. Wendy and her friend did not distance themselves from the National Front, unlike many of those who talked in similar tones. For example, a police-men's daughter at a fee-paying school thought that the National Front were far 'too extreme'. She herself would never vote for such 'lunatics'. But something ought to be done about 'immigration': 'The gates are still open and they're pouring in.' Similarly, the Young Conservative members studied by Billig (1986b) thought that the National Front was a bunch of unpleasant and violent extremists; but (and as so often there was a 'but') some of what they said should be taken note of. Even unambiguous denun-ciations of fascist parties are not necessarily accompanied by similarly unambiguous declarations of tolerance. A young SDP supporter was strong in his denunciation of 'idiots', 'trouble-makers such as the NF'. He continued: 'I pray that the National Front or the British Movement never get in power – Britain would become a dictatorship.' On the question-naire used by Cochrane and Billig, even he could not bring himself to agree that 'It is good that there are both black and white people living in Britain now.'

In this way the symbols of racism can be forthrightly rejected, but not its assumptions. If sharp differences of opinion did not occur within the ranks of the reasonably prejudiced, then the reasonably prejudiced would often turn upon National Front supporters in their discussion groups. For example, Kay kept rounding on the skinhead British Movement supporter in her group. Groups like the British Movement and the National Front cause 'a lot of violence and all that'. A rudimentary psychological explana-tion of their behaviour was offered: 'They think they're big walking around with swastikas on.' When the skinheads made their unashamedly racist remarks, she countered with comments such as 'They're all the same as we, only they've got different coloured skin.' It was wrong to pick on non-whites: 'There's some good in everybody and there's some bad in everybody.' Her brother was married to a Pakistani and 'Our mother went and chucked 'em out and says "I don't want them smelly things in here." I mean, it's a shame.' Yet, for all the undoubted sincerity of these declarations, and in particular the rejection of her mother's harsh unreason-ableness, the abstractions of reasonable prejudice would still be made. The division between 'them' and 'us' was still accepted as axiomatic. At one point, she was opposing the skinhead's view that all non-whites should be expelled from Britain. She declared: 'Let them stop in this country but stop them from coming in. But they ought to move into their own areas instead of letting them mix in the same schools.'

If the concept of 'prejudice' was often used to imply that the prejudiced are the psychological cause of their prejudices, then the reasonably prejudiced stressed the psychological irrationality of the extremists. The prejudiced were violent, idiots, lunatics, people who need to think themselves big, and so on. It is as if those who overstep the bounds from reasonable to unreasonable prejudice display their own psychological irrationality. The Conservative MP, proud of his reputation for demanding strict immigration controls, caught this assumption when he called his fellow MP 'bone-headed' for using racial abuse. The term 'bone-headed' may not be found in psychological textbooks, but it is a lay equivalent of a psychological concept: it suggests that only those with too little grey matter in their cortical areas would use the language of outright prejudice. In other words, the judgement expressed by the 'bone-head' lacks rational justification. Of course, all these lay psychological terms, as used by the reasonably prejudiced, are not merely descriptive. Their psychologizing serves as a moral condemnation, and in this way psychological abuse is directed against those who hurl racial abuse. By so doing, the reasonably prejudiced make claims for their own psychological reasonableness.

The reasonably prejudiced may be caught in the dilemma of possessing contrary ways of talking about 'them', drawing upon opposing themes of tolerance and prejudice, sympathy and blame, nationalism and internationalism. In this sense their discourse, and indeed their thinking, possesses a dilemmatic quality. The unreasonable know no such dilemma. Many of the National Front supporters in Cochrane and Billig's discussion groups were delighting in their own prejudices, freed from any restraining reasonableness. There were few expressions of regret in their claims that 'they' (or worse) should be expelled in order to relieve the level of unemployment; instead, they would employ the violent language of 'kicking out', 'booting out', 'getting rid of' to describe an event to which they looked forward. The unambiguously prejudiced had few inhibitions about name-calling. In fact they frequently played their undilemmatic parts in order to taunt the sensibilities of the reasonably prejudiced, as well as to express their own strong feelings. One skinhead insisted upon repeating the catch-phrase 'BM [British Movement] boys are big and brave, each deserves a nigger slave.' Others would twist every conversation around to joky remarks about 'Pakis' and the smell of curry, so sabotaging the themes of reasonableness. Psychological condemnation seemed to be invited by violently expressed obsessions: 'Wogs smell like six-month-old shit; Pakis smell like curry which has been mixed with shit and piss; their breath stinks like the local fucking sewers; all our teachers are bastards.'

It would be tempting to presume that this is the 'real' voice of racism: the protective coating of liberalism has been removed, with the unconscious aspects of racism, freed from the superego of tolerance, becoming conscious. However, there is one aspect of this unashamed racism which should be noted. It is no more 'real' than the liberal themes of the reasonably prejudiced are 'unreal' strategies of self-presentation. In fact the unabashed prejudice lacks reality, for it is unbelievable, even to the believer. As Sartre noted in his essay 'Portrait of the anti-semite', extreme bigots do not fully believe their own bigotry, and constantly seem to be operating at a level of ferocious joking. The same joky quality has been noted in extreme fascist propaganda (Lowenthal and Gutterman, 1949; Billig, 1978: 169).

The remarks made by the skinheads about 'slaves' and 'sewers', and the constant references to 'curries', are not intended to be taken literally. Instead, freed from the dilemmas of 'reasonableness', the extreme bigot is free to play consistently and unambiguously in an area which is beyond reality but which taunts reality. There is no need to hedge and qualify statements in order not to pass a seemingly unreasonable judgement. Bigots do not have to believe that non-whites literally smell like six-month-old excrement, for the bigots have chosen a metaphorical mode for their thinking and have removed their thinking from the constraints of reality. It is in this sense that their thinking has a joky quality. Saying this does not imply that the joke is in any way funny. Nor does it imply that the style of thinking is frivolous. On the contrary, it possesses a deadly seriousness, for the unreal metaphors and the loud aggressive laughter tend towards a violence which is only too real. Yet this mentality is very different from that of the reasonably prejudiced, whose reasonableness the unambiguous prejudice serves to confirm. The reasonably prejudiced have not been freed from the demands of reality, or from the heritage of prejudice. They pick their way through the contrary themes of this heritage, for they live within a society in which prejudice is a reasonable reality and tolerance a reasonable hope.

'Still we ought not to burn them'

The skinheads who enjoyed their untrammelled racist obsessions were not troubled by the dilemmas of prejudice. For the reasonably prejudiced, on the other hand, the dilemmas were clear: prejudice was to be avoided, but there were 'problems' to be faced; 'they' (the immigrants, the non-whites, the Asians, the blacks, the foreigners) were the problem, but of course 'they' had 'their' problems too. The language of prejudice and that of the avoidance of prejudice continually conflict. Conjunctions such as 'but' or 'still' show how these opposing themes can coexist grammatically and dilemmatically within the same sentence. In this ambivalent discourse there are both individual or psychological themes, and group or sociological ones.

Speakers become lay psychologists when they make characterizations about the personal qualities of the 'others', especially when employing stereotypes. They switch to become lay sociologists when they discuss how these same 'others' suffer social disadvantages. As Katz, Wackenhut and Hass (1986) write about the attitudes of American whites, 'Apparently, blacks tend to be seen as both *disadvantaged* (by the system) and *deviant* (in the sense of having psychological qualities that go counter to the main society's values and norms)' (pp. 41–2; italics in original). The discourse of the lay sociologist in this context is a discourse of sympathy, whilst that of the lay psychologist is one of blame (Edelman, 1977). However, the discourse of prejudice does not solely consist in blaming the system or the individual. In addition, there is the discourse of 'prejudice' itself, and this contains overt psychological themes. Those who fail to use the lay sociological discourse of sympathy, but who constantly use the psychological discourse of blame, are to be categorized as 'prejudiced'. Not only do the prejudiced use the psychological mode in their discourse, but their prejudice itself is to be psychologically explained, whether in terms of an irrationality of personality, bone-headedness or whatever. In this sense, the concept of 'prejudiced' is closely linked to lay psychological discourse. However, in addition to the psychological theme in the use of 'prejudice', there is also a covert sociological sense. It is sociological because the concept is used to defend a way of life – 'our' way of life – whilst criticizing 'theirs'.

There is the belief that 'prejudice' is one of 'our' concepts, indicating 'our' tolerance and liberality. Such an assumption is shared by Americans citing the virtues of the American creed. As Myrdal found, even whites from the deep south, committed to the practices of racial segregation, were proud of American tolerance. There is similar pride in Britain, as tolerance is given a national interpretation: 'we' are a tolerant country with an ancient tradition of tolerance (for examples from the mass media of the tolerant country mythology see Barker, 1981; Gordon and Klug, 1986). The unreasonably prejudiced do not bother with such claims. For instance, a claim to the value of tolerance is not to be found in the pages of *Mein Kampf*, whose form of nationalism brutally rejects liberal traditions. Nor were the violent skinheads overly concerned to arrogate the niceties of toleration.

Linked to the concept of 'prejudice' is the notion of equality, for to be unprejudiced is to treat all people equally. It is of the nature of prejudice that the prejudiced show an unequal, and unjustifiably unequal, bias against certain others. In consequence, the reasonably prejudiced must uphold the values of equality, even as they formulate their unequal views. One strategy for expressing the dilemma is to add the ethnocentric theme. Equality and tolerance are the property of 'us', and these historic values are being threatened by 'them'. In America the survey research of the new racism, conducted by McConahay, Sears and their colleagues, has shown that this theme emerges in the attitudes of many white Americans. Opposition to black political demands is expressed in terms of the traditional value of equality: 'they' are getting special privileges, which run counter to the fundamentally egalitarian values of 'our' American way. In this way the victims of prejudice are translated into the enemies of tolerance.

This theme ran strongly through the comments of Wendy and other school children taking part in the research of Cochrane and Billig. Very early in the discussion, Wendy asserted that 'Some things aren't fair, like those Indians who ride on the bikes without crash helmets.' Many others mentioned disapprovingly the fact that Sikhs, who wear turbans, can be exempted from wearing crash helmets. Wendy also complained that Asians at school are given special lessons to learn English, and some can bring sandwiches rather than eat the normal school lunches. At first sight, these complaints seem to be driven by the same combination of envious worries which Sennett and Cobb (1977) have described in their study of the American working man. Forced to submit to unpleasant disciplines and deprivations themselves, working men resent those who seem to be able to receive benefits, especially of a financial sort, without such self-denial. The comments about school lunches might be thought to fit this pattern, but the more often repeated complaints about crash helmets and turbans seem rather different. The complaints are expressed at an impersonal level. The complainant does not seem to be expressing resentment because others are doing something which the complainant, consciously or unconsciously, wishes to do, for there is no suggestion that the complainant actually wants to ride motor cycles whilst wearing turbans.

Yet there is an animus that special privileges are being given to circumvent general rules. It is not any rules which are being circumvented but, at an obvious level, the complaint is linked to a nationalist theme. The rules are 'our' rules. This is 'our' country and, if 'they' want to come here, 'they' must abide by 'our' rules, which constrain 'us'. If 'they' obtain special privileges, then 'they' will be receiving unequal treatment. A fifteen-year-old son of a tax inspector put it this way:

> I feel very strongly about immigration; if immigrants come to this country, then they should have no immunity to some of our laws, like religious daggers and the failure to wear crash helmets. If an employer doesn't wish to employ a black, then surely he must hold the choice. After all if a white person is refused a job, he can't go running to the nearest court.

In this way, an employer's freedom to discriminate against a black is defended in the name of equality and fairness. This type of complaint provides a justificatory reason for prejudice by claiming simultaneously to defend nationalism and equality. The nationalist and/or racist themes can be used by the unreservedly bigoted, but the egalitarian theme is liable to cause problems for the unreasonably prejudiced. For example, the following was spoken by a girl who claimed to be a member of the British Movement and who did not shrink from racist abuse: 'I think that in Britain today there are too many niggers.' There was also the claim of unfairness: 'Whites get the blame a lot more than blacks do.' Then followed the confusion between a complaint presented as being based on a non-racist and egalitarian criterion, and unabashed racism which did not justify itself in terms of anything: 'If they stay in Britain, they should at least dress and speak British, if not go home; they should go home anyway.'

The reasonably prejudiced person cannot take this last step: if 'they' are to go 'home', it must be for 'fair' reasons and not merely because they should 'anyway'. In invoking the concept of 'fairness', reasonable racists such as Wendy are implying that they ('we') have been unfairly treated. Not only is it claimed that 'we' are discriminated against, but especially that 'we' are prevented from being prejudiced whilst 'they' are not. In this, they are casting themselves as the victims of prejudice, and it is the others ('they') who are the truly prejudiced. Her friend declared that 'They [blacks] call us names, but if we turn and say "nigger", then they can go and they can report us and we're in trouble, because they can call us names.' Therefore the assertion of 'our' reasonableness is bound up with the assumption of 'their' unreasonableness and the unfairness of it all.

There was a further point in Wendy's friend's complaints. Her point did not rest with name-calling. She could hardly object to restrictions on name-calling, having agreed that such abuse was itself unfair prejudice. However, she made a more general and thereby depersonalized point about language:

> We've had to change names from golliwog. People can't put a sign in their shop window 'Golliwogs for sale', because people think 'Ah, coloured prejudiced'. Nigger-brown, the old nigger-brown – they have to call it chocolate brown now, because of the Jamaican people: you know, that's prejudice to them. It's always been called nigger brown.

Thus the truly 'prejudiced' are forcing 'us', by accusing 'us' unfairly of being prejudiced, to change 'our' language. And how could 'our' language have been prejudiced, when the words described such neutral things as colours and dolls? It is at this point that the sociological theme in the concept of 'prejudice' is becoming apparent. 'Prejudice' is not merely a property of crazy or disturbed individuals. It also relates to ways of life or cultures. 'Our' language, our reasonable and traditional ways of life are being threatened by an unreasonable way of life, a prejudiced way of life. A refusal to conform is indicative of a desire for privileges. As Barker (1981) has suggested, the new racism involves a redefinition of prejudice: 'You are racially prejudiced if you refuse to adopt the characteristic life style of the country in which you have chosen to live' (p. 17). Moreover, if that life style is held to be inherently unprejudiced, because it is heir to all manner of nationally unprejudiced traditions, then the desire to be different is itself a threat to this unquestioned reasonable 'tolerance'. In this spirit, the Young Conservatives of Billig's (1986b) study were at pains to point out that it was the Asians and the blacks who were really racially prejudiced; 'their' mentality had not reached the level of unprejudiced reasonableness. Thus 'their' very way of life was a threat to the tolerant fairness which 'we' all, except for the lunatics in the National Front, staunchly support.

The linking of nationalist, or ethnocentric, themes with the concept of 'prejudice' should not be seen merely as a recent development, occurring since the postwar discrediting of the old racism. It has not been an unfortunate accident of history which has recently mingled the separate, and internally uncomplicated, traditions of liberal and national ideology. In fact, it is not difficult to point to themes within the high points of enlightened rationalism which match the patterns of Wendy's ambivalences. In addition to the psychological critique involved in the concept of 'prejudice', the Enlightenment philosophers were also attacking ways of life, particularly traditional religious ways, which were based upon irrational prejudices. Whole groups of people could be dismissed because their traditions were steeped in irrationality, as opposed to 'our' modern Enlightenment. In this way, the Enlightenment declared its own conditions of life free from prejudice, whilst condemning those of others. Nowhere is this sociological theme more apparent than in Voltaire's comments about the Jews, especially in his *Philosophical Dictionary*.

Time and time again, Voltaire went out of his way to castigate the supposed primitive irrationalities of the Jews, 'the most contemptible' of all nations (p. 88): 'The Hebrews have ever been vagrants, or robbers, or slaves, or seditious' and 'They still are vagabonds upon the earth, and abhorred by men' (p. 92). Such outbursts were not a betrayal of rationalism, but a product of it. Thus Voltaire denied that he was being abusive: he had no personal prejudices. In a letter to the Jews, reproduced in the *Philosophical Dictionary*, he wrote assuringly that 'You ought to know that I never hated your nation.' In fact, 'Far from hating, I have always pitied you' (p. 97). The haters could be dismissed as psychologically prejudiced, but the sociological prejudices of their victims could not be overlooked. Sympathy might be shown to the victims of hatred, but one must pity their irrational backwardness and be aware of the dangers of such primitive unenlightenment.

The very tones of ambivalence are caught in Voltaire's writings. His stereotyping and sociological dismissal of Jews might be far cruder than anything Wendy said. Yet the symbol of enlightened philosophy shared similar ambivalences of 'prejudice' with the young working-class supporter of a fascist party. Above all there was the same two-handedness which expressed, but denied, prejudice. As Voltaire wrote about the Jews, whom we 'tolerate' but from whom 'we' receive nothing but prejudice:

> In short, we find in them only an ignorant and barbarous people, who have long united the most sordid avarice with the most detestable superstition and the most invincible hatred for every people by whom they are tolerated and enriched. Still we ought not to burn them. (p. 94)

8
Gender and Individuality

In selecting examples of dilemmatic aspects of common sense we have focused on contradictions apparent in everyday understandings of human nature: the relationship between mind and body; learning in childhood; individual expertise and human equality; the concept of prejudice as applied to human groups. This chapter will focus on everyday talk about men and women, relating this to the issue of ideological constructs of human nature more generally.

In contemporary Western society we have available to us a number of different ways of talking about ourselves and other people. On the one hand, the very notion of 'human nature' presupposes an identity common to those objects labelled 'human' (based on a capacity for 'rationality' according to the classical liberal theorists). On the other hand, we are also able to refer to the existence of infinite human variation. The assertions 'We are all human' and 'We are all individuals' are both equally and self-evidently 'true'. The potential for contradiction is further enhanced by the existence of a third type of explanation which refers to categories of persons. Not only is it true that we are all human and all individuals: it is also accepted as a fact of life that we are all either male or female (see Kessler and McKenna, 1978). The notion of 'types' of persons, of whatever kind, is opposed in some senses both to the adage that all human beings are essentially 'the same' and also to the assertion that all individuals are essentially 'different'. The collision of these various available notions of human nature may result in a dilemma between categorization and particularization, summed up by the question 'How far can we generalize?'

The use of gender categories

Social psychologists have long been concerned with the way in which people use gender categories when thinking about themselves and other people. Although theorists have differed in their approach to this issue, they have been united in a common tendency to presuppose consistency in the use and in the meaning of gender categories (see Condor, 1986 for a detailed account). Currently, academics have been concerned to document the content of gender categories (so-called 'sex stereotypes'). Social psychologists working in this area often presuppose that gender categories are stable, universal, cognitive structures which can be traced to 'real differences' in the external environment: 'The human race can be divided rather easily into two groups of males and females. *A consequence of this fact* is the development of cognitive categories to describe and process gender-related information' (Deaux et al., 1985: 145; our emphasis). In conducting sex stereotype research, the social psychologist usually accepts gender categorization as a prior fact, and simply requests that respondents describe the given category labels 'men' and 'women'. Not only do studies of sex stereotyping tend to overlook the possibility of alternative discourses (for example, those asserting individual difference), but they also assume consistency in the meaning associated with gender categories. Moreover, in re-presenting their findings, researchers tend to overlook their own role as agenda-setter, and present gender categorization as an ubiquitous schema employed by their 'subjects' (see Condor, 1986).

An alternative perspective attempts to trace themes of 'gender', 'individual difference' and 'common human nature' to discrete belief systems. Just as academics have attempted to delineate separate, internally consistent, ideologies of education (see chapter 4), sociologists have distinguished 'differentiating' from 'non-differentiating' ideologies of gender (Holter, 1970). From this perspective, 'traditional' positions are identified with gender-based generalization, and 'non-traditional' positions are identified with discourses of 'common human nature' and 'individual difference'. Feminists, concerned to construct contradiction-free theory, may go further and attempt to subclassify 'types' of feminism on the basis of whether or not a particular perspective opts for a gender-categorical account. Hence, McFadden (1984) categorizes feminist theories into 'minimizers' (those which seek to unite male and female under a common 'human nature') and 'maximizers' (those which articulate difference and the unique perspective of the female).

Social psychologists may present talk about 'gender' or of 'individual differences' and 'common human nature' as reflecting stable, internally consistent 'sex role attitudes' espoused by particular individuals (for example Osmond and Martin, 1975; but see the criticisms of Wetherell, Stiven and Potter, 1987). A similar attempt to account for variation in the use of gender categories in terms of stable individual differences is also apparent in Bem's (1981) suggestion that people vary in the extent to which they interpret the world in terms of a prepacked 'gender schema' (cf. Wetherell, 1986).

The tendency to regard notions of 'gender', 'individuality' and 'common human nature' as distinct positions, which may be used as a reliable means by which to classify 'different' belief systems, necessarily minimizes the coincidence of these different themes *within* accounts. Notwithstanding her attempts to pigeon-hole feminist theories in terms of whether or not they adopt notions of gender distinction, McFadden (1984: 497) concedes that 'Many thinkers [seem] to vacillate on the question, so that it is often hard to discern their mature position.'

In this chapter we shall suggest that an acceptance of the reality of gender, far from representing a ubiquitous aspect of social cognition, or being characteristic of a discrete belief system, may coexist with competing constructs of human nature. The consequence is that vacillation may not be confined to formal feminist rhetoric, but may rather represent a common feature of talk about men and women. In fact, such vacillation can sometimes be seen in psychology textbooks themselves. For example, Weinreich (1978: 19), in a chapter on 'sex role socialization', first suggests: 'The [psychological] evidence does not justify the stereotypical beliefs which exist in our society about major sex differences in ability and personality.' However, she subsequently goes on to consider the effect of such stereotypes in actually producing the sex differences which the psychological evidence does not supposedly justify: 'There are stereotypical myths about sex differences which, despite their inaccuracy, are reflected in behaviour. These myths influence beliefs about what sex roles should be, and in particular they influence the agents, content and process of socialization' (p. 20).

As this example illustrates, notions of common human nature and gender difference may be so closely related in talk that it is difficult to regard them even as separate 'positions' or discourses, let alone as aspects of discrete ideologies or attitudes. The use of different, and potentially contradictory, notions of human nature may pass unrecognized. On other occasions, however, demands for consistency may mean that the simultaneous recognition of gender distinction and a 'common human nature' come to be regarded as a problem. In the words of a psychology lecturer: 'I find myself saying silly things like, "Of course men and women are different, but they are not really."'

Theories of human nature and notions of fairness

In chapter 3 we noted the prevalence of the ethos of individualism in contemporary Western thought. Individualism involves an assertion not only of fact (that we are 'all different') but also of value (the moral prescription to appreciate the rights and liberty of the individual). Individualism questions both the validity and the morality of categorical thought. Authors of social psychology textbooks make it clear that 'prejudice' is to be deplored not only because of its associations with irrationality. 'Prejudiced thought', which focuses on social categories such as 'race' or gender, also contravenes the intellectual and moral prescription to recognize and value the unique qualities of the individual (see chapter 7). Data on psychological 'sex differences' is often presented in terms of two only slightly overlapping normal distribution curves, in order to illustrate the reality of individual variation and the limited validity of gender-based generalization.

Human variation is regarded not only as a fact which 'ought' to be appreciated, but also as a goal to be achieved in a 'fair' society. The notion of human variation is associated with the Aristotelian notion of distributive justice, which takes into consideration differences in deserts and needs in the allocation of rights, duties and resources (equity). In so far as gender categories obscure individual variation, they can be seen to constitute an obstacle to the achievement of a 'fair' social hierarchy.

It is not, however, simply the case that we value notions of 'individual difference' and devalue alternative notions of human nature. The construct of 'common human nature' also has a moral, as well as a factual, status. This is reflected in the ambiguity of the term 'equality', often used, in formal theory as in everyday talk, both as an assertion of fact and as a value (see Williams, 1962). In fact, individualism hinges upon values of equality, since the autonomy of the individual can only be attained and maintained by an appreciation of 'equal liberty' and 'equal opportunity'. Talk about 'men' and 'women' not only contravenes the value of individuality: it also contravenes the value of human equality. This time the objection is that gender imposes (rather than obscures) differences between human beings.

The moral tension between on the one hand values of individualism and equality, and on the other hand the assertion of gender distinction, is expressed most clearly in debates utilizing the construct of 'sex role socialization'. The argument that particular forms of gender distinction reflect the practice of a 'sex role socialization' or 'conditioning' – understood as an unfair external constraint upon the full development of individual potential – will be familiar to the modern reader of psychology textbooks. The construct of 'socialization' is often used to imply that, in so far as gender distinction has been (unfairly) imposed from without, differences between males and females cannot be construed as 'real'. In J.S. Mill's words: 'What is now called the nature of women is an eminently artificial thing – the result of forced repression in some directions, unnatural stimulation in others' (1970). Similarly, Weinreich's contradictory statement concerning the 'existence' of sex differences (see above) is based on an assumption that, in so far as gender difference can be atttributed to external social influence, this difference is not 'real'.

However, despite the fact that values of human equality and individuality can both be used to question the validity and legitimacy of a categorical treatment of persons as 'male' and 'female', the problem cannot be resolved once and for all by simply denying the reality and significance of human gender. Although liberal feminists such as Bem (1978: 21) may look forward to a time when 'gender no longer functions like a prison', there remains the problem of how to construe this ideal 'gender-free' humanity. A prior assumption of the fact of human equality might lead us to assume that gender distinction would not exist in the absence of 'forced repression' or 'unnatural stimulation' (see Jaggar, 1983). At the same time, however, the notion of gender distinction constitutes a ubiquitous intellectual and moral lens through which we perceive and evaluate the world. Ethnomethodologists have pointed to the existence of a 'natural attitude', a moral and intellectual demand that we attribute gender to persons

(Garfinkel, 1967). The common-sense assumption that every individual *must* be either 'male' or 'female', and that it is essential to determine which, is as apparent in biological and psychological 'science' as in everyday thought (see Kessler and McKenna, 1978). Whenever we think about human nature we are caught on the horns of a dilemma. On the one hand, values of individualism and equality suggest that talk about 'men' and 'women' is neither valid nor fair. On the other hand is the common-sense assumption that all people are, and must be, either male or female.

The dilemma between asserting human similarity and difference, summed up in the question 'How far should we generalize?', implies that there may be problems construing values of equity and equality as discrete or individual standpoints (cf. Rasinski, 1987; Sampson, 1975). Rather, notions of human similarity and values of equality may jostle for priority with notions of human variety and values of equity when deciding what is 'fair'. As Ginsberg (1965: 7) notes: 'The statement that equals should be treated equally and unequals unequally throws no light on what is to be done to or for equals and unequals. Nor, indeed, does this dictate what qualifies as equality.' The coincidence of beliefs and values in *both* a fundamental human equality and an infinite human variety means that the extent of similarity or difference between persons always constitutes a potentially contestable issue.

In everyday talk as well as formal theory it is important to acknowledge the range of contestability, both with respect to constructs of human nature ('How far should we generalize?') and with respect to notions of 'fairness'. Notions of 'gender', 'individual difference' and 'human equality' can all be used to support different rhetorical ends, and the meanings associated with the values of liberty and equality may vary. Mary Wollstonecraft's arguments, far from demonstrating a 'natural' affinity of notions of equality with feminist rhetoric, actually represented a conscious corruption of existing liberal discourse in which the slogan of 'equality' was used to justify female subordination. Notions of equality may still be used as a component of an essentially conservative discourse (see, for example, the discourse of 'equal but different' as described by Dworkin, 1983). An assertion of equality as a fact can, by denying the existence of power relations, foreclose a debate for social change ('Now that we have sex equality...'). Moreover, as we shall see later, the acceptance of equality as a fact can be used to portray feminist arguments as ('unfairly') limiting individual freedom and the 'right to choose'.

How far should we generalize? Gender categories in conversation

Up to this point we have been focusing on the use of gender categories in the abstract language of political and 'scientific' theory. Let us now turn to consider the use of gender categories in conversations which may more closely mirror 'everyday' talk about 'men' and 'women'. In the following conversation five female students are discussing the way in which people choose their university course. In this excerpt they are talking about women and science. (Slashes are used to indicate pauses, with double slashes indicating a pause greater than one second.)

Colette: Like women all become// well not// a lot of women/ still er/ are less likely to do scientific jobs/ which is why I mean obviously/ at the moment everyone is trying to persuade women to do scientific/ jobs but// um say if you go along to a French lecture or something like that you see that it is mostly females/ and/ and sort of fewer males whereas if you go along to a physics lecture you are likely to see more blokes.

Sue: Why do you think that is?

Jill: Because it is conditioning isn't it?

Jane: It's the effects of school isn't it?

Jill: Yea.

Colette: A lot of schools I mean when I was at school

Jane [interrupting]: And your parents

Colette: the people who were at the top of the maths groups and the top of the physics and chemistry group were all were about three or four girls and then you had a sort of mixture of girls and boys and then another group of girls. But sort of you know mixed in together obviously more or less but the people who were actually best at it were girls funnily enough.

Jane: They must have been just discouraged when they were young.

Jill: Yea.

Sarah: Your parents discourage kids.

Jill: Yea.

Jane: And the teachers do.

Colette: It isn't possible to generalize at all/ but not in// um/ well you can't generalize in the sense that/ when you say that/ girls are better at one because of the way their brains work its just that// um/ it is conditioning isn't it?/ But there was some theory or other that I read somewhere which was that um/ the female in the female brain the two hemispheres are fused together more/ so that women are better at/ general thinking.

Jane: Yea.

Colette: We're just brilliant at everything.

This conversation may be seen to illustrate a dilemma over how far one may generalize about women; Colette hesitates and qualifies the generalizations she makes, from 'all' to 'a lot' or 'about three or four'. This is a dilemma which involves a clear confrontation of values as well as a quandary over facts.

The dominant tendency in the conversation is to deny or explain the 'reality' of sex differences, by accounting for women's failure to take up scientific subjects in terms of social pressure: 'It is conditioning isn't it?', 'It's the effects of school.' The assumption reigns that if sex differences are attributable to social pressure then they are not 'real': girls have been '*just* discouraged'. In her penultimate statement, Colette suggests that if the behaviour of women is due to 'conditioning' then 'you can't generalize'. Throughout the conversation (and beyond the quoted extract), the participants continually pitted generalizations against a recognition of human variation. They also showed commitment both to a principle of equality, and also to a competitive individualism which assumes that some people are better than others, the issue being that of determining who are better and at what. Indeed, the conversation provides an interesting reflection of a contradiction which Jaggar (1983) identifies within liberal forms of feminism in which emphasis on the social bases of character ('socialization', 'conditioning') threatens to undermine coexisting notions of abstract individualism which regard human nature as 'basically' presocial.

Even an acceptance of gender-based generalization does not appear to activate a prepackaged 'gender schema' which leaves these young women with nothing more to ponder. Colette starts out by talking about female inferiority: asserting that women 'are less likely to do scientific jobs' or to take up scientific subjects at university. However, in her second statement she notes a distinction between her own personal experience and the generalized statement which she has just made: 'funnily enough' when she was at school, it was girls (or, at least some of them) who were *better* at science. In her last statement, notions of female inferiority or specialism ('mostly females' do French at university) give way to notions of generic female superiority: 'We're just brilliant at everything.'

Our short conversational extract illustrates a range of contradiction implicitly denied by most social psychological theories of sex stereotyping or sex role attitudes. Rather than sex simply constituting a 'salient' aspect of social perception, there is a *tension* between talking about sex differences and an acknowledgement of human variation. When generalization is accepted there is a tension between regarding differences as 'real' and as socially constructed. Even when differences are accepted as 'real', the interpretation of difference is not constrained by rigid stereotype templates. Rather, there is a problem in ascertaining the place of women in the comparative meritocracy. Does difference mean that women are worse or better than men?

Contradictory themes do not, in this case, appear to be the property of distinct belief systems or to constitute distinct individual standpoints. Contrary ideas may be articulated by the same individual. This is most apparent in Colette's third statement, in which her initial suggestion that 'It isn't possible to generalize at all' is followed by the observation that 'It is conditioning isn't it?' Both statements are then contradicted ('but') by generic reference to brain lateralization. We have already noted how humour may reveal tensions by emphasizing the less privileged pole of a contradiction in an unqualified, parodied manner (chapter 5). This seems to be the case with Colette's final statement, in which the shift to an apparently unqualified acceptance of the 'reality' of gender and of female superiority ('We're just brilliant at everything') is marked by a jocular simplicity and manner of delivery.

Competing notions of gender and individual difference: opting for 'an answer'

Conversations such as the one we have just considered pose the researcher something of a problem: this is related to the distinction between implicit and explicit conflict outlined in chapter 2. In the students' discussion, contrasting themes may be identified, but contradiction is either unrecognized by the speakers or left largely unchallenged ('funnily enough'). In one sense it is, of course, legitimate that the researcher 'read' contradictions in transcripts. However, on the other hand there are problems in allowing ourselves the power of interpretation when we would (as social scientists) wish to say something about the meanings intended by, and the motivations of, the speakers themselves (see Parker, in press). Of course, it is not always the case that contradictions can be ignored or shrugged off with passing reference or humour. In many situations in our everyday life, contradiction poses an explicit dilemma of choice.

Although we may be content to use contrary themes in our everyday talk, occasions arise in which we are required to opt for a *single* 'answer'. *Men and Women: How Different Are They*? asks John Nicholson in the title of his book, and the psychologist's attempt to quantify 'sex differences' is, of course, a good example of an attempt to resolve the 'How far can you generalize?' dilemma. The need to opt for a single answer is not, of course, a problem facing the academic psychologist alone. Take, for example, the following advice given to a woman who finds that her 'kind and loving' husband has been hoarding pornography: 'Either you have to decide that all men are foul, that your husband has the mind of a psychopath in the body of a beast, making nonsense of his 33 years of tender devotion to your well-being. Or you have to agree that he himself is the victim of sexual shyness' (Phillip Hodson in *She* magazine, September 1986). The answer is phrased in terms of a *choice* between generalization ('all men are foul') and particularization ('he himself').

It is important to remember that although we may be encouraged to opt for a single explanation, answers need not represent a final resolution to any dilemma. An assertion of similarity or difference between human beings may remain essentially contestable even after the option has been made. In fact, rather than it being possible to establish a 'mature position', the distinction between assertions of human similarity, absolute variety and (gender) difference may be regarded as *inherently* unstable. Billig (1985, 1987) notes that categorization presupposes particularization and, conversely, particularization presupposes categorization. We might, on this basis, argue that people only use one type of account through a recognition of the possibility of alternatives. Statements to the effect that there exist no essential sex differences would be both unnecessary and essentially meaningless, were it not for the implicit or explicit recognition of the alternative contention that differences do exist. Furthermore, to talk of 'men' and 'women' as distinct categories reminds us that ('however') it is *also* true that 'We are all human', and that 'We are all individuals.'

The meanings associated with any choice of explanation are, as we have already noted, also open to negotiation and to criticism. Since the woman who wrote to the *She* problem page is presumably a thoughtful individual, she could doubtless think of other possible solutions, not admitted by Phillip Hodson. She might, for example, choose to alter the allocation of blame by regarding men (in general) favourably but her husband as an (exceptional) bestial psychopath.

Some of these considerations are illustrated in the following extract from a conversation among six university students who were asked to provide a joint solution to a current social psychological sex role attitude scale. The experience of being 'subjected' to social psychological attitude research is an example (albeit a rather unusual one) of an everyday situation in which we may be confronted with an ostensibly simple choice. The following transcript has been taken from a study which investigated the range of contestability in 'sex role attitudes' by asking groups of 'subjects' to discuss, and reach a joint decision on, items drawn from Parry's (1983) British version of the Attitudes Toward Women scale. This particular transcript has been taken from a more detailed analysis of the 'sex role attitude' issue (Condor, 1987a and in submission). The question the students are considering is:

> There are some jobs that men can do better than women.

The extract starts at the beginning of the discussion, and finishes at the point at which the students began to negotiate which point of the scale to choose as their answer.

Peter: Yes there are some.
Julie: Some.
Marie: Yes some.
Harriet: And there's a lot of jobs that women can do better than men.
Peter: Precisely. But even that's variable cos take a job that *in general* men can do better than women you're bound to find some women who can do the job just as well or better than the men.
Marie: Yes.
Harriet: Yes.
Peter: And vice versa you know.
Harriet: There's an exception to everything.

Raymond: There will/ there will be jobs that men can do better/ possibly/ *possibly* physical jobs.

Peter: Um.

Raymond: Men in general have twenty-five per cent more strength or so the books say/ but/

Harriet: Maybe for things like

Raymond [*interrupting*]: But that's not all/ in terms of manipulative skill in fact in terms of manipulative skill they're superior.

Peter: But surely it all depends on the individual though.

Marie: Well/ I think that men have less potential to do work that women do because women have more potential to do work that men do/ in general.

Peter: Why?

Marie: Because/ men don't have the sensitivity in general that women have. Like the nurturing faculty which is necessary in caring for people.

Cathy: I think it depends on the individual don't you?

Marie: The majority though I think in the majority sense

Peter [*interrupting*]: Also of course everybody always goes on about/ women are oppressed but of course surely to a great extent those particular aspects of men are quite repressed as well.

Harriet: Yea quite.

Peter: You know by upbringing because they've got to be tough little soldiers and they've got to be you know they've got to be men and masculine and all the rest of it like me of course but um

[*Laughter*]

Peter: You know what I mean? It's probably because it's repressed rather than being natural.

Marie: But with regard to jobs at the moment I think that women in general

Peter [*interrupting*]: and yet saying that a lot of the women I have met who are in social work etcetera are often very very hard very cold. And yet the men I've met they're extremely sort of warm and kind and all the rest of it you know.

Marie: But this isn't answering the question is it?

Harriet: Well there are many jobs.

Raymond: We'll have to say how many there are.

Julie: I wouldn't say there were many. There might be a few.

Peter: Many I suppose puts across the idea that there's more than half.

Julie: We need to qualify this statement.

Peter: But of course you can't do that with these things.

An analysis of conversation (which allows 'subjects' to 'show their working') reveals the presence of ideological dilemmas which may be obscured by the usual social psychological procedure of focusing on 'the answer'. Once again, we may identify a tension between generalization (the agreement that there are some jobs that men and women are able to perform differentially) and individuation. The fact that the discussants have been asked to come up with a single (unqualified) answer leads to a more direct confrontation with contradiction than was apparent in the earlier transcript. Although the framing of the question would appear to impose gender categorization, the discussion is characterized by a generalization–particularization chain reaction, with each categorical statement sparking off a reference to individual difference. Initial agreement with the question is immediately qualified: 'But even that's variable', 'There's an exception to everything.' Raymond returns to the generalization theme, but provokes Peter to suggest 'But surely it all depends on the individual.' Marie then generalizes, but her statement is countered by Cathy: 'It depends on the individual.' Although the flip between sides of the argument is most apparent between speakers, particular individuals do not appear reliably to employ one theme rather than the other. Peter, in particular, is prepared to assert that there are some jobs that men can do better than women, but also to refer to individual variation. This comes out most clearly when he parodies his own generalization about the repression of male emotionality (the demand 'to be men and masculine and all the rest of it') by ironically including himself ('like me, of course').

Again, the problem of generalization is accompanied by an argument concerning what to make of gender difference. The 'natural difference' versus 'socialization' polarity is again apparent in this debate. Raymond suggests that there may be physical reasons why men can do some jobs better than women, and Peter accounts for men's lack of nurturance in terms of repressive upbringing 'rather than being natural'.

Even when generalization is accepted as valid there is still the problem of interpreting what this means. Although the discussion begins with a (qualified) agreement with the question, speakers tend to dissociate their own use of a gender generalization theme from a simple agreement that 'There are some jobs that men can do better than women.' Rather, the meaning as well as the viability of generalization is subject to debate. In particular, attempts are made to dissociate a recognition of difference from an assumption that men are, therefore, 'better'. Harriet suggests that 'There's a lot of jobs that women can do better than men' and Raymond follows with a comment about men's superior physical strength, but then switches focus to the more contentious domain of 'manipulative skill'. This direction is taken up by Marie, who further switches from the physical to the psychological aspects of difference and suggests that women can do more jobs than men because of their superior 'sensitivity' and 'nurturing faculty'. Marie's focus on the psychological characteristics of men and women is taken up by Peter, and the argument is again inverted, this time in a counter-stereotypic assertion, that in his experience 'a lot' of female social workers are 'very, very hard, very cold'.

In opting for 'an answer' to the ostensibly simply question posed to them, the choice which the discussion group had to make was not a simple one as implied by the usual request that respondents define their answer in terms of a particular point on the continuum between strong agreement and strong disagreement. The issues raised in our second conversational extract parallel some of those in the first. There is again a dilemma over how far generalization is warranted given the fact of individual variation. And again this is no sterile debate about the descriptive validity of generalization, but an argument based on the ideological dilemma that talk about sex differences contravenes the prescription to appreciate individual differences. At the same time, it is recognized as impossible to reject entirely the 'fact' of gender. The individualistic ethos also brings with it the assumption that some people *are* better than others and, in so far as men and women do differ, it is necessary to ascertain who is better at what.

Freedom and control

One important aspect of liberal ideology which puts into question the morality of gender-categorial thought is the value of individual liberty. However, there is no straightforward equation whereby 'liberty' is assigned unambiguously to a positive pole and 'control' to a negative. One dilemma which has surfaced on several occasions in this book is the pull between recognizing the liberty of the individual and appreciating legitimate authority.

We shall now consider another transcript, taken from another discussion by the same students, which illustrates a tension between two notions of 'freedom': first, the notion of 'freedom *from*' external control; and secondly, the notion of 'freedom *to*' act. The particular issue we will consider is that of the individual 'right to choose'. These two notions of freedom are, of course, interconnected. Individuals must be *free from* external pressure before they can be deemed *free to* choose. However, predictably, things are not this straightforward. In the example we shall be considering a contradiction which is in some respects similar to the problem characterized in chapter 5 (on expertise) as a 'dilemma of democracy'. In this case, the dilemma can be broken down into two stages.

The first problem relates to the constructs of the 'free' and the 'socialized' individual. This involves the question of the extent to which an individual can be considered sufficiently free from external constraint to be fairly deemed able to exert freedom of choice. The second aspect of this problem concerns the limits of freedom of choice. Formal liberal theories tend to avoid making substantive claims concerning the nature of human desires or interests (the 'good'), and reject the legitimacy of any external agency or expert to do so. It is assumed that each individual is expert in defining his or her own interest. The prioritizing of the 'right' (individual freedom of choice) over the 'good' (which involves a definition of what is desired) has been termed the 'deontological perspective' in contemporary liberal thought (Sandel, 1982). A problem arises when the value of individual freedom of choice conflicts with the value of 'right' as the basic requisite of a 'fair' society. What happens when an individual, who is deemed free to choose, chooses against freedom?

In order to illustrate that these issues are not merely esoteric problems chewed over by formal political theorists, but may also provide food for everyday thought, we will consider the students' discussion of the question:

> Women are better off having their own jobs and freedom to do as they please rather than being treated like a lady in the old-fashioned way.

Again, this extract starts at the beginning of the discussion.

Cathy: Depends what they want.

Marie: Yes it depends on the individual.

Harriet: It does really/ It's hard// It's an awful question.

Peter: I mean why can't you have both you know?

Cathy: Yea.

Peter: I mean it's/

Cathy: So what do you think/ disagree or agree?

Harriet: I agree.

Cathy: You agree?

Peter: Sorry what was the question again?

Harriet: Women are better off having their own jobs and freedom to do as they please rather than being treated like a lady in the old-fashioned way.

Cathy: I agree but I don't agree 1 or 7 or whatever it is.

Julie: I agree cos if they carry on being treated like a lady in the old-fashioned way how are they going to

Marie: Yes but isn't it also

Cathy: Maybe if they have their own jobs and freedom to do as *they* please and what pleases them is to be treated/ in the old-fashioned way/ then

Julie: But if they are treated in the old-fashioned way how will they get freedom to do as they please?

Harriet: But if they want to be treated in the old-fashioned way that's up to them, really. We can't just decide for them. That's not fair.

Julie: But the question says 'better off'. Women might be better off having jobs/ even if some women *want* to be treated

Cathy: But then you are suggesting that they have to have jobs/ even if they don't want to. That's not fair.

Julie: But women often do *have* to be treated in the old-fashioned way./ If they don't want and that's not fair either.

Cathy: It should depend on the individual.

Harriet: But what if they don't know what's best for them?

Cathy: I agree. But a woman should be allowed to decide.

Peter: Can anybody truly be allowed to do as they please? Can anybody really truly be allowed to do as they please? To do anything they like? To be really horrible to everybody?

Julie: Well with a job they've got freedom of choice haven't they? Whereas/ the old-fashioned way they haven't got

Raymond: It must be up to the individual.

Paul: It's the right of the individual to choose.

Julie: Questions like this are really difficult/ because they only look at your results not/ they don't take into account all this discussion which went beforehand.

Harriet: Yea.

Peter: Exactly.
Julie: and it's the discussion that's the most important.

It is important to consider how the themes of this discussion are set by the question. The value of 'freedom to' (do as they please) is juxtaposed at the outset with a notion of 'freedom from' external pressure (*'rather than* being *treated* like a lady...'). Speakers wrestle with the idea that women both 'are' and 'are not' free individuals. On the one hand, as human beings, women have a right to equal liberty. The individual 'right to choose' is upheld. Cathy and Marie start off the discussion by suggesting that it is up to the individual to decide for herself. Later Cathy suggests that 'a woman should be allowed to decide', Raymond asserts that 'it must be up to the individual' and Peter agrees that 'it's up to the individual to choose'. On the other hand there is a recognition (particularly as stated by Julie) that women are *not* at present sufficiently free from external pressure for their choices to be valid reflections of their own self-interest: 'If they are treated in the old-fashioned way, how will they get freedom to do as they please?'

As socialized individuals, how far are women able to assess their own needs? 'What if they don't know what's best for them?' As Julie notes, the question poses 'better off' as an abstract concept. Women might be better off having jobs even if some women do not want them.

In opposing the imposition of rational authority (asserting the value of liberty) against a democratic respect for the opinions of others, this dilemma is similar to that addressed in the chapter on expertise. The dilemma is 'What if they don't want freedom to do as they please?', and the question is unanswerable. To allow women to choose against freedom is to contravene the value of freedom as an inalienable human right. On the other hand, to impose freedom is to deny the ability of the individual to choose not to be free, to impose 'unfair' constraints on individual freedom: 'We can't just decide for them' says Harriet, 'That's not fair.' Cathy remarks to Julie, 'You are suggesting that they have to have jobs even if they don't want to. That's not fair.' However, as Julie replies, the question is not whether or not women are free to choose, since women are already subjected to constraints on their freedom which are 'not fair either'.

Julie's suggestion that women in general might be 'better off' having jobs even if some women do not want them illustrates a quandary over the value of individual freedom versus the general good. This is also expressed by Peter in his rhetorical question, 'Can anybody, truly, be allowed to do as they please?'

'That is no lady: that is my wife': resolving the gender/ individual-difference contradiction

In this final section we shall be focusing on one particular tension which has run through this discussion: how can we square the existence of gender with the existence of infinite human variety? Although we shall still focus on the presence of dilemma in talk and in written text, some of the examples we shall be citing point to practical issues relating to the ways in which we are able to make sense of our everyday lives, as individuals and as men and women.

At various stages in this chapter we have noted how the moral pressure to talk of individual differences is such that, even when *opting* for a categorical explanation (in terms of 'men' and 'women'), there is often a tendency to acknowledge the truth of alternative accounts. In some cases this acknowlegement may be implicit in the conversation, as when a statement is qualified with 'but. . . ' or 'and yet, saying that. . . '. In other cases this may be explicit, as in the first transcript in which Colette introduced her comment on brain lateralization with an acknowledgement that 'It isn't possible to generalize at all.' It is also worth noting how, in social psychological research, statements of gender distinction may be accomplished by initiating the research conversation with a disclaimer. Take, for example, Williams and Bennett's (1975: 329) instructions to their respondents:

> We are interested in studying what we have termed the typical characteristics of women. It is true that not all men are alike (e.g. some men are more aggressive than others) nor are all women alike (e.g. some women are more emotional). However, in our culture some characteristics are more frequently associated with men than with women. . . The attached answer sheet contains a list of 300 adjectives which are sometimes used to describe people. . . For each adjective you are to decide whether it is more frequently associated with men rather than women, or more frequently associated with women rather than men.

Another way in which generalization may be maintained is by redrawing category boundaries in such a way as to make difference appear exceptional (a process which Gordon Allport termed 'refencing'). An example of this was apparent in our first transcript, in which Colette treats the achievement of some girls as a 'funny' exception which does not affect the general rule that women fail to do well in scientific subjects. Other examples of refencing can be seen in the following quotations in which women talk about their relationship to other women (Condor, 1986):

> I've got a lot of things in common with other women. Interests and such like. Of course, by 'other women', I mean wives and mothers like me. Women with family commitments, not career girls or Greenham women who neglect their families or anyone like that.

> When I talk about 'women', I am taking it for granted that you understand that I am talking about women with careers outside the home.

> When I talk about 'women', obviously, what I mean is normal ordinary women. I don't mean lesbians or prostitutes or people like that. They are quite different.

Refencing does not, however, constitute any final resolution to the dilemma 'How far can we generalize?' The maintenance of generality by the exclusion of exceptions conflicts with notions of a universal human nature which dictates that everybody 'must' be attributed to one (and only one) gender (Kessler and McKenna, 1978). On the one hand, lesbians and prostitutes are 'quite different'. On the other hand, the fact that they 'are' women ('like me') cannot be denied.

Although, as we have seen, statements concerning individual difference may be *juxtaposed* with generalized statements about 'men' and 'women', we may also attempt to resolve contradiction by a deconstruction of the gender/individual-difference distinction. Theoretical attempts to resolve apparent contradictions between individualism and generalization have been identified as a prominent feature of 'modern' forms of formal liberalism (Gaus, 1983). For present purposes we may identify three ways in which the gender/individual-difference distinction may be managed in everyday talk.

The first example, 'androgyny', gives priority to the notion of individual differences and is consistent with liberal values of the 'full development' of the individual. The contemporary notion of psychological androgyny involves combining masculinity and femininity within the individual self (for example Bem, 1974). The location of the androgyny construct within a wider cultural ethos of self-contained individualism has been discussed in some detail by Sampson (1977; see also chapter 2). Although there is no need to repeat this argument here, it is worth noting that it provides a good illustration of the way in which competing notions of gender and individuality are located in a wider moral discourse which, through its relation to notions of fairness, may serve to legitimate certain forms of social action. Social psychologists' talk of the 'androgynous personality' is not merely a descriptive, but also a *prescriptive* device, as evidenced by the developing practice of 'counselling for androgyny' (see Cook, 1985).

A second example, the notion of 'unity in diversity', gives priority to the category as opposed to the individual. Feminists' autobiographies provide good examples of what Gergen and Gergen (1987) term 'unification myths': a progressive narrative from individuality to unity. However, an emphasis on unity as an end state need not imply, as Gergen and Gergen suggest, that themes asserting individuality therefore have been dropped. Rather, themes of relationship may be *blended* with those of individuality in a single explanation:

> Objectively speaking, there are a lot of ways in which I am very different from other women. However, although I am not oppressed like, say, gay women, or my oppression is not as obvious as say, prostitutes, I feel that their problems are really a reflection – or a magnification –of the problems facing all women.

> Being a [women] creates links between us all, but the day-to-day reality of my life is vastly different and more privileged than say a working-class single parent on [supplementary benefit] let alone black women in Third World countries. (Condor, 1986)

A third type of solution focuses on the heterosexual *couple* (rather than the independent individual) as the basic social unit and emphasizes complementarity between male and female (Condor, 1986). Contrary to Sampson's (1977) suggestion that an emphasis on interdependence is characteristic of a 'different historical perspective' to that which upholds the values of individual self-sufficiency, it is clear that an emphasis on human interdependence in general, and male–female interdependence in particular, is prevalent in 'modern' liberal accounts of human nature (see Gaus, 1983).

Rawls, for example, notes the impossibility of any individual realizing all of his or her potential capacities and emphasizes intermeshing of differences and the need for individuals to look to others to 'complete their nature': 'It is a feature of human sociability that we are by ourselves but parts of what we might be. We must look to others to attain the excellencies that we must leave aside, or lack altogether.' (1971: 529). That formal liberal theories emphasize *both* the value of full individual development and interdependence is, in fact, often exemplified in discussions of gender:

> The function of society being the development of persons, the realization of the human spirit in society can only be attained according to the measure in which that function is fulfilled. It does not follow from this that all persons must be developed in the same way. The very existence of mankind presupposes the distinction between the sexes; and as there is a necessary difference between their functions, there must be a corresponding difference between the modes in which the personality of men and women is developed. (Green, 1890: 201)

We can see, again, how notions of male–female complementarity may represent more than an attempt to resolve a 'mere' intellectual puzzle. These images of human nature are related to moral notions of fairness and exchange and serve as the basis for explicit prescription for activity. Complementarity through marriage has long represented the basis of 'good advice' to young people:

> We are foolish, and without excuse foolish, in speaking of the 'superiority' of one sex to the other, as if they could be compared in similar things. Each has what the other has not: each completes the other, and is completed by the other: they are in nothing alike, and the happiness and perfection of both depends on each asking and receiving from the other what the other only can give. (Ruskin, 1883: 90–1)

Gergen and Gergen suggest that notions of 'connectedness' of male and female may represent one of the most common forms of unification myth in Western society. The prevalence of this theme in common-sense understanding is perhaps unsurprising given its prominence in advice books, which may be viewed as representing a form of mediation between formal and common-sense ideologies. Take, for example, the following extract from *The Girl that You Marry* (subtitled 'A book for young men about young women'):

> Girls are built and designed to do certain things and boys to do different things. Girls excel in some things and lag behind in others just as boys do ... Biologically speaking, girls and boys have been designed to act in pairs. Thus, nature has devised a very helpful arrangement, and if a husband and wife will recognize each other's relative abilities and disabilities, they can make a very effective team. If, on the other hand, they bicker over these differences, the load they can pull together will be smaller and they spoil a natural advantage. (Bossard and Boll, 1961: 14)

As an aside, it is worth noting the opening sentences of this book: 'The girl that you marry is not a man. To keep this in mind goes far towards making a marriage happy' (p. 7).

This 'happy ever after' solution, however, does not provide any permanent resolution to the dual moral pressure towards gender categorization and individuation. We have already suggested that unification myths may coexist with (and may, in fact, only exist with reference to) individuating themes. Although we may wish to focus our attention on marital unity, an alternative individuating discourse is always waiting in the wings. In contemporary Western society, the existence of a 'free market' interpersonal economy brings the unifying and individualizing discourses into direct opposition. People may, and do, express with pride how their partner is 'different from all the others' (Condor, 1986).

As an example, let us consider ('22-year-old model') Mandy Freedman's account of a meeting with ('Hollywood heart-throb') George Hamilton, as reported by Neil Wallis in the *Sun* newspaper (23 March 1987):

> 'We really got on well. He told me that I was like a breath of fresh air, so different from the hard-faced, bleached blonde Hollywood bitches he usually spent time with. I really got to like him. He was interested in me, particularly my stories about going to school in London's East End. He said that was real life, as distinct from the candyfloss world of Hollywood that he lived in.'
> It was dawn when George asked her back to his Belgravia mews cottage. 'By that time I really liked him,' Mandy says. 'He didn't seem blasé like so many of the stars I meet through my job. He appeared interested in something other than himself. . . *me*. I was having fun and wanted it to continue. He kept saying, "I've never met a girl like you before."'

The mutual attraction is accounted for in terms of the unique qualities of the individual. George had 'never met a girl' like Mandy before, and Mandy, in her turn, found George to be unlike 'so many' other film stars. At the same time, however, it is unlikely that either Mandy or George would contend that the other was not 'all' or 'a real' man/woman. In order to fulfil their side of the male–female synthesis the individual must both exemplify his or her sex, and also 'stand out' (be 'so different'). This contradiction is illustrated elegantly in a cartoon published in *Punch* magazine in 1919. A disappointed suitor who laments: 'I shall never find anyone else like you. You see, you're so different from other girls,' receives the reply: 'Oh, but you'll find lots of girls different from other girls.'

9

Theoretical Implications

The previous chapters have presented examples of the dilemmatic aspects of everyday thinking. These examples, taken from a number of research settings, have suggested that ordinary people do not necessarily have simple views about their social worlds and about their places in these worlds. Instead, their thinking is frequently characterized by the presence of opposing themes. These are not the oppositions which might be associated with a careless lack of thought. Rather they are the opposing themes which enable ordinary people to find the familiar puzzling and therefore worthy of thought. It has been a constant theme of the substantive chapters that ordinary people do find the familiar puzzling and talk about the contradictory themes in ordinary life.

The teachers in the classroom are operating in familiar surroundings. For many years teachers might hang their coat on the same peg, tell the same stories in the same classroom and sigh with exaggerated exasperation as the same mistakes are made. They might be completely at ease with the cries of school children and feel at home in the routines of the staff-room. Yet these same teachers, so at ease with the familiar, can also be perplexed by the strangeness of their profession. As was seen, they can puzzle over the quandary of the limitations and the unlimitedness of children's potential. Women students, confident of their awareness of the opportunities and restrictions of gender in the modern world, can puzzle over what can be said about women like themselves. Their answers do not spill out like well-learnt formulas, but their discourse shows the hesitations and contrary themes which characterize dilemmatic thinking. Similarly, white working-class school children are puzzled by their own views on non-whites, not because the non-whites are unfamiliar, but because they are so familiar. We should not be prejudiced, they say, but we are, or rather we are not really. And because the responses are not formulaic, we can observe people thinking in their discourse about the strangeness of the ordinary.

The dilemmatic nature of ordinary thought might be said to reveal that people possess contrary linguistic repertoires for talking about their social lives (Potter and Wetherell, 1987). Prejudiced and tolerant themes lie to hand and are sometimes mingled together in the semantics of the same concepts. Thus the concept of 'prejudice' itself can be used to express theme and counter-theme in a way that criticizes and justifies racism. Teachers and experts possess an egalitarian and an authoritarian discourse, or, rather, their discourse blends both egalitarian and authoritarian themes.

The discourse on gender oscillates between judgements of similarity (categorization) and those of individuality (particularization). The availability of both ensures the continuation of the dilemma of generalization ('How far can you go?'). Similarly, the discourse of health and illness possesses its own internal ambivalences. At first sight, little could seem simpler than an unambiguous equation of illness with undesirability and health with desirability. Yet the ways of talking about health involve assumptions of illness and vice versa.

If there are opposing themes, this does not mean that the opposition is equally balanced. One theme might be the more dominant in particular discourses. Its terms might be the taken-for-granted ones, whose forms are unmarked. Health might be conceived as being normal, as opposed to illness. Whiteness or maleness might be assumed unless blackness or femaleness is specified (Guillaumin, 1972). Nevertheless, the counter-theme is recoverable, for it is frequently present in the major theme. Thus if health is to be equated with freedom, as opposed to the necessities of illness, then nevertheless the maintenance of health implies the subordination of freedom to a healthy regime. In this way the language of freedom includes within itself the language of necessity, just as the dialectic of prejudice includes both tolerant and intolerant themes, and as the former are being expressed so the latter are revealed.

The presence of contrary themes in discussions is revealed by the use of qualifications. The unqualified expression of one theme seems to call forth a counter-qualification in the name of the opposing theme. There is a tension in the discourse, which can make even monologue take the form of argumentation and argument occur, even when all participants share similar contrary themes. A statement about the individuality of all women invites a qualificatory generalization, as the speaker gives truth to the lie, and lie to the truth, that all women are the same or are different. The same teacher who expresses the progressive view of education is able to provide the counter-balancing 'on the other hand', with stories from everyday experience about the 'intelligence' or 'unintelligence' of various pupils. Too many stories of this ilk can then be countered by the progressivist discourse and its own experienced stories. As regards prejudice, the unashamed bigots refuse such balancing in order to live unambiguously within their bigotry. They might succeed in evacuating the dilemmatic aspects from their thinking, but the perceived nature of everyday reality is altered. Instead of being puzzling, it becomes unreal in its simplicity. The bigotry is experienced in a way that is unbelievable to the bigots themselves, but, of course, all too real to those who suffer the bigotry.

The dilemmatic aspects do not only concern contrary ways of talking about the world; they exist in practice as well as in discourse. Above all, the dilemmatic aspects can give rise to actual dilemmas in which choices have to be made. In its starkest form, the coronary patients had to choose how to structure their own lives and how to conceive of their own simultaneous health and illness. The choice here could literally be one of life and death. The teachers in the classroom were constantly faced in each lesson by dilemmas: the teacher must choose when to ask a question, when to provide the answer and so on. Educational philosophy might claim to determine how questions are asked and answered. Yet there is no one dominant philosophy in practice. As one teacher stressed, there must be room for both educational philosophies – the progressive and the traditional. The room is not found by literally laying aside separate class-rooms or even separate times. The teachers, with the daily problem of imparting and eliciting knowledge, meet the demands of the classrooms with strategies which simultaneously give room or expression to both philosophies. Cued elicitation, whose daily forms the children must learn to recognize, is a routine expression of the daily dilemma. Similarly, the chairperson at the committee meeting of experts has worked out a routine greeting for encouraging the contributions of the less expert. A display of friendly equality must be made, but not to such an extent that the authority of expertise is undermined. If the greeting has become as routinized, or as skilled, as the experienced teacher's cued elicitation, this does not mean that the dilemmas which have given rise to the routine have been resolved. Nor does it mean that the contrary thoughts, which themselves might give rise to the dilemmas of practice, have become any less puzzling.

It was possible to read into routines of cued elicitation, and those of the committee greetings, underlying dilemmatic aspects. One might say that these dilemmatic aspects involved the clash of contrary values. In this respect we are not dealing with values in general but with ideological values in particular, for it was possible to see ideological values in the operations of these everyday rituals. Similarly ideological values are involved in the discussions about gender, race and health and illness. In all instances some of the grand themes of ideology can be seen to flow through the thoughts of routines of everyday life. In this way, the history of ideology affects contemporary thoughts and routines, and thus this history is daily continued in everyday life. It is this historical dimension which distinguishes our analyses from most other social psychological analyses. Those social psychologists who might study the routines of everyday life seldom try to link the content of routines, or of cognitive schemata, to the processes of history. By contrast, we have sought to draw attention to the continuing ideological history of liberalism, and of the Enlightenment, in the comments of our respondents.

This inevitably raises a methodological problem, which cannot be resolved here. It might be argued that we have been able to find ideological elements in our data because we have selected our slices of everyday thinking in order to prove the point. Discussions about gender or race would seem to call out for ideological themes, for they invite talk about the nature of the individual and the nature of the social group. It would be hard to see how people could discuss these issues without involving representations, in some form or another, of major ideological themes. On the other hand, it has been possible to read such themes into less overtly promising enterprises, such as the behaviour of the teacher in the classroom or the chairperson in the committee room. Of course, this cannot rule out the possibility that there might be many other activities into which it would be much harder to read ideological themes. And, of course, we have attempted no class comparisons. The flow of liberal ideology might have been reduced to a feeble trickle had we specifically looked at the routines of the underprivileged, rather than concentrating on the Niagara of liberalism in our middle-class teachers and committee members.

What is important is the form of ideology which has been detected in these discourses and incidents. Ideology is not seen in terms of single images, or even single values. We see the impact of the classic liberal values of individualism, freedom and equality, but not in isolation. The values are understood in relation to conflicting counter-values, so that ideology does not imprint single images but produces dilemmatic quandaries. In this respect the dilemmas are ideological ones, rather than dilemmas which might arise from conflicts between age-old commonsensical maxims. The teachers are heirs to the Enlightenment, and are reproducing Enlightenment traditions, not only because they share Rousseauesque notions about progressive education, but also because theirs is a practical philosophy to be applied and tested in the classroom. Moreover, the philosophy is not experienced as an abstract system. The progressive notions are continually conflicting with authoritarian ones, as room must be found for both themes. The experts in the child development unit are guided by rationalism and egalitarianism in the best Enlightenment traditions. The nursery nurses and the physiotherapists, the psychologists and the paediatricians, may or may not be familiar with eighteenth-century *philosophes*, but the dilemmas of Enlightenment philosophy run through the practices of the unit. Their answer to the dilemma of authority and equality might bear a resemblance to the solution of Durkheim, except that hard-pressed members of the unit know that no magical solution is possible in practice. Instead, each day new solutions have to be found to the problems, which are continually reconstituting themselves.

In the discourse on gender, egalitarianism also appears as an embattled value, conflicting with the demands of individuality. Similar conflicting themes are woven into the discourse of race, as egalitarianism is asserted and qualified at the moment of its assertion. Here also individual freedom finds itself conflicting with the demands of social necessity, for the discourse draws upon lay psychological themes which stress the freedom of the agent, and lay sociological ones which emphasize iron laws of social necessity. Again both themes can trace their heritage to the Enlightenment.

A similar opposition is detectable in the discourse on health and illness. The person is seen as an agent, with the healthy freedom of agency. Yet the person is simultaneously under the thrall of bodily movements, which are prey to the necessities of disease. Again the oppositions can be traced to common ideological roots, as modern notions of health and illness can be seen as part reflections of the Enlightenment tradition, which simultaneously declared the ethical freedom of the individual's human nature and the material necessity of the individual's bodily being. Just as the philosophical problem of free will and material causation is not readily soluble in abstract theory, so it is reproduced in everyday discourse about bodily disease and what can be done about it.

There is a further theme to be detected in the examples of the previous chapters. The democratic and egalitarian motivations seem to indicate an embarrassment with power. At times it is as if power were a social obscenity, whose naked limbs need to be chastely covered. At times the teachers talk as if power were absent in the classroom, and they and their charges were interacting in democratic equality. Educational theorists have even reinterpreted the history of philosophy so that drapes can be placed over the form of power. Socrates's quizzing of the slave in *Meno* has become the epitome of free educational dialogue, when it is the slave, of all the characters in the Platonic dialogue, who shows sullen obedience to his social better. The modern experts have to be experts in human relations, and this means presenting themselves in a non-authoritarian manner, as if they were the friends of the non-experts. However, the friendliness is itself a part of their expertise, and, as such, a part of their egalitarianly presented authority. Perhaps a parallel can be drawn with the uncomfortable comments of the white working-class teenagers, who wished to be reasonable in their prejudices. Their racism was not a simple expression of a belief in social or genetic superiority. In fact, far from expressing any superiority, these speakers felt the need to recast themselves as the victims of prejudice. It was as if they would be embarrassed to declare overtly that they wished for the unequal privilege to which their racial views implicitly laid claim. Similar themes were also detectable in the lives of the men recovering from coronaries: the more that authority was claimed over the lives of their wives, the more that it would be denied. Again authority, in this case authority within the family, needed to present itself as if it were egalitarian.

In all this we can see the operation of what has earlier been called, following Edward Shils, the 'equalization' of personal relations. However, the society in which this equalization must occur is not an equal one. Thus the dilemma between equality and freedom cannot be wished away, nor can an individual decision resolve the socially constituted dilemma. The child development unit, in true egalitarian spirit, attempted to create a haven of rationality from which the irrationality of rank would be expelled.

Yet the more that egalitarianism was reinforced within the unit, the stronger that the unit unwittingly cast the shadow of authoritarianism. The gulf between the unit and the non-experts outside was widened. The egalitarian motivation, operating within an inegalitarian social reality, had its unintended authoritarian consequences: the motivation on its own was not sufficient to overcome the socially rooted counter-tendencies. Similarly, one might predict that the dilemmas of tolerance and prejudice are not to be resolved merely by goodwill. The social conditions which underlie the realities of discrimination are not to be wished away by individuals striving to order their own thoughts in a rational manner.

The example of prejudice raises a further issue which must be faced. The present approach links dilemmas to the nature of thought. Ideology, in presenting dilemmas rather than systematized schemata, ensures that the ideological subject is a thinker. Thus we do not look forward to the end of dilemmas, and towards a pure consistency of thinking, for that would be to look forward to the end of thought. From this, a critic might conclude that our position does not hope for, or even envisage, any change to the present dilemmas of thinking. However, this would be a misreading of our position. This can be illustrated by taking the example of prejudice. Our position might be interpreted as suggesting that it is inevitable that people will talk about other nations and other races in the way that our National Front sympathizing respondents did. In other words, we might be interpreted as suggesting that the contemporary dilemmas of prejudice are inevitable, and, therefore, that social action to reduce prejudice, or any other unwanted ideological theme, is a waste of time.

Nothing, however, is further from our intention. Such an interpretation would ignore the stress which has been placed throughout the present work upon the ideological, and historical, nature of dilemmas. Dilemmas may be constant within society, but our present dilemmas will reflect our present society. That being so, it becomes entirely feasible to pursue social action to change the basis of society, not in order that dilemmas will be removed *tout court*, but so present dilemmas might be replaced by others. In short, this means seeking to change opinions by changing what people might talk, argue and think about. Prejudice is to be dispelled when the underlying conditions, on which prejudice depends, are changed and the terms of present discussions are altered. When such changes have been successfully brought about, it can be predicted that people will talk about different things than they do now. Present-day discussions about races and nationalities will then seem as remote as do medieval discussions on the intricacies of courtly chivalry, or as strange as those earnest eighteenth-century discussions on the issue of whether Africans were truly members of the human race. They will seem strange, not because people will have stopped talking and arguing amongst themselves, but because they will have found other topics for their discussions. In this sense, one of the goals of social action or of social reform is to win a present argument, in order to change the agenda of argumentation.

This view implies a different conception of ideology, and indeed of social action, than that found in many contemporary social theories. On a general level, it implies that thinking is necessary for society, and that a society without thought is either an impossibility or a totalitarian nightmare. Therefore, utopian aspirations should not dream of a silent society, in which all dilemmas have been resolved and whose members, in consequence, have nothing to deliberate about. The stipulation that thought is necessary to society does not mean that all societies must think about the same things. Nor does it mean that all societies must think in the same way as do people in late-twentieth-century Britain. That would be a most arrogant, and unscholarly, assumption. It might be assumed that all societies must possess their own dilemmatic themes, but this does not mean that present-day dilemmatic themes are universal. In fact, if the dilemmatic aspects of thinking are ideologically created and the products of history, they can hardly be universal. From these assumptions, a number of critical, indeed technical, comments can be made about theories of ideology.

Contradictions and ideology

The main body of this book has undertaken some initial investigations into the nature of real and concrete dilemmas which confront individuals and groups in the flow of everyday life in our own contemporary society, whether it be at work, at school, at home or in the community. Of course these discussions have not claimed to be exhaustive. They play the role, rather, of key illustrations of some of the issues and problems which are brought to light when, instead of asking abstract or theoretical questions about 'action' or 'choice', we investigate dilemmas in terms of everyday practice and experience.

This book, then, has begun to examine the social elements in the dilemmatic character of thought and argument. It is launched within a particular intellectual tradition (Western rationalism applied to social phenomena) and background socio-political culture (Western parliamentary democracy). In this and the following sections it is time to reflect upon some of the implications of our investigations. It may be that this will in part result in a critique of contemporary psychological and social theory: for much of what is presented as 'interactional' or 'dialectical' social psychology and sociology, said to be inspired by a project in which the negotiations between social groups and classes is meant to be the central focus of interest and explanatory principle, has failed to fulfil the objective of examining social 'interaction' as expressing social dilemma. As will be argued, even the main forms of 'post-structuralist' theory have, in their attacks on dominant methodological tendencies, only produced new theoretical monologues, not displaced them with a perspective in which the truly dialogic principle and its necessary conditions are of prime concern. In short, argument is downgraded in modern sociology and philosophy.

There is, we suggest, a consistent avoidance of examining social life as dilemmatic, and in this section we look at some of the principal ways in which this avoidance takes place. First of all we do not subscribe to the view that what has fundamentally deflected the development of analysis of the structures of argumentation is the development of scientific reason itself (understood as a new totalitarianism – an image that knowledge grows without human argument, out of either a special method or the special type of mind of the 'genius'). So many views of this kind, which are generally called 'positivist' doctrines of science whether in the social sciences or philosophy, simply reproduce old myths about the nature of the sciences as absolutist and dogmatic. It is hardly necessary to develop a sophisticated analysis of the practices of the sciences to grasp that much if not most of what is produced in theoretically structured experimentation is only made meaningful by an argumentative context. Neither is science a string of unambiguous truths, although no doubt what is aimed at is the discovery of incontrovertible law: the truth of the phenomena studied. Problems only arise when this goal is thought to be the only and easily attainable goal, or one where 'incontrovertible' means 'unchallengeable'. Nothing is gained by suggesting that no such ambition should be entertained, and that researchers should not – at one crucial stage – aim at presenting, in the most detached manner possible, the 'most plausible' demonstrations to an audience of the uninitiated. Whatever scientists say about their method, scientists will rightly expect such presentations to be met in a spirit of argumentation and contradiction (Billig, 1987). However, the idea that scientists and some philosophers of science present of scientific logic and practice, perhaps in order to argue against the idea that knowledge is relative to social experience and condition, is that it aims and in general achieves an order of validity beyond the constraints of social interest and power.

More erroneous still is the view that scientific method can be detached completely from controversy, either scientific or ideological, and, as extreme rationalists would say, is the only way to truth. The suggestion that all other forms of human knowledge are tainted as 'false' knowledge, as 'ideology', is to point analysis and research in the wrong direction. It will be suggested here that, to some degree, social science's avoidance of the analysis of the dilemmatic character of social argument may be traced to the simple application of some versions of 'scientific method' to the analysis of social phenomena. But what is curious is that those traditions which have most conspicuously eschewed 'positivistic' methods, for example existentialist and interactionist perspectives, have also failed to develop the means to analyse social argument. There is precious little that can be cited in modern social theory which even hints that there is a problem here, let alone that the problem is crucial. This is all the more surprising since most modern anti-positivist social theory is inspired by a thoroughgoing rationalist approach to the study of social interactions.

But these difficulties are also registered in ordinary everyday discourse, where words like 'ideological' and 'political' are often used to identify a form of argument as having overtones of bias and duplicity, implying sometimes that judgements are not derived from an examination of the facts or evidence but are deduced from principles or, worse, from dogmas. One conclusion drawn from this is that social science methodology should try to separate out and dispel matters of value or resign itself to the position that disagreements that involve a clash of values cannot be logically resolved. Thus a conception of logic itself is invoked: truth is free from logical contradiction. One recent philosopher has remarked: 'If contradiction is tolerated, then, in a very literal sense, anything goes. This situation must itself be totally intolerable to anyone who has any concern at all to know what is in fact true' (Flew, 1975: 17). It is easy to see that it is but a short step from this to the view that the significantly dilemmatic and contradictory nature of everyday social life produces only forms of untruth and that philosophy must be hostile to it.

There is, of course, another philosophical tradition, that of dialectical philosophy, which claims to find a positive place for contradiction. But even here it is noticeable that the place of argument has been supplanted by that of 'dialectical logic', a logic which does not remain on the ground of human interaction but which has, within this tradition, emerged as universal if not cosmic. Hegel, the most important philosopher in this tradition, for instance, does not really value the logic of dialogue as such but rather the mysteries of its circles and negations of thought. That one should take the concept of life, he suggests, in order to oppose it to the concept of death is quite natural but false. 'Life involves the germ of death, and...the infinite, being radically self-contradictory, involves its own self-suppression.' Not only this, he says, 'Every abstract proposition of understanding, taken precisely as it is given, naturally veers round into its opposite.' The dialectic he suggests is found also in nature, for example the planets: they are in one place but are also moving (Hegel, 1975: 117–18). It was the last view which was to be taken up in the later writings of Engels in the formative period of dialectical materialism. The essential conclusion is that the dialectical tradition, instead of placing the real historical and social processes of dialectic at the centre of its concerns as was projected in the early writings of Marx and Engels (in for example *The German Ideology*), eventually allowed an abstract logic to take the stage.

One of the important elements of our argument is precisely that it is an argument. A significant part of this book is critical, but not for the sake simply of controversy itself; a key objective is the revitalization of the study of ideology. Although the concept of ideology has been the subject of prolonged debate there is a widespread sense that much of the discussion has not been as fruitful as was hoped. One of the aims of these final sections will be to investigate some of the principal contributions to the debate and to attempt to show how a once promising field of inquiry has become a quagmire. Certainly the objective here is not at all to produce an exhaustive survey of work on ideology; it is rather to question leading representative schools or traditions of research and to begin to indicate new lines of inquiry which might reinvigorate this problem area, which is so central to the social sciences as a whole.

The argument in its broadest sense may be stated as follows. The major studies of ideology, with few notable exceptions, though acknowledging the importance of 'dialectic' and 'contradiction', have tended to treat ideology as one relatively coherent and internally consistent social structure or layer contained within a wider social whole. Where there is some acknowledgement of social conflict or antagonism, the modification to the basic approach has been to say that there is more than one ideology in the society and that one of them is dominant. But this does not go far enough and therefore does not recognize the complexity of everyday life as it has been revealed in the earlier chapters of this book; for example, there is no straightforward way for an expert to practise in a society in which egalitarian principles have a prominent place. Some previous lines of inquiry even point to the ideological layer specifically as the site in society where social contradictions are sorted out and resolved. In opposition to these suggestions the discussion in this work has in effect developed the idea that Marx was wrong to formulate the question as concerning 'ideological forms in which men become conscious of. . .conflict and fight it out' (1971: 21). It is necessary to conceive of human consciousness as arising as part of and implicated in, from the beginning, social oppositions (and consciousness is not only consciousness of something, for to begin to be conscious also implies the existence of inner oppositions which form the preconditions of inner reflection and deliberation). It is also necessary to question the highly rationalist assumption that ideological formations ever attain high degrees of internal consistency or that it would ever be desirable that they should.

As was mentioned in chapter 3, there is no single generally agreed conception of ideology in the social sciences. What exists is widely varying usage, not a little confusion and talk at cross purposes. But some principal points of debate can be perceived, for example, in the oppositions supporting many of these debates: between the social ideology or structure and the individual's soul/body or mind/body; between science (truth) and ideology (error); and between ideology (belief) and ritual (action). Some writers would place ideologies within a wider category of 'culture' along with myths, legends, proverbs, even 'mentalities'. Of course there is no reason to demand uniformity of usage here; what is at stake is the conception of the nature of social consciousness itself (whether it be called mind, spirit, collective conscience, cultural system or whatever). Conceptions of ideology which ignore its dilemmatic character seem to encounter significant difficulties sooner or later.

Let us for a moment look at two examples taken from the Marxist tradition. In the late 1960s Sartre looked back over his own writing, and was astonished at some of the oversimple ways in which during his existentialist phase he had assumed that choice was a relatively straightforward issue, and one which could be reformed without difficulty:

> The other day I re-read a prefatory note of mine . . . and was truly scandalized. I had written: 'Whatever the circumstances, and whatever the site, a man is always free to choose to be a traitor or not.' When I read this, I said to myself: it's incredible, I actually believed that!

But Sartre continues by suggesting that within a short time he had moved to an almost diametrically opposed position:

> I later wanted precisely to refute myself by creating a character . . . who cannot choose. He wants to choose, of course, but he cannot choose either the church, which has abandoned the poor, or the poor, who have abandoned the church. He is thus a living contradiction, who will never choose. He is totally conditioned by his situation. (1969: 44)

This very dramatic switch from total freedom to total constraint illustrates the two poles of a modern ideological dilemma, but only by ruling out the very problem of dilemma itself. Even for Sartre it was unsatisfactory, for he went on to acknowledge that, although conditioned, freedom is that

> small movement which makes a totally conditioned social being someone who does not render back completely what conditioning has given him. (1969: 45)

Ultimately, then, Sartre was led to the view that the essential elements of the dialectic were to be found in the actions of individuals and groups in social life. Methodologically, this meant that analysis should always follow the courses of the actions (or praxes) of groups in situation (their projects). The dialectic is the nature of the flux of these groups, the processes of fusions and serialization of groups, not the active process of debate, argument and interlocution.

An alternative, opposing point of view is that of structural Marxism as represented by the writings of Althusser, a theme which we have already touched on in in chapter 3. Here the dominant problem is the difference between science and ideology, first in terms of a clarification of the epistemological pretensions of science (a specific practice), and then in terms of the social functions of ideology (ideological state apparatuses). In criticizing his own former views, Althusser in the 1970s suggested first that the distinction between science and ideology rested on an uncritical acceptance of 'the point of view which "science" holds about itself' (1976: 122), and second that he had

> disregarded the difference between the regions of ideology and the antagonistic class tendencies which run through them, divide them, regroup them and bring them into opposition. The absence of 'contradiction' was taking its toll: the question of class struggle in ideology did not appear. (1976: 141)

Again the discussion develops the theme of contradiction, this time as a complex process of oppositions and displacements, a process occurring in the social body and not one through which social groups argue and consciously engage with one another in real encounters.

Both Sartre and Althusser recognized the limits of their initial perspectives and reflected that, because of rationalist assumptions, their work had failed to begin to grasp something of the contradictory nature of ideological relations. More than this, the very approach which leads to a conception of ideology as a formally consistent total social structure invariably fails to question the ways in which individual subjects and groups struggle to find their paths through the complexities with which they are confronted. Althusser, for instance, was interested in a general theory of ideology as a mechanism which transforms individuals into human subjects (through 'interpellation'). But the way in which his question is asked is implicitly linked to the thesis that each society produces a dominant ideology and a dominant ideological state apparatus. Even those who have questioned the dominant ideology thesis have tended to criticize either the notion of dominance or its rather weak epistemological ground rather than the concept of ideology it implies.

This is not to say that the Marxist contribution to the analysis of ideology is negligible. Althusser is certainly right to point to the weaknesses of pre-Marxist views: (a cynical theory) that there are religions because priests have invented seductive lies in order to maintain themselves in positions of privilege. Marx's critique of these and other similar propositions are recognized as a valuable contribution to modern social theory, which has focused on the structural analysis of functioning 'belief systems'. But in turning to the contributions from sociology it is possible to see that non-Marxist theory suffers from many of the same limitations as the Marxist tradition, indicating much the same kind of reluctance to examine social life as dilemmatic. They have not been able to come to grips with the issues which we have raised in this book. For example, teachers in schools do not simply aim to produce pupils who will be adequately self-disciplined social beings and who will respond to complex ideological instruments of social control and thus social constraint. They also aim to foster human beings who have within them the necessary social and cultural means for self-determination which, as we have pointed out, implies that there are adequate means of self-reflection and thought.

Thus citizens are encouraged to think for themselves within and beyond the limits imposed by the networks of constraints.

Sociology and ideological contradiction

If we now turn to sociological theories of the mainstream tradition as it has been influenced through the German tradition, for example, we can see once again that there seem to be very specific and limiting consequences of the methodological positions adopted. One of the most celebrated works which initiated the sociological study of ideology, Karl Mannheim's *Ideology and Utopia*, explicitly follows the ideas of Max Weber (in the construction of ideal types) and Alfred Weber (in constellational analysis). What this means is that Mannheim's project aims specifically to elaborate ideologies as whole constructs, and then to look at subtypes such as utopian structures: 'that type of orientation which transcends reality and which at the same time breaks the bonds of the existing order' (1960: 173). What Mannheim suggested therefore was something akin to defining common sense as ideology and some forms of ideology as utopian thought. This of course retained the idea of the strain, tension and even contradiction between certain kinds of belief and existing reality. On top of this, Mannheim attempted to reconstruct the main forms and stages of such utopian thinking, proceeding from the anabaptists to communism. It is emphasized in a phrase which quite nicely displaces the idea of the real:

> We will be concerned here with concrete thinking, acting, and feeling and their inner connections in concrete types of men . . . no individual mind, as it actually existed, ever corresponded completely to the types and their structural interconnections to be described. (1960: 189–90)

This 'methodological device' has very specific consequences, for it is only with the emergence of socialist-communist utopian thought that Mannheim begins to find a 'struggle' between these structures, a struggle aimed at the 'fundamental disintegration of the adversary's beliefs' (p. 217). In other words all the main utopian forms emerge and develop, and only then do they engage in mutual criticism. In the 'conflict' between Marx and the anarchist Bakunin, Karl Mannheim argues, the more primitive egalitarian, 'chiliastic' utopianism 'came to an end' (p. 219). The social basis of the collapse of this kind of anarchist utopianism is seen as follows:

> Bakunin's advanced guard, the anarchists of the Jura Federation, disintegrated when the domestic system of watch manufacture, in which they were engaged and which made possible their sectarian attitude, was supplanted by the factory system of production. In place of the unorganised oscillating experience of the ecstatic utopia, came the well-organised Marxian revolutionary movement. (p. 219)

It is clear that Mannheim is not really interested in the actual meeting of arguments between Marx and Bakunin, or even between the Marxists and the Bakuninists. Conceived at the level of ideal types, where quite explicitly 'no single individual represents a pure embodiment of any one of the historical-social types' (p. 189), such considerations could only be of marginal interest. The method also in one sense deflects the charge of oversimplification by pointing to the socio-economic forces at work – but this too can only be a suggestion at the level of 'types'. (If Mannheim did indeed intend to argue that ideological and utopian movements are directly determined by economic changes then of course this would require a different kind of analysis from the one he presents, and the example of Marx and Bakunin given here certainly could not stand without further and elaborate substantiation, if only to point to the real complexities of such processes when not considered as types.) No doubt unresolved dilemmas in social thought could be approached using the ideal-type method, but this raises questions of another kind as we shall discuss in a moment.

First, however, we wish to consider another sociological work which has had wide influence, namely *The Social Construction of Reality* by Peter Berger and Thomas Luckmann (1971). Influenced by both Weberian and Sartrean traditions, this work set out to eleborate a theoretical understanding of the ways in which the symbolic systems in modern societies are socially constructed. In its consideration of the general beliefs in society it approached them by examining the processes of conceptual maintenance of the symbolic universe. Four main types of 'machineries' were discussed: mythology, theology, philosophy and science (pp. 127–34). Myth is immediately stigmatized as naive, and its naivety is used to explain its inconsistent patterns. Indeed it is only the relatively more sophisticated systematization of the theological forms which it is argued distinguishes them from naive mythology. Systematization leads to the first real differentiation of forms of knowledge in society, and philosophical and scientific forms are really only further elaborations in the direction of systematization. In order to maintain the dominance of these more systematic thought systems, Berger and Luckmann argue that two further techniques are used: therapy and nihilation. The latter concerns ways in which the legitimacy of the dominant perspectives are secured through the rejection of the threat of alternative views:

> Nihilation involves the more ambitious attempt to account for all deviant definitions of reality in terms of concepts belonging to one's own universe...The deviant conceptions are not merely assigned a negative status, they are grappled with theoretically in detail. The final goal of this procedure is to incorporate the deviant conceptions...and thereby to liquidate them. (p. 133)

Berger and Luckmann move into a discussion of the 'social-structural base for competition between rival definitions', for it is this which will 'affect', if not 'determine outright', the outcome of such struggles. The sphere of social organization of the 'experts' involved in such struggles is paramount, and Berger and Luckmann offer some 'types'. When experts hold an 'effective monopoly over ultimate definitions of reality' – where there is a specific power group which develops its own perspectives in a way which differentiates itself – this gives rise to an ideology proper (p. 141). In modern pluralistic societies where there is a 'shared core universe', experts have to be able to find ways of 'theoretically legitimating the demonopolization that has taken place' (p. 142). The relationship between ideas and institutions is 'dialectial', it is argued: 'Theories are concocted in order to legitimate already existing social institutions. But it also happens that social institutions are changed in order to bring them into conformity with already existing theories' (p. 145). Unlike the discussion which we have presented of the expert (in chapter 5), little in this presentation by Berger and Luckmann seems to indicate the existence of problems or dilemmas for the expert in any practical sense; these exist only for society.

It is clear then that in these examples of the sociology of knowledge, 'belief systems', whether called ideologies or some other term, are conceived as ideational totalities (more or less systematic and systematized) associated with certain kinds of social groups (more or less organized, more or less under strain). And these totalities are presented as a result of a certain way of looking at society: not as an aggregation of individuals, but as an outcome of typification by the sociologist. Somehow, in the process of constructing these ways of looking, the sociologist seems to have become predisposed to treat 'ideologies' or 'beliefs' as structures which possess remarkable degrees of inner coherence – even, it may be said, primitive ones. Conflicts, in so far as they are dealt with, seem to revolve around inter-ideological issues. These orientations have their complements in other discussions in modern sociology: from those views which see at the heart of any society a 'common conscience' or common value system which society has to protect if it is to survive, to those which see ideology in metaphorical terms as a 'social cement', even to those who see in ideological formations the principal ways in which social tensions and conflicts are not so much 'fought out' as resolved through (unconscious) structural transformations.

There is, however, a major writer who should also be considered here, for, in one sense, the work of the sociologist Talcott Parsons has as its basis the idea that social life must be analysed as a series of dilemmas which have to be decided in any social process. Out of a synthesis of the writings of major nineteenth-century and early-twentieth-century writers, whose thoughts, Parsons argued, converged in an anti-positivist theory of action, he developed an action frame of reference into which was posed what he called basic 'pattern variables'. These were a limited set of oppositions which could form the means for analysing the pattern of all social action. He argued that there were only five of these ideal-typical dilemmas: affectivity and affective neutrality; self or collectivity orientation; universalism or particularism; achievement or ascription; and finally specificity or diffuseness (Parsons, 1951: 58–67). These were turned into criteria for the classification of societies and for the analysis of processes.

An illustration of Parsonian analysis is his celebrated analysis of the modern medical process (1951: chapter 10; for a commentary see Devereux in Black, 1961). For Parsons the situation of the doctor is one of achievement, technical expertise, affective neutrality, functional specificity and collectivity orientation, while that of the patient or someone occupying the 'sick role' is one of relative need and helplessness often accompanied by problems of affective adjustment, and one of technical incompetence in the face of these problems. When Parsons comes to analyse the process itself he immediately admits that the logical model does not really operate at all (1951: 470). First of all, the knowledge system is radically incomplete and the technical means are highly limited. More than this, in order to make effective the techniques he does possess, the medical practitioner has had to build up an elaborate social mechanism for handling a number of crucial doctor–patient problems: access to the body of the patient, access to private knowledge of the patient, and so on. The outcome has been the development of the medical professional institutions and legal immunities, with specific rights and obligations which are built up to facilitate the technical tasks of the physician and the defence of the patient against exploitation and of the status of doctors and their profession. The specific dilemmas which Parsons examines, after a consideration of the 'sick role' as a significant legitimization of a possible deviant category within the social system, centre on the fallible expert in the face of limited knowledge and technique, and the strong desires of the sick and of friends and relatives who are exploitable (in more than one sense) and yet who, if there is an unfortunate outcome, may blame the doctor. (The doctor may indeed be guilty of malpractice – but who is to judge but the reluctant technical expert, who will throw the first stone?) Parsons insists that it is the modern professional institution which emerges specifically to resolve these dilemmas for the doctor, who then is subject to its beneficent discipline. Even the patient benefits, he suggests, from the reluctance of the physicians to judge themselves; for without this reluctance they would not take risks in their profession, which would then simply ossify.

A number of criticisms of Parsons's position have become well known, and seem telling (see Black, 1961). Most significantly here, the 'pattern variables' have been heavily criticized on several counts: their level of generality; whether they are 'choices' or 'dilemmas' at all; whether they are exhaustive; whether, indeed, they are even required for such forms of analysis. Certainly Parsons seems to find it useful to identify the 'sick role' and the institutional complex through them. When he begins his analysis, however, he immediately begins to find concrete historical and social inconsistencies, discrepancies and illogicalities which appear to surprise him. As we have seen in chapter 6, the notion of the sick role is an oversimplification because of the complex interrelation of ideological dilemmas over health and illness. Indeed Parsons's own analysis develops in this direction when he considers the tensions in the medical process and the strains in its ideology.

At bottom, however, there are some remarkable misconceptualizations: the pattern variables are not 'dilemmas' in any sense of the term which can refer to acting agents or subjects. On the other hand, when he does talk of a medical practitioner as being in a dilemma, say a clash between scruples and advantage, or emotional involvement inhibiting technical competence, the battery of pattern variables seems redundant. Moreover it is not clear that this theoretical apparatus helps us to understand the nature of the situation of the expert in a democratic society as discussed in chapter 5. Parsons's claim then that his theory is founded on the dilemmatic character of social ideologies is thus quite misleading; the most that could be claimed is that at some points in his work, as with the work of other major thinkers, some elements of the real complexity of modern life are evoked, and symptomatically these are the elements which we have termed dilemmatic. That is why the type of discussion presented in this book is so different from that of Parsons. For example, neither the discussion of health, nor that of the expert, nor that of the dilemmas which confront teachers assumes that there are any dilemmas which can be identified through the application of ideal-type categories. Nevertheless it does appear to be the case that on analysis certain quite different but common and recurrent dilemmatic themes are discovered. Maybe it will be the case that some dilemmas will continue be found to be more important to social life than others, or to have significant implications for problems of social control or social reproduction; but these are not known in advance. Again looking at Parsons's own analysis, it is not really obvious that his empirical analysis has in any way benefited from the application of these Parsonian ideal-type dilemmas, and it could certainly have been carried out with an altogether more modest set of instruments as has been the case in this book.

Theoretical oppositions

It may help the reader to grasp the main theoretical orientation adopted here if we attempt very briefly to situate the ideas relative to some important contemporary dilemmatic currents in the social sciences. The way in which our position can be expressed most clearly involves making some oppositions, but in considering these it is important to remember that the realities to which they relate are not quite so clear cut. Nevertheless, two sets of oppositions can be identified: the polarity of humanism and structuralism; and an epistemological polarity between absolutism and relativism (indifference). These all combine in different ways, but it is useful to identify them separately.

Humanism and structuralism
Humanist approaches such as that developed in the existentialist and interactionist traditions, as represented by a writer like Sartre, tend to focus on praxiology: they assume communication to involve the exchange of meanings formed prior to linguistic structures, the latter being only vehicles for the exchange. Acts translate such meanings into the physical world as projects. Everything is thus dependent on understanding original and derived meanings, which are seen as rich in meaning.

Structuralism, as represented by Althusser for example, can be seen as a response to humanism because it rightly stresses the necessity of theorizing the media of communication and investigating their effects on messages. But such approaches tend to go further and analyse the content of messages in terms of infrastructures which are independent of such media – and in social theory these infrastructures are thought of as being related to or transformations of social structures. This leads to attempts to simplify individual meanings in order to identify structures which exist between social groups. This endeavour is said by critics to lead to 'thin' descriptions of individual experience (as discussed for example in the work of Geertz (1975) or E.P. Thompson (1978)).

In the light of post-structuralism it can be seen that what these two approaches have in common is that they overemphasize the harmonic integration of action and structure in some posited unifying meaning in the individual or society. We go along with this critique. An important implication of this criticism is that the idea that investigation can find whole, seamless structures of meaning which somehow hold the social world together is not well founded.

Absolutism and relativism
Epistemologically, absolutist investigations, for example Durkheimian sociology, assume that there can be established a single truth about a phenomenon, either through a literary or historical method or through a logical or geometric method. These approaches rarely consider the position of the observer except in terms of an evolution of the rationalist spirit.

Relativists or indifferentists, for example symbolic interactionists or ethnomethodologists, in fact tend to be pale versions of absolutists in order to avoid the problems involved. Relativism, with its suggestion that knowledge can never attain high degrees of objectivity because of the social rootedness of the observer (a doctrine which nevertheless claims that its own knowledge is objective and true), is safer or more palatable politically (because democratic) without this dilemma itself becoming an issue.

The way of dealing with the inevitable difficulties of this opposition seems to us to lie in developing two important forms of reflexivity: an understanding of the ways in which knowledge structures itself in relation to its own development (historical consciousness), and a recognition of knowledge as a social force. Both of these aspects have to be understood within 'argumentative' contexts, that is from the recognition of the dilemmatic character of knowledge and belief.

There is an important problem, however, if this line of argument is counterposed to the general thrust of post-structuralism, in the sense that the critique of these two sets of oppositions has been developed by post-structuralism in its attack on the idea that the goal of social science should be to discover determined structures. Post-structuralism, we think rightly, puts the stress on the fact that things can come apart in unexpected ways, for both the subject and the object of analysis. It stresses the discrepancies between structure and infrastructure, between sender and receiver of messages. While the ethnomethodologist gets round this by talking of contingency and the post-structural Marxist by social reproduction mechanisms overdetermined by class struggle, it seems to us that some process akin to rhetorical engagement in dilemmatic ideological formations is being acknowledged here. For example, Michel Foucault once explicitly formulated the problem admirably as follows:

> History . . . is intelligible . . . and should be analysed . . . according to the intelligibility of struggles, of strategies and tactics. Neither the dialectic (as logic of contradiction) nor semiotics (as structure of communication) can account for the intrinsic intelligibility of confrontations. The 'dialectic' is a way of avoiding the always hazardous and open reality of this intelligibility, by reducing it to the Hegelian skeleton; and 'semiology' is a way of avoiding its violent, bloody and deadly character, by reducing it to the pacified and Platonic forms of language and dialogue. (In Morris and Patton, 1979: 33)

If what is in part aimed at by such approaches is that they consider textual and social strategies, we would also add that any such project must, as well as posing theoretical questions as to the nature of ideology, also recognize the necessity of grasping, within a social analysis, the play of ideologies as born and developed in social action and counteraction.

Studying dilemmas

It is now possible to turn to what we think is required in any adequate contemporary approach to the examination of the dilemmas of everyday life, and to sketch out some of the prospects for such a project.

First of all, it is evident after the brief survey of social science literature provided in this book, that many of the traditional methods seem particularly weak as means to think about these problems and analyse social reality. In our presentations and analyses we have demonstrated that our preferred forms of approach are qualitative and interpretative, and have indicated that too early theoretical or empirical closure in the direction of social system thinking or cognitive consistency thinking makes it difficult to recognize the real object of investigation. In line with much contemporary thinking in the social sciences it is recommended that social life is viewed as complex and open; closed system thinking should for the present stage of research remain in suspension. This has implications for the image presented both of a person, here regarded from the point of view of a subject capable of argument (indeed dependent on argument), and of a society in which many of the resources for argument are produced in the complex nature of its demands and opportunities.

This must not be misunderstood as an appeal for a certain dose of confusion or illogicality in thought and analysis. It is however in line with a strong theme of modern social analysis which is that personality and society be considered as complex phenomena, as containing within them themes and structures which are contradictory in principle. If this theme has been developed most noticeably in the French tradition (for example in Durkheim and Foucault), as well as in the Marxist one, complexity has often meant formal logical complexity in which the structural principle of complexity is invoked. In this work, however, the idea of complexity which has been developed is that of historical and ideological complexity of the social world, where people have to grapple with issues which are rarely clear cut and where they have to struggle to come to terms with problems because there is not and cannot be a ready formed authoritative solution. The attempts to close down the world by programming or sacred formulas only explode in the face of the unforeseen surprises of everyday life and the fact that human life is vulnerable.

It is not suggested, however, that the social world is so complex it cannot be thought about. The progress that may have been made in the present work has been possible on the basis of a relatively modest reorganization of the problematics of ideology. It has been implied that social and social psychological analysis must be liberated from any principle of inherent or demiurgic logical dialectic. If there is a dialectic this will be structured into the argumentative context of real historical interaction as either explicit or implicit dilemmatic matrix. Neither is there any urgent need for a consideration of ideal communication forms (such as those examined by Habermas), since the only ones which are of interest for analysis are those which have played a significant role in the continuing problems of everyday life. Here, none has essential privileges. In the discussions in previous chapters, we have presented the voices of ordinary people in conversation and debate in order to reveal the tactics and strategies of dealing with recurring and novel difficulties of everyday judgement. Sometimes these have been generalized into a discussion of an occupational role, for example, but not through the application of a prior set of formal 'dilemmas' to it in the manner of Parsons. It is not suggested that role conflicts do not exist. Rather, for the style of analysis developed here, these conflicts are of interest from an altogether different objective: not to find how they might be institutionally resolved or functional for the social system, but to show how they give rise to both problems and opportunities for reflection, doubt, thought, invention, argument, counter-argument. Hence our conception suggests that in everyday thought the individual is a lay philosopher, not a marionette dancing to the desires of a great design.

Thus we return to the nature of dilemma. If in the initial discussions we began the examination by looking at what appear to be simple dilemmas, for example, 'the wolves or the precipice', our analyses have shown that what is involved is clearly not a straightforward issue of choice, of alternative courses of action, or on the other hand a matter of intellectual puzzles or paradoxes. Whether or not to buy item A or item B is not in itself a dilemma (nor incidentally is whether to buy or steal item A). The characteristic of a dilemma which makes it significant for social analysis is that it is more complex than a simple choice or even a straightforward technical problem (even the existence for a doctor of barriers to access to the body is not a dilemma, it is simply an obstacle). Again the fact that actors may not be in possession of complete or adequate knowledge, or may have conflicting knowledge, is not a sufficient condition of either insecurity or dilemma. If we have begun to examine dilemmas as ideological, as social situations in which people are pushed and pulled in opposing directions, it is because they are also seen to impose an assessment of conflicting values. The technical problem is perhaps inescapably interwoven with problems concerning the involvement with or 'management' of clients. In this way the characteristics of dilemmas are revealed as fundamentally born out of a culture which produces more than one possible ideal world, more than one hierarchical arrangement of power, value and interest. In this sense social beings are confronted by and deal with dilemmatic situations as a condition of their humanity.

References

Abercrombie, N. (1980) *Class, Structure and Knowledge*. Oxford: Basil Blackwell.

Abercrombie, N., S. Hill and B.S. Turner (1980) *The Dominant Ideology Thesis*. London: Allen & Unwin.

Adorno, T.W., E. Frenkel-Brunswik, D.J. Levinson and R.N. Sanford (1950) *The Authoritarian Personality*. New York: Harper & Row.

Airey, C. (1984) 'Social and moral values', in R. Jowell and C. Airey (eds), *British Social Attitudes: the 1984 Report*. Aldershot: Gower.

Allport, G.W. (1954) *The Nature of Prejudice*. Garden City: Anchor Books.

Almond, G.A. (1954) *The Appeals of Communism*. Princeton: Princeton University Press.

Altemeyer, R. (1981) *Right-Wing Authoritarianism*. Manitoba: University of Manitoba Press.

Althusser, L. (1971) *Lenin and Philosophy and Other Essays*. London: New Left Books.

Althusser, L. (1976) *Essays in Self Criticism*. London: New Left Books.

Aristotle (1909) *Rhetoric*. Cambridge: Cambridge University Press.

Armstrong, D. (1983) *Political Anatomy of the Body: Medical Knowledge in Britain in the Twentieth Century*. Cambridge: Cambridge University Press.

Aron, R. (1977) *The Opium of the Intellectuals*. Westport: Greenwood Press.

Aronson, E. (1976) *The Social Animal*. New York: Freeman.

Bach, K. and R.M. Harnish (1979) *Linguistic Communication and Speech Acts*. Cambridge, Mass.: MIT Press.

Bacon, F. (1858) *Of the Dignity and Advancement of Learning* (1605). London: Longman.

Bagehot, W. (1965a) *Historical Essays*. New York. Anchor Books.

Bagehot, W. (1965b) *The English Constitution* (1867). London: Fontana.

Bagley, C. and G.K. Verma (1979) *Racial Prejudice, the Individual and Society*. Farnborough: Saxon House.

Barker, M. (1981) *The New Racism*. London: Junction Books.

Bateson, G. (1971) 'The cybernetics of "self": a theory of alcoholism', *Psychiatry*, 34: 1–18.

Becker, H. (1968) *Making the Grade*. Chichester: Wiley.

Bem, S.L. (1974) 'The measurement of psychological androgyny', *Journal of Consulting and Clinical Psychology*, 42: 115–62.

Bem, S.L. (1978) 'Beyond androgyny', in J.A. Sherman and F. Denmark (eds), *The Psychology of Women*. New York: Psychological Dimension.

Bem, S.L. (1981) 'Gender schema theory: a cognitive account of sex typing', *Psychological Review*, 66: 354–64.

Bennett, S.N. and A. Jordan (1975) 'A typology of teaching styles in primary schools', *British Journal of Educational Psychology*, 45: 20–8.

Berger, P. and T. Luckmann (1971) *The Social Construction of Reality*. Harmondsworth: Penguin.

Berkeley, G. (1872) 'Prejudices and opinions', in *Chambers's Readings in English Literature*. Edinburgh: William & Robert Chambers.

Berlak, A.C., H. Berlak, N.T. Bagenstos and E.R. Mikel (1975) 'Teaching and learning in English primary schools', in M. Hammersley and P. Woods (eds), *The Process of Schooling*. London: Routledge & Kegan Paul.

Bethlehem, G. (1985) *A Social Psychology of Prejudice*. Aldershot: Gower.

Billig, M. (1978) *Fascists: a Social Psychological View of the National Front*. London: Academic Press.

Billig, M. (1981) *L'Internationale Raciste: de la psychologie à la 'science' des races*. Paris: Maspero.

Billig, M. (1982) *Ideology and Social Psychology*. Oxford: Basil Blackwell.

Billig, M. (1985) 'Prejudice, categorization and particularization: from a perceptual to a rhetorical approach', *European Journal of Social Psychology*, 15: 79–103.

Billig, M. (1986a) *Thinking and Arguing: Inaugural Lecture*. Loughborough: Loughborough University.

Billig, M. (1986b) 'Very ordinary life and the Young Conservatives', in H. Beloff (ed.), *Getting Into Life*. London: Methuen.

Billig, M. (1987) *Arguing and Thinking: a Rhetorical Approach to Social Psychology*. Cambridge: Cambridge University Press.

Billig, M. (1988a) 'Social representation, objectification and anchoring: a rhetorical analysis', *Social Behaviour*, 3: 1–16.

Billig, M. (1988b) 'Historical and rhetorical aspects of attitudes: the case of the British monarchy', *Philosophical Psychology*, 1: 83–103.

Billig, M. (1988c) 'The notion of "prejudice": some rhetorical and ideological aspects', *Text*, 8: 91–110.

Billig, M. (in press) 'Studying the thinking society: social representations, rhetoric and attitudes', in G. Breakwell and D. Canter (eds), *Empirical Approaches to Social Representations*. Oxford: Oxford University Press.

Black, M. (ed.) (1961) *The Social Theories of Talcott Parsons*. Englewood Cliffs, NJ: Prentice-Hall.

Bloch, M. (1975) *Political Language and Oratory in Traditional Society*. London: Academic Press.

Bossard, J. and E. Boll (1961) *The Girl that You Marry*. London: Darwen Finlayson.

Brown, R. (1965) *Social Psychology*. New York: Macmillan.

Bruner, J.S. (1957) 'On perceptual readiness', *Psychological Review*, 64: 123–51.

Bruner, J.S. (1986) *Actual Minds, Possible Worlds*. London: Harvard University Press.

Burnstein, E. and A. Vinokur (1975) 'What a person thinks upon learning he has chosen differently from others: nice evidence for the persuasive arguments explanation of choice shifts', *Journal of Experimental Social Psychology*, 11: 412–26.

Burton, G. (1979) *Interpersonal Relations: a Guide for Nurses*. London: Tavistock.

Cartwright, D. (1971) 'Risk taking by individuals and groups: an assessment of research employing choice dilemmas', *Journal of Personality and Social Psychology*, 20: 361–78.

Cartwright, D. (1973) 'Determinants of scientific progress: the case of research on the risky shift', *American Psychologist*, 28: 222–31.

Cochran, M. (1986) 'The parental empowerment process: building on family strengths', in J. Harris (ed.), *Child Psychology in Action*. Beckenham: Croom Helm.

Cochrane, R. and Billig, M. (1984) 'I'm not National Front, but...', *New Society*, 68: 255–8.

Colman, A. (1982) *Game Theory and Experimental Games*. Oxford: Pergamon.

Condor, S. (1986) 'From sex categories to gender boundaries: reconsidering sex as a "stimulus variable" in social psychological research', *Newsletter of the Social Psychology Section of the British Psychological Society*, Spring.

Condor, S. (1987a) 'Sex role "attitudes" in conversation', paper presented at the Annual Conference of the British Psychological Society (Social Psychology Section), Oxford, September.

Condor, S. (1987b) 'Towards a feminist analysis of sex-role "attitudes"', paper presented at the Psychology of Women Conference, Manchester, June.

Condor, S. (in submission) 'On adopting little orphans: an analysis of the expression of "sex role attitudes" in conversation'.

Cook, E.P. (1985) *Psychological Androgyny*. New York: Pergamon.

Cosin, B. (1972) *Ideology*. Milton Keynes: Open University Press.

Court Report (1976) *Fit for the Future:* Report of the Committee on Child Health Services. Department of Health and Social Security. London: HMSO.

Cox, C.B. and Boyson, R. (1975) *Black Paper 1975: The Fight for Education*. London: Dent.

Curtis, M.A. and M.E.A. Boultwood (1965) *A Short History of Educational Ideas* (4th edn). London: University Tutorial Press.

Davis, F. (1963) *Passage Through Crisis: Polio Victims and their Families*. Indianapolis: Bobbs-Merrill.

Dawe, A. (1970) 'The two sociologies', *British Journal of Sociology*, 21: 2.

Dawes, R.M. (1973) 'The commons dilemma game: a *N*-person mixed motive game with a dominating strategy for defection', *ORI Research Bulletin*, 13: 1–12.

Deaux, K., W. Winton, M. Crowley and L.L. Lewis (1985) 'Level of categorization and the content of gender stereotypes', *Social Cognition*, 3: 145–67.

de Tracy, A. Destutt (1827) *Élémens d'idéologie*. Paris: Madame Lévi.

Diderot, D. (1966) *Encyclopédie ou dictionnaire raisonné* (1757). Stuttgart: Friedrich Frommann.

Diogenes Laertius (1972) *Lives of Eminent Philosophers*. London: Loeb.

Doise, W. and S. Moscovici (1984) 'Les décisions en groupe', in S. Moscovici (ed.), *Psychologie Sociale*. Paris: Presses Universitaires de France.

Dreyfus, H. and S. Dreyfus (1986) *Mind over Machine: the Power of Human Intuition and Expertise in the Era of the Computer*. Oxford: Basil Blackwell.

Dummett, A. (1973) *A Portrait of English Racism*. Harmondsworth: Penguin.

Duncan, B.L. (1976) 'Differential social perception and attribution of intergroup violence: testing the lower limits of stereotyping blacks', *Journal of Personality and Social Psychology*, 34: 590–8.

Durkheim, E. (1956) *Education and Sociology*. New York: Free Press.

Durlak, J.A. (1979) 'Comparative effectiveness of paraprofessional and professional helpers', *Psychological Bulletin*, 86: 80–92.

Dworkin, A. (1983) *Right Wing Women*. London: Women's Press.

Edelman, M. (1977) *Political Language*. New York: Academic Books.

Edwards, A.D. and V.J. Furlong (1969) *The Language of Teaching*. London: Heinemann.

Edwards, D. and N.M. Mercer (1987) *Common Knowledge: the Development of Understanding in the Classroom*. London: Methuen.

Edwards, D. and D.J. Middleton (1986) 'Joint remembering: constructing an account of shared experience through conversational discourse', *Discourse Processes*, 9: 423–59.

Edwards, D. and D.J. Middleton (1987) 'Conversation and remembering: Bartlett revisited', *Applied Cognitive Psychology*, 1: 77–92.

Festinger, L. (1957) *A Theory of Cognitive Dissonance*. London: Row Peterson.

Flew, A. (1975) *Thinking About Thinking*. London: Fontana.

Fodor, J.A. (1975) *The Language of Thought*. New York: Thomas Y. Crowell.

Forbes, H.D. (1986) *Nationalism, Ethnocentrism and Personality*. Chicago: University of Chicago Press.

Forsyth, D.R. (1987) *Social Psychology*. Belmont: Brooks/Cole.

Fraser, C. and D. Foster (1984) 'Social groups, nonsense groups and group polarization', in H. Tajfel (ed.), *The Social Dimension*. Cambridge: Cambridge University Press.

Freire, P. (1972) *Pedagogy of the Oppressed*. Harmondsworth: Penguin.

Friedman, M. and R. Rosenman (1974) *Type A Behavior and Your Heart*. New York: Alfred Knopf.

Froome, S.H. (1970) *Why Tommy Isn't Learning*. London: Stacey.

Furnham, A. (1982) 'Why are the poor always with us? Explanations for poverty in Britain', *British Journal of Social Psychology*, 21: 311–22.

Furnham, A. and A. Lewis (1986) *The Economic Mind*. Sussex: Wheatsheaf.

Gadamer, H.-G. (1979) *Truth and Method*. London: Sheed & Ward.

Gane, M. (1983) 'On the ISAs episode', *Economy and Society*, 12: 431–67.

Gane, M. (1988) *On Durkheim's Rules of Sociological Method*. London: Routledge & Kegan Paul.

Garfinkel, H. (1967) *Studies in Ethnomethodology*. Englewood Cliffs, NJ: Prentice-Hall.

Gaus, G.F. (1983) *The Modern Liberal Theory of Man*. London: Croom Helm.

Geertz, C. (1975) *The Interpretation of Cultures*. London: Hutchinson.

Gergen, K. and M. Gergen (1987) 'Narratives of relationship', in R. Burnett, P. McGhee and D. Clarke (eds), *Accounting for Relationships*. London: Methuen.

Ginsberg, M. (1965) *On Justice and Society*. London: Heinemann.

Gliedman, J. and W. Roth (1980) *The Unexpected Minority: Handicapped Children in America*. New York: Harcourt Brace Jovanovich.

Goffman, E. (1963) *Stigma: Notes on the Management of Spoiled Identity*. Englewood Cliffs, NJ: Prentice-Hall.

Golding, P. and S. Middleton (1982) *Images of Welfare*. Oxford: Martin Robertson.

Gordon, P. and F. Klug (1986) *New Right, New Racism*. London: Searchlight.

Green, T.H. (1890) *Prolegomena to Ethics*. Oxford: Clarendon Press.

Greenberg, J. H. (1966) *Language Universals*. The Hague: Mouton.

Greenwald, A.G. (1980) 'The totalitarian ego: fabrication and revision of personal history', *American Psychologist*, 35: 603–18.

Grice, H.P. (1975) 'Logic and conversation', in P. Cole and J. Morgan (eds), *Syntax and Semantics* vol. 3. New York: Academic Press.

Guillaumin, C. (1972) *L'Idéologie Raciste: genèse et langage actuel*. Paris: Mouton.

Guthrie, W.K.C. (1975) *A History of Greek Philosophy*. Cambridge: Cambridge University Press.

Hamilton, D. (1979) 'A cognitive-attributional analysis of stereotyping', in L. Berkowitz (ed.), *Advances in Experimental Social Psychology* vol. 12. New York: Academic Press.

Hamilton, D. (1981) 'Stereotyping and intergroup behaviour: some thoughts on the cognitive approach', in D. Hamilton (ed.), *Cognitive Processes in Stereotyping and Intergroup Behavior*. Hillsdale, NJ: Lawrence Erlbaum.

Hamilton, D. and T.K. Trolier (1986) 'Stereotypes and stereotyping: an overview of the cognitive approach', in J.F. Dovidio and S.L. Gaertner (eds), *Prejudice, Discrimination and Racism*. Orlando: Academic Press.

Harding, J., B. Kutner, H. Proshansky and I. Chein (1969) 'Prejudice and ethnic relations', in G. Lindzey (ed.), *Handbook of Social Psychology*. New York: Addison-Wesley.

Hawthorn, G. (1987) *Enlightenment and Despair*. Cambridge: Cambridge University Press.

Hazlitt, W. (1934) 'Prejudice' (1830), in *The Complete Works* vol. XX. London: Dent.

Head, B.W. (1985) *Ideology and Social Science: Destutt de Tracy and French Liberalism*. Dordrecht: Martinus Nijhoff.

Heath, A. (1986) 'Do people have consistent attitudes?', in R. Jowell, S. Witherspoon and L. Brook (eds), *British Social Attitudes: the 1986 Report*. Aldershot: Gower.

Hegel, G.W.F. (1975) *Logic*. Oxford: Clarendon.

Herzlich, C. (1973) *Health and Illness: a Social Psychological Analysis*. London: Academic Press.

Herzlich, C. and J. Pierret (1985) 'The social construction of the patient: patients and illnesses in other ages', *Social Science and Medicine*, 20: 145–51.

Hewitt, J.P. and R. Stokes (1975) 'Disclaimers', *American Sociological Review*, 40: 1–11.

Hewstone, M. and R. Brown (1986) *Contact and Conflict in Intergroup Encounters*. Oxford: Basil Blackwell.

Hobbs, J.R. and D.A. Evans (1980) 'Conversation as planned behaviour', *Cognitive Science*, 4: 349–77.

Holter, H. (1970) *Sex Roles and Social Structure*. Oslo: Universitetsforlaget.

Horobin, G. (1983) 'Professional mystery: the maintenance of charisma in general medical practice', in R. Dingwall and P. Lewis (eds), *The Sociology of the Professions*. London: Macmillan.

Hume, D. (1964) *A Treatise of Human Nature*. London: Everyman. (Original, 1740.)

Jacobson, S.K. (1985) 'Resistance to affirmative action: self-interest in racism?' *Journal of Conflict Resolution*, 29: 306–29.

Jaggar, A.M. (1983) *Feminist Politics and Human Nature*. Sussex: Harvester.

Janis, I.L. and L. Mann (1977) *Decision Making*. New York: Free Press.

Jodelet, D. (1984) 'Représentation sociale: phénomènes, concept et theorie', in S. Moscovici (ed.), *Psychologie Sociale*. Paris: Presses Universitaires de France.

Johnson, T.J. (1972) *Professions and Power*. London: Macmillan.

Jowell, R., S. Witherspoon and L. Brook (1986) *British Social Attitudes: the 1986 Report*. Aldershot: Gower.

Katz, I., J. Wackenhut and R.G. Hass (1986) 'Racial ambivalence, value duality and behavior', in J.F. Dovidio and S.L. Gaertner (eds), *Prejudice, Discrimination and Racism*. Orlando: Academic Press.

Keenan, E. (1975) 'A sliding sense of obligatoriness: the poly structure of Malagasy oratory', in M. Bloch (ed.), *Political Language in Traditional Society*. London: Academic Press.

Kennedy, E. (1978) *A 'Philosophe' in the Age of Revolution: Destutt de Tracy and the Origins of 'Ideology'*. Philadelphia: American Philosophical Society.

Kessler, S. and W. McKenna (1978) *Gender: an Ethnomethodological Approach*. New York: Wiley.

Kinder, D.R. and D.O. Sears (1981) 'Prejudice and politics: symbolic racism versus racial threats to the good life', *Journal of Personality and Social Psychology*, 40: 414–31.

Kogan, N. and M.A. Wallach (1964) *Risk Taking: a Study in Cognition and Personality*. New York: Holt.

Lane, R.E. (1960) *Political Man*. New York: Free Press.

Larrain, J. (1979) *The Concept of Ideology*. London: Hutchinson.

Larrain, J. (1983) *Marxism and Ideology*. London: Macmillan.

Lawrence, E. (1970) *The Origins and Growth of Modern Education*. Harmondsworth: Penguin.

Layton-Henry, Z. (1985) *The Politics of Race in Britain*. London: Allen & Unwin.

Lenin, V.I. (1961) 'What is to be done?', in *Collected Works* vol. 5. Moscow: Foreign Language Publishing House.

Lerner, M.J. (1977) 'The justice motive: some hypotheses as to its origins and forms', *Journal of Personality*, 45: 1–52.

Levinson, S.C. (1983) *Pragmatics*. Cambridge: Cambridge University Press.

Lowenthal, L. and N. Gutterman (1949) *Prophets of Deceit*. New York: Harper and Row.

Lukacs, G. (1971) *History and Class Consciousness*. London: Merlin.

Lukes, S. (1969) 'Durkheim's "Individualism and the intellectuals"', *Political Studies*, 17: 14–30.

Mannheim, K. (1953) *Essays on Sociology and Social Psychology*. London: Routledge & Kegan Paul.

Mannheim, K. (1960) *Ideology and Utopia*. London: Routledge & Kegan Paul.

Marriott, S. (1985) *Primary Education and Society*. Lewes: Falmer Press.

Marx, K. (1971) *A Critique of Political Economy* (1859). London: Lawrence & Wishart.

Marx, K. and F. Engels (1968) *The Communist Manifesto*, in *Selected Works*. London: Lawrence & Wishart. (Original, 1848.)

Marx, K. and Engels, F. (1970) *The German Ideology*. London: Lawrence & Wishart.

McConahay, J.B. (1981) 'Reducing racial prejudice in desegregated schools', in W.D. Hawley (ed.), *Effective School Desegregation*. Beverly Hills: Sage.

McConahay, J.B. (1982) 'Self-interest versus racial attitudes as correlates of anti-busing attitudes in Louisville: is it the buses or the blacks?', *Journal of Politics*, 44: 692–720.

McConahay, J.B. (1986) 'Modern racism, ambivalence and the modern racism scale', in J.F. Dovidio and S.L. Gaertner (eds), *Prejudice, Discrimination and Racism*. Orlando: Academic Press.

McConahay, J.B., B.B. Hardee and V. Batts (1981) 'Has racism declined in America?', *Journal of Conflict Resolution*, 25: 563–79.

McConahay, J.B. and J.C. Hough (1976) 'Symbolic racism', *Journal of Social Issues*, 32: 23–45.

McFadden, M. (1984) 'Anatomy of difference: towards a classification of feminist theory', *Women's Studies International Forum*, 7: 495–504.

McFadyen, R. and Wetherell, M. (1986) 'Categories in discourse'. Paper presented at Social Psychology Section, British Psychology Conference, Sussex.

McLaughlin, M.L. (1984) *How Talk Is Organized*. Beverly Hills: Sage.

McLellan, D. (1986) *Ideology*. Milton Keynes: Open University Press.

Mehan, H. (1983) 'The role of language and the language of role in institutional decision making', *Language in Society*, 12: 187–211.

Meighan, R. (1981) *A Sociology of Educating*. London: Holt, Rinehart & Winston.

Merton, R.K. (1976) *Sociological Ambivalence and Other Essays*. New York: Free Press.

Middleton, D.J. and D. Mackinlay (1987) 'Gossip and titbits in teamwork: conversation as an instrument of multi-disciplinary practice in child development centres', in Y. Engeström (ed.), *Activity, Work and Learning*. Helsinki: Proceedings Nordic Society for Educational Research.

Miles, R. and A. Phizacklea (1985) *White Man's Country*. London: Pluto.

Mill, J.S. (1970) 'On the subjection of women' (1869), reprinted in A.S. Rossi (ed.), *John Stuart Mill and Harriet Taylor Mill: Essays on Sex Equality*. Chicago: University of Chicago Press.

Morris, M. and P. Patton (1979) *Michel Foucault*. Sydney: Feral.

Moscovici, S. (1976) *La Psychanalyse, son image et son public*. Paris: Presses Universitaires de France.

Moscovici, S. (1981) 'The coming era of social representations', in J.-P. Codol and J.-P. Leyens (eds), *Cognitive Approaches to Social Behaviour*. The Hague: Nijhoff.

Moscovici, S. (1984a) 'The phenomenon of social representations', in R.M. Farr and S.Moscovici (eds), *Social Representations*. Cambridge: Cambridge University Press.

Moscivici, S. (1984b) 'The myth of the lonely paradigm: a rejoinder', *Social Research*, 51: 939–67.

Myrdal, G. (1944) *An American Dilemma*. New York: Harper.

Newton, K. (1969) *The Sociology of British Communism*. London: Allen Lane.

Nicholson, J. (1984) *Men and Women: How Different Are They?* Oxford: Oxford University Press.

Nietzel, M.T. and S.G. Fisher (1981) 'Effectiveness of professional and paraprofessional helpers: a comment on Durlak', *Psychological Bulletin*, 89: 555–65.

Nilson, L.B. (1981) 'Reconsidering ideological lines: beliefs about poverty in America', *Sociological Quarterly*, 22: 531–48.

Osmond, M. and P. Martin (1975) 'Sex and sexism: a comparison of male and female sex-role attitudes', *Journal of Marriage and the Family*, 37: 744–58.

O'Sullivan, N. (1983) *Fascism*. London: Dent.

Parker, I. (in press) 'Deconstructing accounts', in C. Antaki (ed.), *Analysing Everyday Explanation: a Casebook of Methods*. London: Sage.

Parry, G. (1983) 'A British version of the attitudes towards women scale (AWS-B)', *British Journal of Social Psychology*, 22: 261–3.

Parsons, T. (1951) *The Social System*. London: Collier-Macmillan.

Pepitone, A. and R. Kleiner (1957) 'The effect of threat and frustration on group cohesiveness', *Journal of Abnormal and Social Psychology*, 54: 192–9.

Perelman, C. and L. Olbrechts-Tyteca (1971) *The New Rhetoric*. Notre Dame, Ind.: University of Notre Dame Press.

Perlman, D. and P.C. Cozby (1983) *Social Psychology*. New York: Holt, Rinehart & Winston.

Peters, R.S. (1966) *Ethics and Education*. London: Allen & Unwin.

Peters, R.S. (1969) 'A recognizable philosophy of education: a constructive critique', in R.S. Peters (ed.), *Perspectives on Plowden*. London: Routledge & Kegan Paul.

Pettigrew, T.F. (1979) 'The ultimate attribution error: extending Allport's cognitive analysis of prejudice', *Personality and Social Psychology Bulletin*, 5: 461–76.

Piaget, J. (1970) 'Piaget's theory', in P.H. Mussen (ed.), *Carmichael's Manual of Child Psychology*. New York: Wiley.

Plato (1926) *The Laws*, trans. R.G. Bury. Cambridge, Mass.: Harvard University Press.

Plato (1930–35) *The Republic*, trans. P. Shorey. Cambridge, Mass.: Harvard University Press.

Plato (1956) *The Meno*, trans. W.K.C. Guthrie. Harmondsworth: Penguin.

Plato (1959) 'Crito', in *The Last Days of Socrates*. Harmondsworth: Penguin.

Plowden Report (1967) *Children and Their Primary Schools*. Central Advisory Council for Education. London: HMSO.

Potter, J. and I. Litton (1985) 'Some problems underlying the theory of social representations', *British Journal of Social Psychology*, 24: 81–90.

Potter, J. and M. Wetherell (1987) *Discourse and Social Psychology*. London: Sage.

Potter, J. and M. Wetherell (1988) 'Accomplishing attitudes: fact and evaluation in racist discourse', *Text*, 18: 51–68.

Radley, A. (1978) 'Deliberation and awareness in personal conduct', *Journal of Phenomenological Psychology*, 8: 181–202.

Radley, A. (1979) 'Construing as praxis', in P. Stringer and D. Bannister (eds), *Constructs of Sociality and Individuality*. London: Academic Press.

Radley, A. (1988) *Prospects of Heart Surgery: Psychological Adjustment to Coronary Bypass Grafting*. New York: Springer.

Radley, A. and R. Green (1986) 'Bearing illness: a study of couples where the husband awaits coronary graft surgery', *Social Science and Medicine*, 23: 577–85.

Rasinski, K.A. (1987) 'What's fair is fair – or is it? Value difference underlying public views about social justice', *Journal of Personality and Social Psychology*, 53: 201–11.

Rawls, J. (1971) *A Theory of Justice*. Cambridge, Mass.: Harvard University Press.

Reeves, F. (1983) *British Racial Discourse*. Cambridge: Cambridge University Press.

Richards, C. (1979) 'Belief, myth and practice', in K. Shaw and M. Bloomer (eds), *Innovation and Constraint*. Oxford: Pergamon.

Rokeach, M. (1960) *The Open and Closed Mind*. New York: Basic Books.

Rueschemeyer, D. (1983) 'Professional autonomy and the social control of expertise in R. Dingwall and P. Lewis (eds), *The Sociology of the Professions*. London: Macmillan.

Ruskin, J. (1883) *Sesame and Lilies* (1865). Orpington: Allen.

Samelson, F. (1978) 'From "race psychology" to "studies in prejudice": some observations on the thematic reversal in social psychology', *Journal of the History of the Behavioral Sciences*, 14: 265–78.

Samelson, F. (1986) 'Authoritarianism from Berlin to Berkeley: on social psychology and history', *Journal of Social Issues*, 42: 191–208.

Sampson, E.E. (1975) 'On justice as equality', *Journal of Social Issues*, 31: 45–64.

Sampson, E.E. (1977) 'Psychology and the American ideal', *Journal of Personality and Social Psychology*, 35: 767–82.

Sandel, M.J. (1982) *Liberalism and the Limits of Justice*. Cambridge: Cambridge University Press.

Sartre, J.-P. (1965) 'Portrait of the anti-semite', in W. Kaufmann (ed.), *Existentialism from Dostoevsky to Sartre*. Cleveland: Meridian Books.

Sartre, J.-P. (1969) 'Itinerary of a thought', *New Left Review*, 58: 43–66.

Schank, R.C. and R.P. Abelson (1977) *Scripts, Plans, Goals and Understanding*. Hillsdale, NJ: Lawrence Erlbaum.

Schon, D.A. (1983) *The Reflective Practitioner: How Professionals Think in Action*. London: Temple Smith.

Schonbach, P. (1981) *Education and Intergroup Attitudes*. New York: Academic Press.

Seidel, G. (in press) 'We condemn apartheid, *but*. . .: a discursive analysis of the European Parliamentary debate on sanctions', *Sociological Review*.

Selznick, G. and S. Steinberg (1969) *The Tenacity of Prejudice*. New York: Harper.

Sennett, R. and J. Cobb (1977) *The Hidden Injuries of Class*. Cambridge: Cambridge University Press.

Sherif, M. (1966) *Group Conflict and Co-operation*. London: Routledge & Kegan Paul.

Shils, E. (1975) *Center and Periphery*. Chicago: Chicago University Press.

Skinner, B.F. (1971) *Beyond Freedom and Dignity*. Harmondsworth: Penguin.

Snyder, M. (1981) 'On the self-perpetuating nature of stereotypes', in D. Hamilton (ed.), *Cognitive Processes in Stereotyping and Intergroup Behavior*. Hillsdale, NJ: Lawrence Erlbaum.

Sontag, S. (1979) *Illness as Metaphor*. Harmondsworth: Allen Lane.

Soucie, R. (1979) 'Common misconceptions about nonverbal communication: implications for training', in A. Wolfgang (ed.), *Nonverbal Behaviour: Applications and Cultural Implications*. London: Academic Press.

Tajfel, H. (1969) 'Cognitive aspects of prejudice', *Journal of Biosocial Science*, 1: 173–91.

Tajfel, H. (1981) *Human Groups and Social Categories*. Cambridge: Cambridge University Press.

Tajfel, H. (1982) *Social Identity and Intergroup Relations*. Cambridge: Cambridge University Press.

Tannen, D. and C. Wallat (1986) 'Medical professionals and parents: a linguistic analysis of communication across contexts', *Language in Society*, 15: 295–312.

Taylor, D.M. and F.M. Moghaddam (1987) *Theories of Intergroup Relations*. New York: Praeger.

Taylor, S.E. and J. Crocker (1981) 'Schematic bases of social information processing', in D. Hamilton (ed.), *Cognitive Processes in Stereotyping and Intergroup Behavior*. Hillsdale, NJ: Lawrence Erlbaum.

Taylor-Gooby, P. (1983) 'Moralism, self-interest and attitudes to welfare', *Policy and Politics*, 11: 145–60.

Taylor-Gooby, P. (1985) *Public Opinion, Ideology and State Welfare*. London: Routledge & Kegan Paul.

Thompson, E.P. (1978) *The Poverty of Theory*. London: Merlin.

Thompson, K. (1986) *Beliefs and Ideology*. Chichester: Ellis Horwood.

Tomlinson, S. (1981) 'Professionals and ESN(M) education', in W. Swann (ed.), *The Practice of Special Education*. Oxford: Basil Blackwell in association with the Open University Press.

Turner, B.S. (1984) *The Body and Society: Explorations in Social Theory*. Oxford: Basil Blackwell.

Turner, J. (ed.) (1987) *Rediscovering the Social Group*. Oxford: Basil Blackwell.

Van Dijk, T.A. (1984) *Prejudice and Discourse: an Analysis of Ethnic Prejudice in Cognition and Conversation*. Amsterdam: Benjamins.

Van Dijk, T.A. (1986) 'When majorities talk about minorities', in M.L. McLaughlin (ed.), *Communication Yearbook 9*. Beverly Hills: Sage.

Van Dijk, T.A. (1987) 'Discourse and power'. Unpublished paper, Department of General Literary Studies, University of Amsterdam.

Verba, S. and G.R. Orren (1986) *Equality in America*. Cambridge, Mass.: Harvard University Press.

Voltaire (n.d.) *A Philosophical Dictionary* vol. 2. London: E. Truelove.

Voysey, M. (1975) *A Constant Burden: the Reconstitution of Family Life*. London: Routledge & Kegan Paul.

Walkerdine, V. (1984) 'Developmental psychology and the child-centred pedagogy: the insertion of Piaget into early education', in J. Henriques, W. Hollway, C. Urwin, C. Venn and V. Walkerdine, *Changing the Subject*. London: Methuen.

Wann, T.W. (1964) *Behaviourism and Phenomenology*. London: University of Chicago Press.

Warnock Report (1978) *Special Educational Needs*: Report of the Committee of Enquiry into the Education of Handicapped Children and Young People. Department of Education and Science. London: HMSO.

Weigel, R.H. and P.W. Howes (1985) 'Conceptions of racial prejudice: symbolic racism reconsidered', *Journal of Social Issues*, 41: 117–38.

Weinreich, H. (1978) 'Sex role socialization', in J. Chetwynd and O. Hartnett (eds), *The Sex Role System*. London: Routledge & Kegan Paul.

Wetherell, M. (1986) 'Linguistic repertoires and literary criticism: new directions for the social psychology of gender', in S. Wilkinson (ed.), *Feminist Social Psychology*. Milton Keynes: Open University Press.

Wetherell, M. (1987) 'Social identity and group polarization', in J. Turner (ed.), *Rediscovering the Social Group*. Oxford: Basil Blackwell.

Wetherell, M. and J. Potter (1986) 'Discourse analysis and the social psychology of racism', *Newsletter of the Social Psychology Section of the British Psychological Society*, 15: 24–9.

Wetherell, M., H. Stiven and J. Potter (1987) 'Unequal egalitarianism: a preliminary study of discourses concerning gender and employment opportunities', *British Journal of Social Psychology*, 26: 59–71.

Wilden, A. (1980) *System and Structure: Essays in Communication and Exchange* (2nd edn). London: Tavistock.

Williams, B.A.O. (1962) 'The idea of equality', in P. Laslett and W.G. Runciman (eds), *Philosophy, Politics and Society*. Oxford: Basil Blackwell.

Williams, J.E. and S. Bennett (1975) 'The definition of sex stereotypes via the ACL', *Sex Roles*, 1: 327–37.

Williams, R. (1961) *The Long Revolution*. Harmondsworth: Penguin.

Wolfendale, S. (1986) 'Ways of increasing parental involvement in children's development and education', in J. Harris (ed.), *Child Psychology in Action*. Beckenham: Croom Helm.

Wollstonecraft, M. (1792) *Vindication of the Rights of Woman* (reprinted 1978). Harmondsworth: Penguin.

Name Index

Subject Index